Advanced Praise for *Hidden Profit*

"*Hidden Profit* is more than just a book; it's mentorship in your hands. Your journey to financial empowerment and profitability in your business begins right here, and with Jamie as your guide, you're set up for success."

—Amy Porterfield, *New York Times* bestselling author of *Two Weeks Notice* and host of *The Amy Porterfield Show*

"This book will transform your business and your life. If you're sick of drowning in bills, excel sheets, and complex financial jargon, you need this book."

—Pat Flynn, *New York Times* bestselling author of *Lean Learning*

"Jamie has written the book so many of us needed long before we ever called ourselves business owners. As someone who believes financial literacy is how we protect ourselves and our communities, this book reminds us profit is not a dirty word, it is freedom."

—Dasha Kennedy, Financial Activist, creator of The Broke Black Girl

"If you've ever felt intimidated by finance or thought, 'I'm just not good with numbers,' this is the book for you. From making sense of your numbers to making numbers fun, Jamie offers an easy-to-implement road map to finally stop guessing and start thriving long-term—perfect for entrepreneurs ready to take control without a finance degree."

—Joey Coleman, international keynote speaker and *WSJ* bestselling author of *Never Lose a Customer Again*

"*Hidden Profit* is a boot camp for entrepreneurs, run by the smartest, kindest drill sergeant who cares about helping others. Essential reading."

—David Sax, bestselling author of *The Soul of an Entrepreneur* and *The Revenge of Analog*

"This book demystifies the hidden levers that power success, so you're free to enjoy the rewards of running a small business"

—Elaine Pofeldt, author of *The Million-Dollar, One-Person Business*

HIDDEN PROFIT

TAKE CONTROL OF YOUR FINANCES, STOP LEAVING MONEY ON THE TABLE, and CREATE ABUNDANCE IN YOUR BUSINESS

JAMIE TRULL
Founder of POWER IN NUMBERS

Simon Acumen
New York   Amsterdam/Antwerp   London
Toronto   Sydney/Melbourne   New Delhi

SIMON ACUMEN

An Imprint of Simon & Schuster, LLC
1230 Avenue of the Americas
New York, NY 10020

Copyright © 2025 by Jamie Trull

This publication contains the opinions and ideas of its author. It is sold with the understanding that neither the author nor the publisher is engaged in rendering legal, tax, investment, insurance, financial, accounting, or other professional advice or services. If the reader requires such advice or services, a competent professional should be consulted. Relevant laws vary from state to state. The strategies outlined in this book may not be suitable for every individual, and are not guaranteed or warranted to produce any particular results.

For more than 100 years, Simon & Schuster has championed authors and the stories they create. By respecting the copyright of an author's intellectual property, you enable Simon & Schuster and the author to continue publishing exceptional books for years to come. We thank you for supporting the author's copyright by purchasing an authorized edition of this book.

No amount of this book may be reproduced or stored in any format, nor may it be uploaded to any website, database, language-learning model, or other repository, retrieval, or artificial intelligence system without express permission. All rights reserved. Inquiries may be directed to Simon & Schuster, 1230 Avenue of the Americas, New York, NY 10020 or permissions@simonandschuster.com.

Simon & Schuster strongly believes in freedom of expression and stands against censorship in all its forms. For more information, visit BooksBelong.com.

No warranty is made with respect to the accuracy or completeness of the information contained herein, and both the author and the publisher specifically disclaim any responsibility for any liability, loss, or risk, personal or otherwise, which is incurred as a consequence, directly or indirectly, of the use and application of any of the contents of this book.

All rights reserved, including the right to reproduce this book or portions thereof in any form whatsoever. For information, address Simon Element Subsidiary Rights Department, 1230 Avenue of the Americas, New York, NY 10020.

First Simon Acumen/Simon Element hardcover edition October 2025

SIMON ACUMEN is a trademark of Simon & Schuster, LLC

For information about special discounts for bulk purchases, please contact Simon & Schuster Special Sales at 1-866-506-1949 or business@simonandschuster.com.

The Simon & Schuster Speakers Bureau can bring authors to your live event. For more information or to book an event, contact the Simon & Schuster Speakers Bureau at 1-866-248-3049 or visit our website at www.simonspeakers.com.

Interior design by Julia Jacintho

Manufactured in the United States of America

1 3 5 7 9 10 8 6 4 2

Library of Congress Control Number: 2025010909

ISBN 978-1-6680-8208-9
ISBN 978-1-6680-8209-6 (ebook)

To the power women who came before and lit the fire, and to the rebel queens who will fan the flames. Keep breaking barriers, defying limits, and rewriting the rules. Your courage and determination remind us that progress is never passive and the world is shaped by those bold enough to challenge what has always been. Keep that light burning bright.

CONTENTS

Foreword by Amy Porterfield   1
Introduction   5

Part I: Know Your Numbers

Chapter 1: Why Data Matters   13
Chapter 2: Your Financial Statements   21
Chapter 3: When Numbers Lie   39
Chapter 4: Create Your Own Performance Metrics   53

Part II: Set Up Your Management Control Room

Chapter 5: Manage Your To-Do List   65
Chapter 6: Manage Your Cash Flow   79
Chapter 7: Manage Your Budget   91
Chapter 8: Manage Your Risk   107
Chapter 9: Manage Yourself   119

Part III: Find Your Hidden Profit

Chapter 10: Become Profitable   133
Chapter 11: Sell More   137

Chapter 12: Raise Your Prices	143
Chapter 13: Mix It Up	159
Chapter 14: Generate More Value	169
Chapter 15: Cut (Unnecessary) Costs	177
Chapter 16: Pay Less Taxes	191
Chapter 17: Carry Less Debt	207
Chapter 18: Make Big Profits	217

Part IV: Create Your PROFFIT Plan™

Chapter 19: Make a Plan for Your PROFFIT	227
Chapter 20: Build Your P-O-T of PROFFIT	231
Chapter 21: Prepare for the Future	241
Chapter 22: Make It Fun	249
Chapter 23: Make an Impact	259
Conclusion: There's Power in Numbers	267

Acknowledgments	**271**
Notes	**275**
Index	**279**

HIDDEN PROFIT

FOREWORD

by Amy Porterfield

When I first launched my business, I imagined a world of freedom, liberated from the traditional confines of having a boss. I planned to work on projects I was passionate about, do it on my own schedule, and earn money in the process.

But instead of achieving the freedom I envisioned, I ended up feeling more constrained than ever. That's partly because within just two years of starting my business, I found myself $40,000 in debt. I realized then that success requires more than just passion and a plan; it requires a solid grasp of finances.

Over the next few years, I focused on mastering my business finances and crafting impactful marketing strategies. I had quite a few missteps and stumbles in the beginning, but little by little, the changes I made to focus on organic marketing started to produce results. Thank goodness I stuck with figuring out how to market myself while managing costs, because within a few years, I was able to turn my business around and become wildly profitable.

As I moved forward in my entrepreneurial journey, my commitment to understanding my finances only grew in importance. That commitment not only saved me from retreating back to corporate life (never again, please) but also saved me thousands and thousands of dollars. Truly—just take this one story as an example: About five years into my business, during what I'd thought would be a routine tax appointment with my tax accountant, my accountant informed me that I owed the government $250,000. Instantly, my heart sank. Confusion and doubt flooded my mind. I had been meticulous with my financial tracking. I had paid my estimated taxes diligently, and based on my calculations, I expected to owe significantly less than that. As I drove home, the numbers swirled in my head and I kept thinking, *How can this be? Where did I mess up?*

But deep down inside, I knew my numbers, and I knew that something was off. I had been actively engaged in every facet of my finances, from tracking to reviewing to checking data monthly. By the time I pulled into my driveway, I was convinced that the mistake wasn't mine; it had to be his.

I called my accountant from my kitchen and explained the numbers, pointing out the possible error he had made. And after reviewing the figures together, we discovered that he had indeed made a mistake.

I'm incredibly grateful that I took the time to understand and actively manage my business finances, which gave me control when I needed it most. In that moment, I felt capable and confident enough to make that call and have that important conversation. I was able to take care of both myself and my business, and I realized that numbers can actually empower, rather than intimidate.

Understanding your finances isn't just about balancing the books; it's about finding your voice and unlocking your true potential as a business owner. When you have a firm grasp on your numbers, you gain the power to make strategic decisions with confidence, seize opportunities, and navigate challenges with resilience. It enables you to handle economic downturns, unexpected expenses, and market fluctuations with a clear head and a steady heart. It ensures that your business will remain profitable and dynamic in any environment.

Moreover, understanding your finances empowers you to invest in what truly matters. It enables you to allocate resources efficiently, whether that means reinvesting profit, scaling up your operations, or donating to causes you care about. By mastering your financial landscape, you set the stage for sustainable growth, fulfillment, and long-term success in your business.

I understand that learning about and discussing money can be intimidating and overwhelming, especially for women in the business world. However, it's so important to tackle this topic. By having open discussions about money, we can inspire one another and find the freedom we've dreamed of.

Particularly for those near the beginning of their journey, ***mastering your finances is nonnegotiable***. It's essential to become knowledgeable about how you spend, make, and view your money. And to achieve this level of competence, it's important to gather as much financial knowledge as possible from trusted sources.

That's why I felt honored when Jamie asked me to write this foreword. I immediately said yes, excited to kick off this life-changing book and share my journey and insights into business finances with you.

With that said, you, my friend, are making a smart choice by picking up this book today. You're about to learn from someone who blends hard-won financial knowledge with heart and genuine entrepreneurial grit.

I've been watching Jamie teach finances online for years, and I couldn't be prouder of the impact she's making in the world. She's teaching people to prioritize investments, budget effectively, and build businesses that are profitable from the start. She's teaching and transforming lives, while building a profitable business that gives her the time and freedom to be an incredible mom to her kids. And if you ask me what makes her stand out as a teacher, it's how she guides business owners from a place of genuine possibility. She shows people how to align their business finances with a fulfilling life, one shaped by desires rather than constrained by financial limitations and past misunderstandings.

Hidden Profit is more than just a book; it's mentorship in your hands. Your journey to financial empowerment and profitability in your business begins right here, and with Jamie as your guide, you're set up for success.

Amy Porterfield, *New York Times* bestselling author of *Two Weeks Notice*

INTRODUCTION

I own a small service-based business and I'm embarrassed to even admit this, but I'm so incredibly bad with managing money. I wish I had someone to hold my hand on a monthly basis and tell me my budget, tell me what I can pay myself, and help me out of this mess.

I know I'm not dumb, but—I just don't get it.

Since I started a free Facebook group for entrepreneurs in 2019, I have seen many posts just like this by smart, capable people. They are business owners who have created products, set prices, collected money from customers, issued refunds, and paid taxes.

I've seen posts by moms who handle their kids' school schedules and extracurriculars, manage the family budget, got A's in algebra in school, and cook dinner every night while running businesses in their "spare" time.

And by dog walkers who can walk four dogs of different sizes at the same time while making sure that each does its business during the twenty-minute walk time, using various electronic key codes for drop-off and pickup, and calculating their earnings for the day in their head, all while sending off a quick message to each owner with the precise amount agreed upon for each dog's walk.

To remix Taylor Swift, the problem is not you. You are not stupid for not understanding the ins and outs of business finances. Nor are you bad at managing money. But like many of the entrepreneurs I work with, you've been convinced that you are.

Why?

Because we've been told that our whole lives—by the media, by mentors and authority figures, by friends and family, maybe even by ourselves.

Whether we didn't catch on immediately when our accountant dropped jargon or were stereotyped by our racial or gender identity, we believed what people told us about ourselves.

As a small-business owner and a mom who regularly shops small, the idea that entrepreneurs are inept at managing their money just doesn't work for me. And as a certified public accountant (CPA) who is an expert in business finances, I decided to do something about it. After working in corporate finance for over a decade, I launched my own business, Balance CFO, in 2018. The entrepreneurs I work with frequently describe themselves as being "bad with numbers" and blame themselves for hitting financial roadblocks and challenges in their business. But ultimately, it's not their fault—or yours, either.

You *can* learn how to be "good with numbers" and create abundance in your business bank accounts and life. Money doesn't have to vanish every month. You don't need to struggle to pay yourself consistently. And if you're the type who likes to pretend that you don't have bank accounts 360 days out of the year while simultaneously hoping and praying that you'll have enough money in those accounts at tax time—I can help.

I am passionate about helping small-business owners who currently make less than $500,000 in revenue understand their finances so that they can grow or simply find more freedom in their businesses and lifestyle. Though I work with all kinds of small businesses and types of entrepreneurs, most of my clients and audience have a marginalized identity. This is no coincidence, as women, people of color, and those who identify as LGBTQIA+ or neurodiverse are often left out of conversations about finance.

The disparities are clear. Recent data from NerdWallet shows that while women make up 40 percent of small-business owners, the revenue of women-owned businesses accounts for only 4 percent of total small-business revenue in the United States.[1] Businesses owned by Black women make even less revenue, with an average of $24,000 annually compared to $142,900 for all women-owned businesses.[2]

The reasons for these disparities are complex and often systemic in nature and show up in a multitude of ways.

For instance, women still often do a disproportionate amount of household unpaid labor, even when they are the primary breadwinner.[3] Additionally, women and people of color are less likely to be approved for financing for their business (and when they do, the loan size they receive is, on average, 10 percent less than their male counterparts receive).[4]

In addition to the cultural and systemic issues that create and perpetuate disparities, women are also statistically less likely to measure their success based on the attainment of monetary goals. While seemingly noble, some of this can stem from an internalized belief that money and the desire to attain it are inherently bad.

The truth is that money is a tool. And like a screwdriver or a fork, a tool is neither inherently good nor inherently evil. The impact of any tool is based on who has possession of it and how that person uses it. That's part of the reason I want to level the playing field for women, people of color, and other folks who have a marginalized identity. I believe that if we collectively earn more money through our businesses, the world will change substantially for the better.

Money feeds hungry children, gives women the ability to leave dangerous domestic situations, and helps break cycles of poverty and violence, replacing those forces with education, opportunity, even intergenerational wealth. For people who are struggling, money absolutely can buy something even better than temporary happiness; it can buy safety, security, and the hope of a better life.

The positive impact money can have is the reason I want to help *every* business owner succeed. A big part of our success as entrepreneurs is understanding our numbers. Being able to review our revenue, costs, and profit—and understand what decisions to make as a result—can be the difference between thriving and barely scraping by. When you look at the data on small businesses nationwide, it's pretty clear that most small-business owners struggle to generate revenue. Despite all the people online bragging about their million-dollar months, just one in ten entrepreneurs earns a six-figure annual income from their business. In fact, a recent report showed that the average revenue of a business in the United States in 2023 without employees is $46,978—20 percent less than an average salary ($59,428)[5]—and that is revenue, not the money business owners take home after expenses.

Luckily, as a CPA, former fractional CFO, and current business owner, I can tell you that understanding your business finances doesn't require a degree in applied mathematics or thousands of dollars in programs and services. The meat and potatoes of what you really need to know are right here, in this book.

And while there is a learning curve, the best thing you can do for yourself and your business is to learn. It's my goal to show you how to embrace your numbers. I want you to feel the power that comes with becoming your own CFO. What you'll learn in this book will show you how to build a stable and predictable financial foundation, step by step. I will share real, practical, and implementable strategies that will unlock the hidden profit potential in your business and enable you to pay yourself—consistently and well.

Being "good" with numbers isn't about becoming a human calculator or getting it right every single time. When you're feeling tempted to overanalyze (or give up entirely), I want you to remind yourself that *numbers don't have to be perfect to be useful*. You have my permission to make assumptions, guesstimate, and round. In fact, as a business finance expert, I encourage you to!

What you're going to learn in this book is how to understand exactly what you need to know without all the financial jargon and acronyms. (Okay, we do have to use some acronyms, but I promise there won't be any quadratic equations, and there's zero need for a graphing calculator. But if you want to buy a pretty calculator because it feels cool or empowering, be my guest.)

That being said, if you are looking for exact directions that include words such as "always" and "never," you won't find them here. Neither will you find the "right" way to do anything, because in my opinion, there is no singular way to succeed. However, I will help you embrace your inner CFO so that you can trust yourself to find the way forward that best fits you, your business, and your goals. That's ultimately what will help you create the habits you need to build wealth steadily and reliably.

In part I, we begin with the basics. I'll help you understand why data matters and teach you how to read and understand your financial statements. Then I'll go further, explaining how numbers can lie to us (true story) and showing you how to find the key metrics in your business that can make it more profitable. By the end of this section, you will understand how to organize your money.

In part II, I'll introduce you to your Financial Control Room and guide you through the financial duties every successful business owner should understand—even if you plan to outsource some of those responsibilities. I'll explain exactly what you need to do to be compliant, including how to file your taxes without losing your mind (70,000 pages of tax law has a way of doing that!). I'll offer ways to better manage your cash and make smart financial decisions, as well as show you how to manage the tasks of a CFO together with everything else you're juggling. We'll also discuss the differences among profit, cash flow, and what's showing up on those financial statements your accountant or bookkeeper (or software) puts together. Last, I'll discuss the reasons why it's not necessary for your business to have a budget (yes, really!).

Once you know all that, we can talk about you. It sounds simple, but every entrepreneur and every person is different. I'll show you how to figure out what *will* work for you, not what some social media influencer or talking head says *should* work for you. I'll help you discover your personal risk tolerance when it comes to things such as taxes and debt, and what that means for you and the decisions you make. To help you understand your money habits better, I've provided a quiz that reveals your money personality, also called your Sacred Money Archetype®. This system, created by Kendall SummerHawk, allows us to transform our relationship with money by working with our innate personality, rather than against it.

Part III is all about finding the profit that is already hiding in your business. And yes, you (probably) have profit. You'll discover ways to grow that hidden cash through the Profit Levers™, my unique way of creating more money in your existing business through eight independent strategies. Over the next several chapters, I'll dive deeper into how "pulling" each lever can help you generate more revenue, spend fewer dollars on costs without scrimping, and pay less on taxes and debt. Last, I'll sum up the entire section with guidance on what lever to pull and when.

Best of all, in part IV, I'll show you how to use my unique PROFFIT Plan™ to manage your cash so that you can cover emergencies, take advantage of opportunities that come your way, plan for the future, and have a ton of fun along the way. By the end of this book, you'll have not only a plan for your money but a clearer vision of where you are headed and how to get there.

Before we jump into all the numbers and strategies in this book, there's just one more thing we need to do. If you're reading this, you've probably tried to regain control of your money before. You've likely read other books, taken advice from friends, and resolved that *this time* you're finally going to succeed and make some big shifts.

I appreciate that energy, I do. But I also know that once we get into the nitty-gritty, that energy will most likely fade. You can't rely on the motivation you feel at this moment to keep you on track, and life will most definitely get in the way. So before we get to the practical step-by-step stuff, you need to think about your *why*:

- Why do you want to gain control of your business finances?
- Why do you want to make more profit?
- Why is this something that needs to be prioritized when there are a million fires springing up that urgently need to be put out?

When you are determining your *why*, I suggest you include a motivation for helping others. What I've found after working with thousands of entrepreneurs and on my own journey is that we are often quicker to give up on a goal when the outcome benefits only us. When what we're working for benefits us *and* others, we tend to keep moving.

Give a long, hard think about your *why*. Get out a journal (yes, really!) and go deep. Keep asking "Why?" until you feel it in your soul of souls. Don't judge or overanalyze what you come up with; just write it all down. And most importantly, don't worry about the "how" right now. That will come later.

Once you have your *why* (or *whys*—it's okay to have more than one!), it's time to start finding the profit that's hidden in your business and unleash the power in numbers.

PART I

Know Your Numbers

Where do I even start?

This is the most common first question I get. And it makes sense. With so many to-dos on your list, it can be hard to know what to tackle first.

But here's the easy answer: Whether you've had your business for thirty years or thirty minutes, you can always benefit from going back to basics. In this section, we're going to talk about data; specifically: why data matters, how we can use data in our business to make decisions, and the pitfalls to watch out for. You'll also get a crash course in financial statements, including how to read (and understand) a P&L and Balance Sheet. We'll even talk about why and how to get your finances organized, even if things feel messy right now.

By the time you finish this section, you'll know how to use data to propel your business forward.

CHAPTER ONE

Why Data Matters

As a mom of two young children, I know how to calm my kids down when they are upset. Based on tons of past experience (aka meltdowns), I know that my son tends to need reassurance, hugs, and to talk it out, whereas my daughter almost always just needs a little downtime and a snack (she and I have a lot in common that way).

How do I know all this? Data. Even if you don't consider yourself an "analytical" person, you're still processing data all around you, all the time. In this chapter, I'm going to help you learn how to embrace the data from your business, even if you are someone whose nightmares involve spreadsheets.

All data is ultimately a record of what happened in the past. Every time we make a decision, we are subconsciously using the data we've collected as humans living life. For me, the data I use with my kids is my past experience. Similarly, the data you can use in your business is what you've already experienced. We usually think that data = numbers, but data is actually way broader than that.

Consider this: When you decide what time to leave for work based on traffic, you're relying on patterns of data you've noticed. When choosing a new recipe, you might remember how similar dishes turned out or how your family feels about certain ingredients to guide your decision (mayo = a no-go for the Trull fam). Even when picking a vacation spot, you likely consider past experiences, your friends' recommendations, or even reviews you've read—none of which is pure numbers. These examples show how data is much more than numbers; it's the everyday observations, patterns, and memories that shape our decisions.

When we ignore data, we almost always expend more energy than we need to get the result we want (if our desired result occurs at all). Going back to the parenting example, I would spend way more emotional energy trying to calm down my daughter with my words than handing her a pack of mini muffins. Paying attention to data and interpreting it correctly will save you time, money, and emotional headaches in the future.

A lot of the time, analyzing data can feel intimidating because it seems foreign and difficult. But our brains are constantly using data to live efficiently—without us even consciously realizing it. That's why I know it's possible to teach your brain how to analyze your business data with the same level of effortlessness. All it takes is some education (which you have in this book) and some practice.

For now, what you need to know is that there are two different types of data: the subjective kind that I just talked about and the actual "hard" data that involves numbers.

In most businesses, "numbers data" includes past sales and costs, profit margins, and specific metrics (sometimes called Key Performance Indicators, or KPIs, which I'll talk about more in chapter 4) that show what's really going on. As you can probably guess, there is no shortage of "hard" data points to look at in business. But in my opinion, the single *most important* data to track in your business is the data that indicates your level of **profitability**. At its most basic, profitability is a super simple math equation utilizing a few high-level data points:

Revenue (money you made) - Expenses (money you spent) = Profit (or loss, if this number is negative)

When your revenue goes up, your profit goes up. When your business expenses (also known as *deductions*) go up, your profit goes down. As a business owner, you pay taxes on profit, not revenue (thank goodness). Unfortunately, this fact can lead business owners to prioritize the wrong things.

Here's a good example. I was sitting in the chair at my hair salon with foil on my head when a stylist proudly declared that she "got her profit down to zero" and wouldn't be paying taxes this year. I had to fight the urge to jump out from under my heat lamp, foil and all, when the other stylists leaned in, eager to learn her secret, which—spoiler alert—was spending a bunch of money on stuff she didn't need to avoid taxes.

By the way: This is not just a stylist thing. I hear this sort of thing all the time.

While it may seem obvious that more profit = better, many small-business owners actually operate as if the opposite is true. Like the stylists, a lot of well-meaning entrepreneurs become so preoccupied with reducing their taxes that they make decisions that don't serve them well. While there are tax strategies that can help you save money, one of the most common I see is to spend money needlessly to "save" on your taxes through deductions.

But that strategy doesn't do anything for you other than reduce money from how much you're able to pay yourself in the end. That's because if you don't have profit (or have a low profit) on paper, you likely also don't have cash in the bank to pay yourself. And that can make for tricky situations later on, such as being able to qualify for a mortgage, car loan, or business loan.

Are there legit ways to reduce taxes without hurting your profitability? You bet. We'll talk about some of those tried-and-true methods in chapter 16. But as business owners, our primary focus when it comes to our finances should be running a healthy, profitable business.

While a business's overall profitability is a super important data point—arguably *the* most important one—that number alone doesn't tell the whole story of your business. Knowing your profitability (or lack thereof) may tell you if there is a problem, but it *won't* tell you what caused it. To get to the root of it, you'll need to dig a bit deeper into your financial data.

As an example, let's evaluate how two business owners could use financial data to inform their decision-making.

Sandra is in her seventh year running a home organization business where she makes $250,000 in revenue annually. She has a few employees to help her so she can focus on other aspects of the business and have more free time. After the cost of her employees and other business expenses, her total profit amounts to $30,000 (before paying herself or taxes).

Monique, on the other hand, is in her fourth year running a home organization business, but she's a solopreneur. She is making $70,000 in revenue annually. But compared to Sandra, she has few actual costs in her business since it's only her. That's why Monique's total profit is $65,000 (again, before paying herself or taxes).

But because she's doing it all on her own, Monique is exhausted. She is struggling to keep her head above water as she juggles the administration and marketing side of her business with her client service duties. She often has to work seven days a week to keep up with it all and regularly turns away new clients because she is at—or over—her maximum capacity.

SANDRA	
Revenue	$ 250,000
Direct Expenses*	120,000
Indirect Expenses	100,000
Total Operating Profit	$ 30,000

MONIQUE	
Revenue	$ 70,000
Direct Expenses*	-
Indirect Expenses	5,000
Total Operating Profit	$ 65,000

*In this example, the Direct Expenses represent the wages of employees who service customers.

Now that we know more about Sandra and Monique, let's take a quick look at their Profit and Loss Statements (P&Ls).

We'll talk more about the P&L (including what constitutes a direct versus indirect cost) in the next chapter, but an important piece of data that *isn't* shown on their financial statements is how much Sandra and Monique were working. Sandra was working an average of thirty-five hours per week, while Monique was working an average of sixty hours per week.

Remember, Monique and Sandra have the same goal: They want to be able to pay themselves more from their business without burning themselves out. It's a pretty universal goal, but the path to get there can vary widely. Their data tells two completely different stories about what they can do to achieve those goals.

How can looking at a P&L really help Sandra and Monique figure out what they need to do? What conclusions can we draw from this snapshot of data? If your P&L just feels like numbers on a page, it can help to do a little simple math, starting with your profit margins. We'll be going deeper into profit margins in chapter 7, but here's a quick example of how this information can help Sandra and Monique determine the next steps to take in their business.

Looking at her P&L, it's clear that Sandra's issue is her operating profit margin, which clocks in at only 12% ($30,000 profit divided by $250,000 in revenue). If she wants to increase the amount she can pay herself, she needs to be looking for ways to increase that profit margin. While there are many ways to do this (I'll be talking more about the Profit Levers in part III), a quick look at Sandra's P&L indicates that reducing costs is likely the easiest place to start. She'll want to spend some time determining which costs are really needed and provide an adequate return on investment and which she can eliminate or reduce.

Monique's operating profit margin is a stellar 93% ($65,000 profit divided by $70,000 in revenue). Focusing on how to cut the small amount of costs she has likely wouldn't be a good use of time and could even backfire. For example, if she decided to cut the $75 per month she pays for a client scheduling tool to reduce recurring costs, she may end up adding *hours* of additional work to her already overloaded week. As I'll discuss more in chapter 16, keeping costs ultralow is great, but *not* if it comes at the expense of your time and sanity.

It's more likely time for Monique to consider investing more of her money back into her business so she can grow it, which would also free up more of her time. She could bring on a part-time or full-time employee to assist her or invest in software that will improve the efficiency of her operations. Doing either or both could add capacity for her business, which would enable her to grow her revenue. Similarly, though her profit margin would decline at first (a typical result of hiring), the overall profit of her business would likely increase over time, even if she cut back her hours. Additionally, the amount of money she would be making on a *per hour* basis could dramatically increase because Monique would be able to work less and pay herself more.

Note that in both cases, if Sandra and Monique didn't pay attention to the data (in this case, their profit margins and capacity), they would probably assume that they just needed to work more to meet their profit target. Most of the time, the default response to not making as much money as we'd like is to chase more sales. But if we do that *before* we fix our business's underlying profitability problems, we risk burning ourselves out and potentially even giving up on our dream.

What I want you to remember is that data is the key to your financial and business puzzles. Without it, we often fall into a cycle of repeating the same things we've always done, even when those efforts haven't yielded the results we desire. Getting really good at understanding and interpreting your data takes time and sometimes a good bit of trial and error. But once you master the skill, it will feel as though you've unlocked a secret cheat code you can use over and over again.

> ### CHIEF FINANCIAL OPINION:
> ### Failure Is Data, Too
>
> If you know me, you know I don't shy away from an opportunity to jump onto my proverbial soapbox regarding something I'm passionate about. Throughout this book, I'll be highlighting these as Chief Financial Opinions (get it?) with some of my personal financial hot takes that I don't want you to miss.
>
> For example, everyone makes mistakes or makes a business decision that doesn't go their way. But what if we saw choices that don't work out not as letdowns but as *data*?
>
> That's right. Every "failure" you have experienced is really just a piece of data revealing what *doesn't* work. It can be tough to look at decisions you regret, but the only real mistake we can make is not to learn from the things that don't go our way.
>
> When we replace the typical "Ugh, I can't believe I messed that up" response with a more scientific "Interesting—what did I learn here?" approach, all of a sudden something that felt discouraging is propelling us toward success. Pretty cool, right?

Take Action

To get started analyzing the data in your business, you'll want to gather up a few basics. Specifically, you'll want to grab:

- Your Profit and Loss Statement
- Your Balance Sheet

If you don't have these yet or you haven't looked at them in a while, don't worry. In the next chapter I'll give you a crash course on what they mean and offer some tips for organizing your financial data fast.

CHAPTER TWO
Your Financial Statements

When I talk about getting your data organized, I'm not talking about business receipts (not yet at least). For most small-business owners, your financial statements are the most critical piece of financial data to have in order. These statements generally consist of a Profit and Loss Statement (P&L) and a Balance Sheet. While there are other financial statements, such as the Statement of Cash Flows, the P&L and Balance Sheet are typically the most common and useful for smaller businesses.

Financial statements present a historical view of your business. They are a record of everything you've earned and spent (the P&L), as well as what you own and owe (the Balance Sheet). If you don't have formal financial statements yet or you have them but don't know how to use them effectively, this chapter can help.

The Profit and Loss Statement

By far the most popular and arguably most useful financial statement is the P&L. Your P&L shows the money your business earned (i.e., its revenue or sales) and the money it spent (i.e., its expenses or costs) during a specific time period. The P&L is also sometimes called the Income Statement or Statement of Operations. (You'll notice that we accountants *love* to complicate things by having multiple names for the same thing.)

Often, P&Ls cover a full year, since that's what's used for tax returns. But you can run a P&L to evaluate your activity during any period you'd like.

Most commonly, P&Ls are run annually, quarterly, and monthly. I highly recommend getting into the habit of reviewing your P&L every month, as it can provide valuable insights into your business. If you don't yet know what to look for, don't worry—I'll cover that.

Remember, your P&L is just a simple math equation. At its most basic, it shows:

Revenue (money you made) – Expenses (money you spent) = Profit (or loss)

FINANCIAL STATEMENTS AREN'T JUST FOR TAXES

Real talk: The majority of business owners don't look at their financial statements regularly. Heck, many don't even worry about pulling them together until tax time is looming. It's why the few months leading up to April 15 are ten times busier for bookkeepers and accountants than the rest of the year. It's also why coffee consumption doubles among these professionals during this time (trust me; I've been there!).

Many entrepreneurs view the P&L process as a "compliance" type of activity (i.e., something they need to do to stay out of jail and in Uncle Sam's good graces). Since tax returns are due only once a year, viewing these tasks from a compliance perspective means that other, seemingly "more pressing" activities such as paying payroll, serving clients, and sales take precedence over staying financially organized. (I'm going to talk about how to stay compliant as a business owner in chapter 5, by the way.)

I'm here to tell you that your monthly financial statements and the underlying data that creates them are a treasure trove of useful information. If you don't yet know how to interpret it helpfully, that's okay. This book will help you build and flex your analysis muscles.

Once you've realized how helpful this data can be *and* how to use it effectively to make more money, you'll be more motivated and have the tools you need to stay on top of your financial organization. Plus, your future self (and your overcaffeinated accountant) will thank you!

My client Nancy runs a print shop making customizable goods such as T-shirts, mugs, and hats and selling them online. Since Nancy runs a product-based business, her P&L includes the cost of goods sold (the cost of the materials she purchased wholesale). In addition to the products she sells, she also does some consulting with aspiring print shop owners and charges consulting fees for this work. She also has software and marketing costs, among other expenses. Nancy's full P&L looks like this:

Nancy's Profit and Loss

NANCY'S PRINT SHOP

ACCOUNT TYPE	ACCOUNT		BEFORE
INCOME	T-shirt Income	$	10,000
	Hat Income		12,000
	Other Product Income		5,500
	Consulting Income		4,000
	Total Revenue	$	31,500
EXPENSES	T-shirt Cost of Goods Sold		2,700
	Hat Cost of Goods Sold		2,000
	Other Cost of Goods Sold		1,100
	Other Direct Expenses		200
	Total Direct Expenses (Cost of Goods Sold)	$	6,000
	Total Gross Profit	$	25,500
	Advertising & Marketing		700
	Website & Branding		1,200
	Legal & Professional Services		350
	Office Supplies & Software		1,000
	Total Indirect Expenses	$	3,250
TOTAL OPERATING PROFIT		$	22,250

Note that while there are a few more lines than in our simple equation, it all boils down to Revenue – Expenses = Profit.

The higher the profit, the more money your business made.

You might be wondering, "But, Jamie, if my P&L is just that simple equation, why is it that my profit on my P&L doesn't match my bank account balance?"

This is a gold star question, my friend. The answer is what I call "accounting funny business." Accounting has specific rules around things such as the timing of when you record sales and expenses that can impact the number on your P&L. This is especially true if you own assets that are being *depreciated* over time or business debt you are paying off; more on these concepts later. For now, you have my permission to ignore all of the "accounting funny business," as it can muddy the water and make it harder to understand what your financial statements are trying to tell you. In chapter 6, I'll dive more into "accounting funny business" and why it can create a disconnect between your cash in the bank and your profit on paper.

The Balance Sheet

Ah, the Balance Sheet. Even if you feel pretty good about your understanding of the P&L, you might still be scratching your head when it comes to the Balance Sheet. You're not alone. The Balance Sheet is the black sheep of the financial statement family, often overlooked and misunderstood. However, it holds some crucial insights into a business's health, so we don't want to gloss over it too quickly.

At its most basic, the Balance Sheet shows you three things:

- What your business *owns* (your Assets)
- What your business *owes* (your Liabilities)
- What your business's *net worth* is (your Equity)

Like the P&L, the Balance Sheet is a simple formula at its core:

Assets − Liabilities = Equity

For a small service-based business, the Balance Sheet may be sparse and not overly helpful. The Balance Sheet is usually relevant for businesses that have assets (other than cash, such as inventory or equipment) and liabilities (such as debt) and for businesses taxed as S corporations (S corps) or C corporations (C corps), which must include their Balance Sheet as part of their business tax return. A Balance Sheet is also essential if you file taxes based on the accrual method (more on this later). Additionally, if you have a product-based business that requires inventory, your Balance Sheet is must-read.

Let's go back to Nancy, the print shop owner. Her Balance Sheet shows that she purchased specific equipment to help her meet an increase in demand for her products. As a result, she needed to add stock of on-hand inventory to offer more product options. To fund both of those purchases, she took out a business loan. Nancy's Balance Sheet (below) reflects what she owns and owes at a given time and gives her a snapshot of her business's financial health.

Nancy's Balance Sheet

NANCY'S PRINT SHOP

ACCOUNT TYPE	ACCOUNT	AS OF DEC. 31
ASSETS	**Current Assets**	
	Cash	$ 15,000
	Accounts Receivable	2,500
	Inventory	4,000
	Total Current Assets	$ 21,500
	Long-Term Assets	
	Machinery	7,000
	Total Long-Term Assets	$ 7,000
TOTAL ASSETS		$ 28,500
LIABILITIES	**Current Liabilities**	
	Credit Card Balances	6,000
	Accounts Payable	1,000
	Total Current Liabilities	$ 7,000
	Long-Term Liabilities	
	Long-Term Business Loan	12,000
	Total Long-Term Liabilities	$ 12,000
TOTAL LIABILITIES		$ 19,000
TOTAL EQUITY (ASSETS - LIABILITIES)		$ 9,500

Nancy's assets (things she owns) consist mainly of her cash balance, her inventory on hand, and her fixed assets (the equipment she purchased). Her liabilities (things she owes) are made up mostly of her credit card and business loan outstanding balances. Her equity (the business's net worth) is the difference between her assets and liabilities. And just as in personal finance, a positive net worth is the goal.

In this case, Nancy has positive equity in the business because her assets exceed her liabilities, which tells her that she is solvent overall. If all of her bills/loans were to come due today, she would be able to cover the amounts owed with her business assets. Additionally, because her short-term assets are higher than her short-term liabilities (short-term = twelve months or less), it means that the company is "liquid" and should be able to cover its financial obligations in the near term.

A key difference between the Balance Sheet and the P&L is that a Balance Sheet reflects *a point in time*, whereas a P&L is run for *a specific period*. Said another way, your P&L shows you the activity that happened *during a specified time range*, whereas your Balance Sheet will be focused on balances *as of a certain date*. A Balance Sheet is useful to see how financially healthy a company is at any point in time. For example, if you run a Balance Sheet report and see that your liabilities exceed your assets, it may indicate that you could have an issue paying your credit card balance next month. While business owners tend to spend more time thinking about their P&L, a Balance Sheet is a popular statement with investors or lenders who want a snapshot of the overall health of your business. A strong Balance Sheet is extremely helpful if you are looking to sell your business, bring on an investor, or apply for debt financing.

How the P&L and Balance Sheet Interact

While they are separate financial statements, the P&L and Balance Sheet are tied together. That's because every time a transaction happens in your business (you make a sale, you pay a bill, or you pay yourself), there are at least *two* impacts on your financial statements from that one transaction. Often, a transaction impacts both the Balance Sheet and the P&L.

While I'm not going to get deep into the world of debits and credits in this book (you're welcome), I will briefly touch on general accounting concepts. While you as a business owner don't need to be well versed in all the principles of double-entry bookkeeping (there are professionals for that), a general overview can help you understand how the P&L and Balance Sheet interact with each other, which will help you make more sense of your financial statements. Let's hop into a few different examples using Nancy's print shop business.

Example 1: Making a Sale

Let's say Nancy makes a $500 sale of a service and collects cash immediately. In this case, she would see the following impacts on her financial statements:

1. An increase in revenue on her P&L
2. An increase in cash on her Balance Sheet

But that's not all. Remember that the P&L and Balance Sheet are formula driven, which means there is a knock-on effect on other accounts on the financial statements as well.

Here's a quick recap of the full impact of this transaction on the P&L (only the line items affected by the transaction are shown in the columns on the right side):

Making a Sale: Profit and Loss

PROFIT & LOSS

ACCOUNT TYPE	ACCOUNT	BEFORE	SERVICE SALE	AFTER
INCOME	T-shirt Income	$ 10,000		
	Hat Income	12,000		
	Other Product Income	5,500		
	Consulting Income	4,000	500	4,500 ↑
	Total Revenue	$ 31,500	$ 500	$ 32,000 ↑
EXPENSES	T-shirt Cost of Goods Sold	$ 2,700		
	Hat Cost of Goods Sold	2,000		
	Other Cost of Goods Sold	1,100		
	Other Direct Expenses	200		
	Total Direct Expenses (Cost of Goods Sold)	$ 6,000		
	Total Gross Profit	$ 25,500	$ 500	$ 26,000 ↑
	Advertising & Marketing	$ 700		
	Website & Branding	1,200		
	Legal & Professional Services	350		
	Office Supplies & Software	1,000		
	Total Indirect Expenses	$ 3,250		
	OPERATING INCOME - PROFIT (LOSS)	$ 22,250	$ 500	$ 22,750 ↑

And here is the impact of that $500 sale on the Balance Sheet:

Making a Sale: Balance Sheet

BALANCE SHEET

ACCOUNT TYPE	ACCOUNT	BEFORE	SERVICE SALE	AFTER
ASSETS	**Current Assets**			
	Cash	$ 15,000	$ 500	$ 15,500 ↑
	Accounts Receivable	2,500		
	Inventory	4,000		
	Total Current Assets	$ 21,500	$ 500	$ 22,000 ↑
	Long-Term Assets			
	Machinery	7,000		
	Total Long-Term Assets	$ 7,000		
TOTAL ASSETS		$ 28,500	$ 500	$ 29,000 ↑
LIABILITIES	**Current Liabilities**			
	Credit Card Balances	6,000		
	Accounts Payable	1,000		
	Total Current Liabilities	$ 7,000		
	Long-Term Liabilities			
	Long-Term Business Loan	12,000		
	Total Long-Term Liabilities	$ 12,000		
TOTAL LIABILITIES		$ 19,000		
TOTAL EQUITY (ASSETS - LIABILITIES)		$ 9,500	$ 500	$ 10,000 ↑

Example 2: Buying Inventory

Now we'll look at the product-based side of Nancy's business, which can be a bit more complex. Let's say Nancy purchases some T-shirt inventory for $1,500. What impact will that transaction have on the financial statements?

Contrary to what you might think, this transaction typically wouldn't affect the P&L at all, at least not just yet. This is because Nancy purchased an asset (inventory), and therefore this transaction will show up initially on the Balance Sheet as an asset, not on the P&L as a cost (because the expense isn't categorized as "cost of goods sold" until the good is actually sold). The value she paid for the inventory will stay there until it is sold to the end customer or is otherwise disposed of (donated, lost, trashed, or determined to be "unsalable"; these determinations are often made during regular inventory counts).

However, on Nancy's Balance Sheet, you'll see a decrease in cash and an increase in inventory related to the purchase, which are both assets. Essentially, she swapped one asset for another (cash for inventory), so the overall effect on equity will also be zero.

Now let's fast-forward to when Nancy *sells* that same inventory. For ease of the example, let's say she sells it all at the same time for $2,500. Here's what the financial statement impact would look like.

To record the sale (similarly to the service-based example):

1. An increase in revenue on her P&L of $2,500

2. An increase in cash on her Balance Sheet of $2,500

That's not the only transaction that needs to be recorded, however. Since an asset was also involved in this transaction (inventory), Nancy needs to remove that inventory from the Balance Sheet, as she no longer owns it.

To remove inventory and record the expense:

1. A decrease in inventory on her Balance Sheet of $1,500

2. An increase in cost of goods sold expense on her P&L of $1,500

Therefore, the ultimate impact on her financial statements from selling the inventory is as follows.

Buying Inventory: Profit and Loss

PROFIT & LOSS

ACCOUNT TYPE	ACCOUNT	BEFORE	PRODUCT SALE	AFTER
INCOME	T-shirt Income	$ 10,000	$ 2,500	$ 12,500 ↑
	Hat Income	12,000		
	Other Product Income	5,500		
	Consulting Income	4,000		
	Total Revenue	$ 31,500	$ 2,500	$ 34,000 ↑
EXPENSES	T-shirt Cost of Goods Sold	$ 2,700	$ 1,500	$ 4,200 ↑
	Hat Cost of Goods Sold	2,000		
	Other Cost of Goods Sold	1,100		
	Other Direct Expenses	200		
	Total Direct Expenses (Cost of Goods Sold)	$ 6,000	$ 1,500	$ 7,500 ↑
	Total Gross Profit	$ 25,500	$ 1,000	$ 26,500 ↑
	Advertising & Marketing	$ 700		
	Website & Branding	1,200		
	Legal & Professional Services	350		
	Office Supplies & Software	1,000		
	Total Indirect Expenses	$ 3,250		
OPERATING INCOME - PROFIT (LOSS)		$ 22,250	$ 1,000	$ 23,250 ↑

Buying Inventory: Balance Sheet

BALANCE SHEET

ACCOUNT TYPE	ACCOUNT	BEFORE	PRODUCT SALE	AFTER
ASSETS	**Current Assets**			
	Cash	$ 15,000	$ 2,500	$ 17,500 ↑
	Accounts Receivable	2,500		
	Inventory	4,000	(1,500)	2,500 ↓
	Total Current Assets	$ 21,500	$ 1,000	$ 22,500 ↑
	Long-Term Assets			
	Machinery	7,000		
	Total Long-Term Assets	$ 7,000		
TOTAL ASSETS		$ 28,500	$ 1,000	$ 29,500 ↑
LIABILITIES	**Current Liabilities**			
	Credit Card Balances	6,000		
	Accounts Payable	1,000		
	Total Current Liabilities	$ 7,000		
	Long-Term Liabilities			
	Long-Term Business Loan	12,000		
	Total Long-Term Liabilities	$ 12,000		
TOTAL LIABILITIES		$ 19,000		
TOTAL EQUITY (ASSETS - LIABILITIES)		$ 9,500	$ 1,000	$ 10,500 ↑

You may have noticed that when your profit goes up, so does your equity (and vice versa!). Your P&L and Balance Sheet are tied together in this symbiotic way. While the rest of this book will largely focus on your P&L and profitability, having a general understanding of how your Balance Sheet plays into the equation is essential for seeing the full picture of your business's health. By understanding your Balance Sheet, including the assets you own, the liabilities you owe, and your overall equity, you will gain insights into your company's stability, liquidity, and ability to grow.

Example 3: Paying Yourself

In this example, we're going to walk through taking a "draw" from your business. Unless you are taxed as a Corporation (which I'll talk about in chapter 16), you'll generally pay yourself with draws from your business profit. Importantly, these draws come from your business's *equity* (as well as your bank account) and won't be found anywhere on your P&L. Why? The P&L is designed to track your business's income and expenses—essentially, what your business earns and spends in its operations. Draws, however, are not operational expenses; they're withdrawals of your ownership share, similar to transferring money from one pocket to another.

Categorizing your owner's draws properly isn't just about following accounting rules; it's also important for tax purposes. Mixing draws with your P&L could lead to inaccurate financial statements and potentially incorrect tax filings. The key is to remember that your P&L is all about how much your business is making and spending. Draws are not part of that; they're simply how you access your share of the profit. The only time a payment to yourself will show up on the P&L is if you own a Corporation and pay yourself a salary as an employee (and issue yourself a W-2 at the end of the year). In general, any other payments to yourself will come from your equity, which represents your share of the profit as an owner.

When you take money out of your business, it has the impact of reducing the overall equity that is still held in your business. Ultimately, your equity is your ownership interest that you haven't distributed to yourself yet. If you have negative equity, that often means the amount you've paid yourself from your business exceeds your cumulative profit since starting the business. Negative equity also means that your existing liabilities exceed your existing assets. As stated above, this could be a negative sign to potential creditors or investors. If you are a Corporation, it can also have negative tax consequences. Increasing your profit and decreasing your liabilities is essential to improving the overall health of a business with negative (or low) equity.

Hidden Profit

Since Nancy's business is an LLC (not taxed as a Corporation), all payments to herself are made from equity. Here's the financial statement impact of her paying herself $5,000 from her business.

Paying Yourself: Balance Sheet

BALANCE SHEET

ACCOUNT TYPE	ACCOUNT	BEFORE	OWNER DRAW	AFTER
ASSETS	Current Assets			
	Cash	$ 15,000	$ (5,000)	$ 10,000 ↓
	Accounts Receivable	2,500		
	Inventory	4,000		
	Total Current Assets	$ 21,500	$ (5,000)	$ 16,500 ↓
	Long-Term Assets			
	Machinery	7,000		
	Total Long-Term Assets	$ 7,000		
TOTAL ASSETS		$ 28,500	$ (5,000)	$ 23,500 ↓
LIABILITIES	Current Liabilities			
	Credit Card Balances	6,000		
	Accounts Payable	1,000		
	Total Current Liabilities	$ 7,000		
	Long-Term Liabilities			
	Long-Term Business Loan	12,000		
	Total Long-Term Liabilities	$ 12,000		
TOTAL LIABILITIES		$ 19,000		
TOTAL EQUITY (ASSETS - LIABILITIES)		$ 9,500	$ (5,000)	$ 4,500 ↓

Should You Use a Spreadsheet or Accounting Software?

If you are just starting out or have a simple service-based business and no employees, a spreadsheet is probably the most economical way to track your income and expenses, at least for now. Personally, I love bookkeeping software and all the extra functionality and ease it can provide, but the monthly cost and learning curve associated with using it properly can be prohibitive. There is no shame in using a spreadsheet to keep track of things.

Remember that you're not just keeping track of your finances for tax purposes; your spreadsheet should be organized in such a way that you can easily see the important financial data that you need. Starting with a P&L template (like the one available at HiddenProfitTheBook.com) is a low-cost way to keep things tidy and helpful.

That said, if you are already using accounting software and have kept up with your bookkeeping, you likely already have a P&L and Balance Sheet that can be generated automagically. Log in and take a look at where you stand. Note that if your accounting software doesn't allow you to run a Balance Sheet, it likely isn't doing official "double-entry" bookkeeping and is just a glorified spreadsheet tracking your income and expenses. This may be fine early on in a business or for a very simple service-based business model, but it likely isn't the best long-term option for those who want to grow and scale up.

In general, as your business grows, you'll need more information. For example, you will need a Balance Sheet if and when you take on debt, buy assets (such as machinery and equipment), try to attract investors, or take on partners. You'll also need one for tax purposes if you plan to be taxed as a Corporation down the line (or if you already are one!).

Accounting software has come a long way. Cloud-based software now allows for automations and integrations, such as pulling your financial information directly from your bank and credit card accounts, and allows collaboration among multiple users in real time, including access from mobile devices. AI features within these programs can also help cut down on manual work and even give you insights into your business's performance.

That said, if you plan to do your own bookkeeping, know that software can take some time to learn and there are common things that can go wrong if it isn't set up properly or you don't know how to use it (such as entering revenue twice or missing expenses).

Overall, the key is to find a system that works for you so that you have ready access to your business data when you need it. Remember, the first step in understanding your financial data is paying attention to it. If you don't have a system to collect and organize that data, you won't be able to utilize it fully, which means that you'll be missing out on potential profit.

Get Support

If this feels like a lot, I get it. As your business grows and becomes more complex, hiring a bookkeeper to keep your financial records straight can be a great investment. What a bookkeeper specifically does can vary based on the provider and the needs of your business, but in general, they can help you organize your financial records and generate accurate financial statements. These days, most bookkeepers use software that gives you real-time access to your financial data.

In my experience, most business owners hold on to their bookkeeping and tax functions *way* longer than they should. There are a few reasons for this. Our business finances feel personal, and letting someone else see everything can feel as though we're stripping ourselves naked in front of a stranger. Fear of judgment and embarrassment are real. But one thing I can tell you with certainty is that your financial records *aren't* the worst that service provider has ever seen. They're probably not even in the top ten. And a good professional will never judge you.

After all, bookkeepers and accountants exist because what they do isn't everyone's forte but numbers are what they are good at and enjoy working with. (Yes, some people *do* enjoy navigating the tax code.) If you are nervous about letting someone see "behind the curtain," that's normal. Spend some time shopping around for the right fit. Being comfortable with someone goes a long way, and you'll also feel more secure asking them questions, which is the best way to learn.

Another reason people tend to avoid outsourcing bookkeeping and tax duties is the belief that it's cheaper to do it yourself. Sure, continuing to do these duties might save you a bit of money in the short run, but in the long run it is likely costing you.

Using qualified professionals for bookkeeping and taxes reduces the risk of errors that could lead to penalties and interest, plus they may find additional opportunities for tax savings you didn't know about. They can also help make sure you stay on top of your financials, especially if you have a tendency to procrastinate (no judgment, it happens to the best of us!).

Not only that, but hiring a service provider helps free up your time as the business owner to focus on more important things that only you can do. What if you could reclaim those arduous hours spent organizing receipts and categorizing transactions and instead channel them back into your business so you could spend more time focused on sales and financial strategy instead of busywork?

Or perhaps you could free up a little bit of your time to spend with the people you care about. There is an opportunity cost every time we choose one activity over another. I'm not sure about you, but I *don't* have endless time, and try as I might, I can't do everything myself. In fact, trying to be a super(wo)man could negatively impact your business potential. It may be time to let go so you can level up!

The easiest (and least expensive) tasks to outsource are the ones that tend to be the most tedious. Professionals are great at keeping you organized and compliant, but you'll still want to keep a close eye on your financials. The great thing is, when you free up your time from some of the nitty-gritty that others are more qualified to do, you will have more time (and up-to-date data) to help you focus on the bigger financial picture. We'll dive more into those financial management duties in chapter 5.

For more resources to help you get organized, including recommended service providers to assist you and special deals on my recommended bookkeeping software, visit HiddenProfitTheBook.com.

Take Action

Now that you know why your financial data is important outside of tax time and have a general understanding of how financial statements work, it's time to get organized.

If you already have a system for tracking your income and expenses, great! You may want to consider improvements based on what you learn throughout this book, but in my opinion, there's no need to mess with what's already working.

That said, if you're like many entrepreneurs I work with and don't have an effective system in place, you've got some decisions to make. Ask yourself:

- Do you want to use a spreadsheet or software?

- Would you like to hire someone to help, or are you comfortable doing it yourself?

For more guidance, you can find my current software and template recommendations at HiddenProfitTheBook.com.

Wherever you land on this, make it a goal to get your finances organized enough to create a Profit and Loss Statement (and possibly even a Balance Sheet for extra credit!). It doesn't have to be beautiful right now (or ever!). Remember—it doesn't have to be perfect to be useful!

As you go through this book, you'll probably have ideas and aha! moments that will impact how you want to organize your data—and that's a *great* thing. Make yourself a fresh cup of coffee, and get started! You'll be glad you did.

CHAPTER THREE
When Numbers Lie

When I worked as a fractional CFO, I was hired by a winery owned by two friends, Dave and Chuck. Dave ran the tasting room, while Chuck was head winemaker. At the time, they were stumped about why their business wasn't making more money, since more people were coming by the tasting room and buying more wine than ever before.

As CFO, I was tasked with figuring out what the heck was going on. I spent days asking Chuck questions, gathering information, and spreadsheeting my little heart out. I ended up breaking down the profit margins by type of wine and how it was sold: in the tasting room for sample pours and wine by the glass or bottled and shipped out.

Eventually, I realized why they weren't making more money: Their chardonnay—Chuck's favorite to make—wasn't profitable. Like, at all.

But I had a plan to make it more profitable, mostly by raising the price of full bottles. When I told the owners about what I had found, Dave nodded. But Chuck went into full fight mode. He argued that their chardonnay was the winery's biggest seller and that if we put the price up even two dollars per bottle, sales would crater. He tried to poke holes in the data, looking for ways to prove it wrong. Unfortunately for him, what I was saying made sense when we looked at the P&L by product. Every other wine was making money—and the buttery, delicious chardonnay simply wasn't.

Because Chuck so badly wanted to support his previous decisions (and avoid feeling as though he had priced the chardonnay too low in the first place), he didn't want to acknowledge what was right in front of him.

Rather than letting the data show him the way forward, he doubled down on his beliefs. At the time, I didn't understand why we make the decisions we do, much less our psychological dependence on past choices. I just knew that I had an answer to their profitability problem and was stumped at why Chuck was so committed to losing money on the admittedly great-tasting wine.

After seeing this dynamic play out over and over again with entrepreneurs, I can tell you from experience that numbers themselves may be emotionless but humans are anything but. In this chapter, I'll help you avoid becoming like Chuck—so stuck in the perception of the way the data *should* be that you avoid the real story.

When Data Lies

In the last chapter, you learned how to read your financial statements. Now it's time to interpret what they are telling us. In his book *The Psychology of Money: Timeless Lessons on Wealth, Greed, and Happiness*, Morgan Housel wrote, "Financial success is not a hard science. It's a soft skill, where how you behave is more important than what you know."[1]

In addition to learning how to read financial statements (a hard skill), you need to learn how best to stay out of your own way (a soft skill). That's what working with small-business owners such as Dave and Chuck taught me. Below, I'm going to talk you through some of the ways numbers can lie to us (or really, how we lie to ourselves) and how we can avoid these pitfalls.

Pitfall 1: Having Disorganized or Incomplete Data

When looking at our business's numbers, we must focus on making sure that our data is *clean*, meaning that it is both *accurate* and *well organized*.

To obtain accurate data, you need to ensure that all data is being pulled in from all relevant sources. If transactions are miskeyed, left out, or double counted, your financial statements won't be accurate. Not only will that affect your ability to make informed decisions about your business, but it can also result in your paying too much or too little in taxes.

And while paying too little may not sound so bad, most of us probably want to stay in the good graces of Uncle Sam without having to worry about interest, fines, and penalties down the road. Using bookkeeping software can make life easier, but it isn't without its own drawbacks. While I love the ease that accounting software can bring to an otherwise tedious task, we mustn't put too much stock in any algorithm to get it right. In my experience, overreliance on automation within software is a leading cause of bookkeeping errors and tax deadline–induced migraines.

How can we make sure that our financial data is accurate?

First, check for **completeness**: Are all transactions being pulled in correctly? Are you missing anything? If you're using bookkeeping software, it can be helpful to understand how information is fed into any integrated systems.

Regularly running a P&L for your business and doing a sense check is critical to finding data problems in a timely manner. It's much easier to pinpoint and fix an error that has been happening for a month versus one that has occurred repeatedly for an entire year. If income or expenses look higher or lower than you had expected, drill into the data and look for the culprit. Often, the discrepancy is pretty evident.

By far the best way to determine if there are errors in your financial statements is to do regular reconciliations. If you just groaned audibly, I'm not judging you. Reconciliations are a giant pain in the backside. But they serve an important purpose, and that purpose isn't just to torture you (believe it or not). At their most basic, reconciliations involve comparing your internal accounting records to external sources such as bank and credit card statements. Reconciliations ensure that all transactions that hit your bank account or credit card statement are also captured in your accounting records. However, *where* these transactions show up on the financial statements can differ based on the type of transaction, and some can impact both the P&L and the Balance Sheet (see the discussion of how these statements work together in chapter 2). The reconciliation process is crucial for verifying the completeness of your bookkeeping and catching any unrecorded transactions or other discrepancies that may affect the accuracy of your financials.

When things don't match up, consider it a giant red blinking warning sign that something is off on your financial statements. If you feel qualified, you can use this information to Sherlock Holmes the issue yourself. However, if you are routinely having reconciliation issues, it's probably time to bring in a professional to help sort things out (and save your sanity).

Let's say you've done your reviews and reconciliations and have confidence that your data is accurate. That's awesome! Now it's time to turn your attention to making sure it is also **well organized**.

Accurate data that is haphazardly organized isn't going to be very helpful when it comes to making business decisions. For example, you may have an accurate laundry list of expenses listed on a spreadsheet, but it's probably not going to be super meaningful for analyzing business performance. Similarly, if you use accounting software to categorize expenses but aren't consistent when allocating expenses into categories, the resulting reports aren't going to be helpful.

Take Erin, a licensed private practice therapist who joined one of my programs. Erin struggled with making decisions in her business and wanted to understand how to use her numbers to help her grow. When I asked her how often she looked at her P&L, she chuckled. She had tried for a long time to understand her P&L, but she couldn't see how it was useful. She told me that it felt like complete "mumbo jumbo."

When I had Erin show me her P&L, I knew immediately why it was unhelpful for her. Her P&L was *five pages* long. *Of course* it wasn't helpful. While the data was accurate, it was anything but well organized.

I explained to Erin that a P&L was meant to be a summary of what had happened in her business over a specified period. Ideally, it would fit on *one* page. As it turned out, she had routinely been creating new accounts whenever she didn't know where to categorize a particular transaction, which had led to an unwieldy (and unhelpful) P&L. Additionally, she was inconsistent with her categorizations; sometimes she'd categorize a particular expense as software, sometimes as marketing expense, and other times as office expense. Her categories were all over the place.

I explained to Eirn that simpler is always better and consistency is key. *Where* she categorized a particular expense on her P&L was decidedly less critical than ensuring that she used the *same category* for the *same expense* the *same way* each time. With a few exceptions (such as meals and entertainment), the tax treatment of an expense is generally the same regardless of where it ends up on your P&L. I explained to Erin that rather than letting taxes dictate how she categorized her P&L, she should instead consider what would be most helpful *for her* to see when making decisions in her business. That shift was huge for Erin, and it can be for you, too.

If your P&L doesn't mean much to you right now and makes you think "Wow, that's a lot of mumbo jumbo," take a step back and look at how it is organized.

- Can you see the key pieces of information you would want to see?
- Is it concise enough to be digested easily?
- Are things categorized consistently period over period?

If there's something you don't understand or that isn't helpful, give yourself permission to change it. If someone else is doing your bookkeeping, have a conversation with them about what data you'd like to highlight. They'll likely be able to work their magic to make it happen for you, including fine-tuning your P&L and setting up supplementary reports with all the useful financial info you need to run your business. Remember, your bookkeeper doesn't typically know what you want until you tell them, so don't be shy when it comes to asking for what you need.

Pitfall 2: Hiding Your Head in the Sand

Denise was a wedding venue owner with a self-professed "phobia" about numbers and finances. She loved to create beautiful moments for her brides but found herself avoiding the numbers side of her business. Just thinking about finances brought up a host of insecurities and worries, so she typically opted to put it out of her mind entirely—at least until she found herself at a "make it or break it" moment that required her to either make her business work financially or sell the venue that she adored.

Avoiding financial problems—or not looking at your numbers in the first place—is one of the most common errors I see when it comes to business. Unfortunately, it sometimes takes a do-or-die moment for people to prioritize their finances. Even then, I often see a focus on finding a short-term fix instead of a long-term solution. Most business owners I've worked with have been more reactive than proactive when it comes to their finances, which means they aren't as prepared as they could be for challenges that may arise.

Imagine you're on a Sunday drive in your car, gliding down the road singing Wilson Phillips at the top of your lungs. Suddenly the check engine light comes on. Total buzzkill, right? You were just at the high part.

You're now kicking yourself for skipping those regular service visits. You know you have a problem that needs to be addressed, but the light itself won't tell you exactly what needs to be done. You could take your chances and continue driving the vehicle with the light on for a while, but that would create risk and added stress, not to mention the possibility of making the damage worse.

We all know what we *should* do: pause our journey, glide on in to a mechanic, cross our fingers, and find out what's up. The same is true for your business. But in the case of your business, *you* are the mechanic. *You* are the expert in understanding how your business runs and what it needs. That means it's *your* job to interpret your numbers and identify what changes you may need to make to get your finances running smoothly again.

For our wedding venue owner, Denise, the check engine light showed up in the form of cash flow problems, a typical warning sign that something is wrong. And like many business owners, she attempted to ignore them, hoping the problem would fix itself. After all, she told herself, she needed just a few more sales and she'd be just fine.

This is called "ostriching"—the practice of deliberately ignoring information by metaphorically burying one's head in the sand. If we don't actively see the threat, we can pretend it isn't there. But we all know from experience that problems only get worse when we hide from them. We also know that the stress of a looming problem will weigh us down, even if we are doing our best to avoid looking it in the eye. We've all delayed the trip to the mechanic and made things worse (at least I have).

However, when we do gain the courage to confront the threat head-on, we usually find that it isn't as bad as we thought. Or perhaps the situation is very, very bad, but at least now we can make a plan of action rather than waiting for a really negative consequence to pop up while our head is buried in the sand.

Eventually, Denise's cash flow crunch got bad enough that she couldn't ignore the problem anymore. She decided to get help (which was where I came in). Ultimately, we had to take drastic measures to bring cash in quickly to save her beloved business. This is unfortunately how ostriching often goes. As someone who teaches business finances, I know that my content is most searched for when times get tough (whether due to a once-in-a-lifetime pandemic or a typical economic downturn). But you *don't* have to wait for the check engine light to come on to get a handle on your finances. Just as with a vehicle, regular attention and maintenance will prevent the vast majority of problems.

Since you're reading this book, you've made the active choice not to hide your head in the sand. This already puts you into the very small category of small-business owners who actively seek out financial guidance. Keep up the good work. As you go through this book, don't forget to check where your head is at. If you're avoiding doing something, I encourage you to breathe for a second and then take action. This is some of the most important work you can do for your business, so keep going! You're on the right track.

Pitfall 3: Ego

Dr. Stelmaszak, my AP Statistics teacher, could have been on *Saved by the Bell*. A zany, high-energy, pocket protector–wearing nerd, he helped foster my love of numbers as a teenager. On the first day of class, he opened with a quote attributed to Mark Twain that inspired this chapter: "There are three kinds of lies: lies, damned lies, and statistics."

The older I've gotten, the more I've been able to see the wisdom of Dr. Stelmaszak's words. People tend to trust information that supports what they already believe, whether it's news filtered through social media or the bottom-line number on their P&L. They also discount or toss away what doesn't line up with their beliefs or way of thinking about the world.

In the winery example, Chuck ignored the data that indicated an issue with the profitability of his beloved chardonnay. In that case, it was more comfortable for him to believe a lie than to come to terms with the fact that he was selling a product for less than the cost to make it. His behavior was confirmation bias at its finest—or should I say, at its worst.

Our brains are evolutionarily designed to pick and choose what data to focus on and what to ignore. And while it's important to have an internal filtration system for determining what is important, our biases often show up when we're dealing with data—especially in our own business. We assume that data that is contrary to our existing beliefs is an anomaly and resist delving deeper. Left to our own devices, we will make any data we are presented with match our existing views. It's psychologically much easier to discount data than wrestle with what it would mean for our ego if we were wrong.

CHIEF FINANCIAL OPINION:
If You Think You're Always Right, Think Again

If you're reading this and thinking about how confirmation bias applies to other people in your life (your parents, your neighbor, or maybe your old boss), I've got news for you: It *also* applies to you.

Confirmation bias is sneaky because when it happens to you, you can't see it. That's the nature of the phenomenon. Yet it is *extremely* evident in others. This can create a false sense that we're always right and others are always wrong, which continues to feed our ego. But no one is always right. And the first step in defeating confirmation bias is to recognize that it exists within ourselves. That said, obviously you're still going to be right *more often* than other folks. *Obviously.* 😉

For business owners, especially those who feel emotionally tied to the businesses they've built, this can show up as ignoring or misinterpreting their financial data—*especially* when we've already invested a significant amount of time or money into something that hasn't panned out as we'd hoped. We want to believe that we've made a good decision. If we bail out, that means admitting to ourselves that we may have wasted precious time or resources. So we stick with something for longer than we should, telling ourselves that we'll eventually get our money's worth out of it—someday.

This is the "sunk cost fallacy" in action, a well-documented human psychological phenomenon. It typically shows up as a bias toward continuing to invest in something that hasn't yielded the expected return. Rather than cut our losses and recognize those past investments as sunk costs (i.e., learning opportunities for the future), we often throw good money after bad to appease our ego.

Let's say you hired an employee and spent time and money training them for their job duties. You've employed them for a year and in that time have realized that they aren't meeting the expectations for the job. After a good-faith effort to help them improve their performance, it's clear that the job duties just don't align with the employee's skill set or interests. What would you do?

If we're being honest, many of us would probably keep that employee longer than we really should. We want to justify our decision to hire them, plus we know that hiring and training another employee to take their place will take even more time and effort on our part. However, we're only delaying the inevitable by continuing to try to make it work and spending more money and time in the long run. We aren't doing the employee any favors, either, as they would be more satisfied in a job that better matched their skill set and interests.

The sunk cost fallacy also shows up as costs that we continue to pay, even though we aren't actively using what we're paying for. Maybe it's a software subscription or a membership we haven't been utilizing. Deciding to pull the plug can create feelings of shame and loss, so we often don't make a decision at all. And so the money continues to be drained from our bank account, despite bringing us minimal or no return.

That said, there is good news. When the business owners I've worked with finally decide to cut their losses and move on from a past decision that didn't work out, they feel tremendously better. If you've ever had to let an employee go, you've likely felt the weight you carried (sometimes for months) lifted off your shoulders as soon as it was done. The same is true when you make a decision to cut a product line that is bleeding money or a cost that you aren't getting a return from. Anxiety grows in anticipation of making the decision, but generally dissipates once you do so.

Consider: What decisions do you need to make sooner rather than later in your business? Where might you need to cut your losses and move forward? You probably have a gut feeling about this already. Go ahead and rip the bandage off. I promise you'll feel better when it's done. I'd like to say that in business, we shouldn't fear being wrong. But because that's hard to do, I encourage you—as I did in chapter 1—to see "mistakes" as data that can help you in the future.

Most successful people have failed more than they have succeeded. The people you admire understand that there is more to learn from being wrong than from being right and almost always attribute their eventual success to those powerful learned lessons. They don't let their ego get in the way of important lessons that will help carry them toward future success.

In her book *The Path Made Clear: Discovering Your Life's Direction and Purpose*, Oprah Winfrey wrote about a time when she was fired from her job as a news anchor in Baltimore. She was told that she showed too much emotion on-screen. She could have let that failure define her and derail her entire career. Instead, that failure helped her realize that her real strength and passion were connecting with people, so she decided to focus on talk shows, where she could connect more personally. She saw that failure as a gift and let it propel her to becoming the media mogul she is today. As she grew her business empire, she continued to see every failure as a stepping stone to success.

We may not be Oprah, but we can still apply these lessons in our own lives. After some initial pushback, Chuck took some time to check (and recheck) my calculations. Eventually, he realized that the numbers weren't lying. Once he accepted the problem in front of him and the data behind it, he was able to channel his energy into figuring out a solution. As it turned out, the winery didn't have to discontinue his beloved chardonnay. It simply took some tweaks in production techniques and a small price increase to fix the profitability problem. Chuck's ego can still rear its ugly head at times (which happens to the best of us), but now he knows why it's better to be profitable than right!

Pitfall 4: Jumping to Conclusions

Back in the day, Dr. Stelmaszak had one other important lesson for our young minds that I've consistently remembered since that teachable moment back in twelfth grade: "Correlation does not imply causation." Said in plain terms, just because two things have a relationship doesn't mean that one *caused* the other. Here's an example. Matt had recently hired a new barber for his barbershop and was looking for ways to bring in more business now that it had more capacity. He decided to offer a discount to returning customers and saw an uptick in repeat business over the next few months. He assumed that it was the discount that had brought the customers back and planned to make it part of his regular strategy.

However, a closer look at the data showed that the returning customers were already highly loyal. When Matt talked to customers about why they kept coming back, they said that Matt's newest hire was the best barber they'd ever had. Many of the returning customers didn't even know about the discount, and it certainly hadn't influenced their decision to return. Price wasn't a factor for most; instead, they cared about the quality of the haircut.

Matt's story illustrates how two things can move in tandem but not necessarily be causally related. If Matt hadn't dug deeper by talking to customers to confirm his interpretation of the financial data, he would have misinterpreted the actual cause of the uptick in customer retention. In fact, he might have assumed that price mattered first and foremost to his clientele, which could have pushed him to sacrifice quality and client experience to lower prices even further. Over time, that strategy would likely have backfired.

It's important to realize that numbers alone won't tell you the whole story. Often, we need to collect more anecdotal data as well, such as customer feedback. Collecting both quantitative and qualitative data will allow for the most well-rounded insights. Rather than over-relying on one or the other, the best observations are the product of looking at both in tandem.

Let's turn back to your business and look at how you might assume a cause-and-effect relationship between two data points, even when one isn't actually causing the other. Say you are analyzing your P&L and notice that months with higher ad spend have higher sales. You may conclude that the additional advertising is what led to the higher sales and use that assumption to justify increasing your advertising budget. But if you look closer, you might notice that you just happened to run more advertising during periods when sales (and therefore discretionary cash balances) were naturally higher.

So how can we know what's really going on? We dig deeper. We test assumptions. We collect qualitative data. We double-check conclusions. We resist the urge to oversimplify our observations. In most cases, the real answer is more nuanced and impacted by a multitude of factors. Just make sure that any conclusions you draw are truly supported by the facts and you aren't jumping to conclusions too quickly.

Getting to the Truth

Every time I run my own numbers, I think about what Dr. Stelmaszak taught me about how data and statistics can lie. Ensuring that your financial data is both accurate and well organized is about more than just avoiding an audit by the IRS. Doing so helps you make key decisions that could be the difference between a thriving business and a failing one. Because of how much psychology is involved, it's important to check that what we think is happening with our data is actually the capital-T Truth.

> **Before drawing conclusions based on data, put it through the "Truth Test" questions:**

Truth Test 1: How was this data collected? How do I know it is complete and accurate?

Truth Test 2: Who collected and/or compiled this data? Do they have a bias that might impact the collection or interpretation of the results?

Truth Test 3: Am I letting an emotional reaction to the data obscure what it's trying to tell me? Am I fighting the results, or preemptively justifying why I can't make a change?

Truth Test 4: Am I jumping to any conclusions when interpreting this data? Are there any other possible explanations for the results I'm seeing?

Take Action

When you have a big business decision to make, consider what you learned in this chapter. To be short and sweet:

1. Is your data organized and complete? Or a hot mess?
2. Are you looking for the truth—or ignoring what's really happening?
3. When you look at the data, are you in your feelings?
4. Have you considered all the possible explanations?

Next, you will want to run the Truth Tests listed above. The answers to those questions, combined with the other sources and kinds of data in your business that I'm about to share in the next few chapters, will help you make smart, data-savvy decisions.

CHAPTER FOUR
Create Your Own Performance Metrics

Lisa owns an e-commerce business specializing in stylish maternity swimsuits. She monitors her sales numbers daily and reviews her P&L from her bookkeeper on a monthly basis. Because of this, she knows how profitable her business is and how sales have been trending. Everything seems good—but the future always feels uncertain. Lisa never knows if her sales will dip suddenly, and she avoids reinvesting into her business out of fear that she'll need the money later. Even though her business is profitable now, she struggles with anxiety about its future. She constantly feels on edge, as if she's waiting for the other shoe to fall.

If you feel as Lisa does, you're not alone. I have felt this way and know several other entrepreneurs who do as well. At times, I've even worried that I'm not cut out for entrepreneurship, despite having built a thriving financial education business from the ground up. As an accountant by background, I'm not exactly wired to throw caution to the wind. Yet when talking with the vast majority of highly successful entrepreneurs I know, I've found that most of them don't consider themselves to be avid risk takers, either. In fact, many long to feel more secure in their business and finances, just as Lisa does.

That caution and wariness make sense. Most of us have families to feed and lives to live. So how do we grow our businesses? How do we know what risks are worth taking? How do we shake the underlying dread we hold in our bodies over what the future holds?

I'm sure my answer won't surprise you: When in doubt, finding the answers comes down to data. But what data should we be looking at?

By now you know that understanding your P&L can give you a great snapshot of how your business is performing over a certain period of time. However, as critical as the P&L is, it only scratches the surface as far as important data goes. Your P&L can tell you if you are on the right track and even give you some insights into potential problems, but it won't give you everything you need. Partly that's because a P&L measures the past. While understanding our past performance is helpful, it isn't always indicative of what the future holds. For that, we'll have to dive a bit deeper, into the world of metrics.

If the last sentence makes you feel tempted to close this book and pour yourself a glass of pinot noir, I understand. The great news is that metrics *don't* need to be complicated. After all, a metric is simply a measure of something. We use metrics constantly in our daily lives without thinking about it. Your car's fuel gauge is a metric showing you how much gas you have left. Your Apple Watch tracking your steps is a metric that tells you how active you've been. Your grades in school are metrics telling you how you are performing in a given class. Metrics are so interwoven into our lives that most of the time, we don't even realize that we're looking at a metric.

What's the difference between data and a metric? Data is generally raw and unorganized; a metric is typically a calculation that uses data but puts it into a more meaningful form. Metrics are generally more specific and have goals attached to them. In essence, data is the ingredients; metrics are the meal.

Anything that can be measured can be turned into a metric. In business, these are often referred to as *performance metrics*. Think about all the things you could measure when it comes to your business. There is probably no shortage of metrics that you could track if you wanted to. In my own business, I could probably come up with a thousand-plus if you gave me all the time in the world (and some strong coffee). Sales conversions, the relationship of budgeted to actual expenses, refund rates, employee productivity, employee turnover, manufacturing time, energy efficiency, customer satisfaction—the list can go on and on (and on).

If we tried to track everything, there's a 100 percent chance that we'd be overwhelmed by the logistics of gathering the data and quit tracking much of anything at all. As the saying goes, when everything is important, nothing is important. While there may be dozens of metrics that could be helpful for your business, there are probably only a handful that are *really* make-or-break.

This is where **Key Performance Indicators (KPIs)** come into play. Essentially, KPIs are what you deem to be your business's most critical metrics. While all KPIs are metrics, not all metrics are KPIs. Starting with five to ten KPIs will help you focus your efforts on what is *most* important. At a high level, a good KPI will be:

1. Insightful into your business and an aid to decision-making

2. Measurable

3. Attached to a goal

Additionally, when selecting KPIs, you'll want to make sure you have both leading and lagging indicators.

- A **lagging indicator** is an indicator of the past that measures how our business has *already* performed.

- A **leading indicator** is an indicator of performance that *predicts* future success.

Put another way, a lagging indicator tells us how our business has previously performed, whereas a leading indicator gives us an indication of what we can expect to happen in the future.

The profit shown on your P&L is a lagging indicator. It shows you the profitability of your business in the past, which may or may not be predictive of the future. While these numbers are good to know and can be helpful for future decision-making, they don't specifically give any clues to what may happen down the road.

Going back to the example of our swimsuit entrepreneur, Lisa, the reason she felt uneasy about the future was because both of the data sets she was relying on—each day's sales and her overall P&L—were lagging indicators. Those data points told her how things had gone before or were going that day but didn't necessarily give her insight into how things were going to go from there. In order to reduce her anxiety about the future, Lisa needed to have a data point that was more predictive.

That was why I advised her to include a few leading indicators as KPIs. Leading indicators function as fortune tellers, giving entrepreneurs a glimpse into the future. For Lisa, the percentage of customers who open her daily email offering new styles often predicts how many swimsuits she will sell that day. Her email open rates were therefore a *leading indicator* to sales. If Lisa sees her email open rates continuously dropping, it's likely that her sales won't be as good in the immediate future.

For many entrepreneurs, the number of new leads coming in or sales calls scheduled is an important leading indicator. Fewer leads (and fewer calls) typically mean fewer sales. Similarly, for entrepreneurs such as Lisa, a leading indicator could also be the number of people who visit her website. How many visits is she getting per month, and how is that traffic trending? Since Lisa knows that most people visit her site three to four times before buying, if she sees an uptick in new website traffic, she can expect to see an uptick in sales, too (and vice versa).

Leading indicators can give you important clues that you can use to make critical improvements. But in order to create clean, easy-to-interpret data, it's important to have both leading and lagging indicators represented in your KPIs in order to get the clearest picture of where you've been and where you're going.

Without leading indicators, you will miss the chance to catch and resolve potential problems before they become major issues. Without lagging indicators, you won't have any historical context to baseline against. Together, all of the indicators can give you a more robust picture of what's happening in your business.

Which Metrics to Pick

Which metrics to pick as your KPIs will depend on the specifics of your business. Sorry—this is another place where there is no "right" or "wrong" answer. However, there is a right question to ask yourself: What data would be most helpful for me to see when making decisions in my business? Don't censor your answer to this question, and don't worry about the "how" right now. Once you've defined what's important, you (or a hired pro) can typically get access to the data you need. The hard part is deciding what you want to track.

I suggest you start by writing down anything that could be helpful to see in your business. If it helps you, feel free to search "KPIs for [insert your business niche here]" on your favorite browser or AI tool. Checking out what other businesses track can be a great starting point, but each business is unique. Any metrics you decide to track should be information you plan to *use* in your business to measure and improve it. If you start tracking a metric and find out it isn't as useful as you thought, there's good news: You're the boss, and you can change your metrics anytime you want!

As a starting point, here are a few common metrics used by small businesses of all kinds.

- **Profit Margins by Product or Service:** What is your gross profit on a per-sale basis for each product or service? (More on this in chapter 7.)
- **Cost per Lead:** How many advertising dollars does it cost to get a lead?
- **Qualified Leads per Month:** How many qualified leads per month are you getting?

- **Conversion Rate:** How many leads are you turning into customers?

- **Customer Loyalty and Retention:** What percentage of customers buy from you again?

- **Cost of Customer Acquisition:** How much does it cost, on average, to obtain a client? (Generally, this can be obtained by dividing total marketing dollars spent by the number of new clients over the same time range.)

- **Customer Lifetime Value:** How much revenue does a customer generally produce for you over the lifetime of being a customer? Knowing your Customer Lifetime Value will also require tracking your Customer Retention. The longer you retain a customer, the higher that person's Lifetime Value. (Hint: You want their lifetime value to be a good bit *more than* your Cost of Customer Acquisition.)

- **Average Transaction Price:** How much does the average customer pay per transaction?

- **Occupancy Rate:** What percentage of appointments is booked? What percentage goes unbooked?

- **Monthly Website Traffic:** How many people visit your website monthly?

- **Email Open Rate:** How many customers open your emails regularly?

- **Days Invoices Outstanding:** How long does it take your customers to pay?

- **Customer Satisfaction** (also called **Net Promoter Score**): How satisfied are your customers, and how willing are they to promote your business and drive its sales? (This could be found out via a survey or other feedback instrument.)

- **Inventory Turnover:** On average, how long does it take to sell your inventory?

Remember, this list is just a starting point. While many of these might seem worthy of tracking in your business, it's best to start with a few and add more later as needed. Something you may notice is that some of these metrics actually require several pieces of information in order to calculate them properly.

For example, to calculate average transaction price, you'll need two data points: your total revenue and your total number of transactions. When you set your KPIs, you'll also want to break down the related pieces of information you'll need in order to calculate the KPI itself. These submetrics may or may not be KPIs themselves, but you'll need to have a way to track that information either way.

Create Your KPI Dashboard

Remember when we talked about clean data in chapter 2? If you recall, one of the requirements for gathering clean data is clear *organization*. If you are anything like me, having an easy-to-read visual representation of your data is key to making sense of it. This is where your KPI Dashboard comes in.

Creating a KPI Dashboard where you record all of the key metrics for your business in one central place can be a game changer. You don't need to buy fancy (and expensive) software for this; you can start by using a simple spreadsheet. If you have KPIs that correspond to specific departments or teams within your business (what I refer to as *departmental KPIs*), each department could keep track of its metrics on its own KPI Dashboard that it can share with the group. The goal is to be able to see what's happening in the business at a glance. If things are going well, the KPI Dashboard will give you insight into what is working well. If things aren't going particularly great, it will show you what may need fixing. A KPI Dashboard also includes metrics related to prior periods, allowing you to see not only how things are going today but also how performance has changed over time.

Metrics you intend to track, including KPIs, should be reviewed at least monthly. You may even decide to give "ownership" of the metric to specific members of your team, who will then compile the relevant data. Having team members present this data at monthly meetings can help others get a feel for the state of the company and also give everyone opportunities to voice ideas for improvement. Some of my team's best ideas have come from discussing performance metrics at one of our team meetings. For example, we track our Conversion Rate closely. If we see these numbers dip, we'll brainstorm how we could improve. Sometimes it's by sprucing up the sales page, adding payment plan options, or implementing a way for customers to reach out to us with questions before they buy. Reviewing metrics at least monthly also gives you insight into whether any changes made after last month's review have made a noticeable impact on your KPIs. Seeing positive results can be a powerful motivator for both you and your team.

Take Action

Ready to have a little fun with metrics? Grab that glass of pinot noir you've been craving, and let's brainstorm some KPIs for your business together! Get out your pen and answer the questions below. I recommend setting a five-minute timer for each question. Give yourself enough time to brainstorm effectively but not enough time to overanalyze.

1. Write down as many metrics as you can think of that would be relevant to your business (whether you know how to find the numbers or not). Don't edit this yet or pick your KPIs; that will come later. Feel free to start with the list in this chapter as a starting point, but don't be afraid to expand on it!

2. Look at the list you just created. Circle five to ten items that would be most useful to track routinely. Ensure that you have selected both lagging and leading indicators. (I recommend that profitability always be one of your KPIs.)

3. Finalize your KPIs. If there are submetrics you need to access in order to calculate them, write these down as well. Brainstorm how you could access this data. Is there a system that already collects some or all of this information? Do you need to change anything about how the data is fed into your system in order to pull the right data out of it? Make a game plan for gathering the data.

4. **Optional:** Come up with tentative targets for your KPIs. You can finalize these later (perhaps after discussing them with your team and reading the rest of this book). Once you have your KPIs and tentative targets, you can create your own KPI Dashboard (or snag our free KPI Dashboard Template at HiddenProfitTheBook.com).

PART II

Set Up Your Management Control Room

As an entrepreneur, you have no shortage of things to manage in your business. You're responsible for making sure that you keep accurate records, file taxes on time, have enough cash on hand to pay the bills, make pricing and budget decisions, manage risk, and forecast the future—and that's just the money side of the job!

If it feels like a lot, that's because it is. But these responsibilities don't have to feel like a chaotic juggling act, with all the tasks threatening to hit the ground at once. In this section, I'll show you how to step up to the challenge and regain control of your time, your task list, and ultimately your mental space.

Imagine that you have your own Financial Control Room, filled with buttons, switches, gauges, and levers, each controlling an element of your business's finances. At first, it might seem a little chaotic. You might see warning lights flashing or hear alarms beeping, alerting you to areas needing attention. But as you familiarize yourself with it, you'll gain confidence and realize that each control has a purpose and a function. In time, the room will become less confusing and less overwhelming, and you'll know how to operate the vessel that is your business with ease and mastery.

In this section, I'll break down the essential financial duties of your business and show you how to manage each efficiently and effectively. Think of it as learning to operate your Financial Control Room: understanding each button, lever, and gauge so that you can confidently steer your business toward success.

By the end of part II, you'll know exactly where to focus your energy, and you'll gain some quick wins that will make managing your finances simpler and easier. This is your opportunity to step into the role of CFO for your business, fully equipped to use your Financial Control Room and chart a clear path to financial health—and growth.

CHAPTER FIVE
Manage Your To-Do List

As a new entrepreneur starting a skin care business geared toward men, Joseph found himself feeling overwhelmed by his financial duties. Between making federal and state tax filings, paying suppliers, navigating banks and credit cards, taking payments from customers, collecting sales taxes, and determining prices for his products, he felt completely out of his depth. His financial to-do list was long and getting longer. Just as soon as he thought he had things under control, he'd get another letter in the mail about some state tax he hadn't paid that he didn't even know existed. At times, he wondered if chasing his dream was worth all the hassle.

Reading this right now, you are probably your business's CEO, CFO, Treasurer, Chief Accounting Officer, and Accounts Payable/Receivable Clerk, among many other things. No wonder you feel overwhelmed! You're carrying out so many duties that it can be tough to be effective at any one of them, much less all of them. Even if you have help to do some of these tasks, it's likely that you're still heavily involved in them.

To curb overwhelm, simplify your to-do list, and free up your mental space, it's helpful to think of your money management tasks in three distinct buckets. I'll call these the "Big Three" financial duties:

- **Compliance:** Filing your taxes and managing your business's risk

- **Cash management:** Having enough money on hand to pay your bills and run your business

- **Strategy:** Figuring out how to make more money and become more profitable

Compliance is what you *have* to do to stay—you guessed it—*compliant* with the rules and regulations of the country, state, or city where you live. Keeping your accounting records (i.e., your "books") up to date and complete and filing taxes in a timely manner and accurately are both compliance activities. In larger Corporations, this department is typically led by the Corporate Controller.

It can be helpful to think of these as "stay out of jail" duties (aka very important activities!).

Cash management is about making sure you have enough cash to run your operations, which may include raising capital or taking on debt. Cash management includes figuring out the optimal timing for making purchases, paying bills, and paying yourself. In the corporate world, you'd typically see these duties falling to the Treasurer.

You can think of these as your "avoid bankruptcy" duties (another must-do!).

And last, **strategy** entails making the big-picture financial decisions around pricing, how much money to reinvest into your business, forecasting future profit, and examining the mixture of products and services you offer. Corporations typically have a Chief Financial Officer (CFO) to oversee this function. Not surprisingly, the CFO is the right hand of the Chief Executive Officer (CEO), who sets the vision for the company. When it comes to finances, the CFO is the head honcho, who calls the shots and drives the financial strategy.

In a small business, this is the work that tends to be overlooked when its owner is overloaded with more immediate concerns (such as staying out of jail and avoiding bankruptcy) and understandably so. At the beginning of your entrepreneurial journey, you're likely just trying to stay afloat, but eventually—for your own sanity and the sustainability of your business—strategy should become a major priority.

For me, strategy work is the fun stuff. But if it's not enjoyable to you (yet), you can think of it as what will keep your business healthy and thriving.

Simplifying your financial to-do list to three main functions versus fifty scattered tasks can help the load feel much more manageable. Understanding these three buckets will give you the context behind *why* to do things and help you assess whether you are spending a lot of time in one or two areas while neglecting another.

Joseph realized that most of the time he spent on his financials related to compliance activities, including dealing with those pesky tax notices. He also spent a good deal of time on cash management, though he was more reactive than proactive, dealing with money issues as they came up rather than planning ahead. He entirely neglected strategy, the very area that would support his long-term business goals the most. His financial to-do list was totally out of whack and needed an overhaul if he was to reach his potential as an entrepreneur. Recognizing this, he decided to take control.

Now let's return to our Financial Control Room.

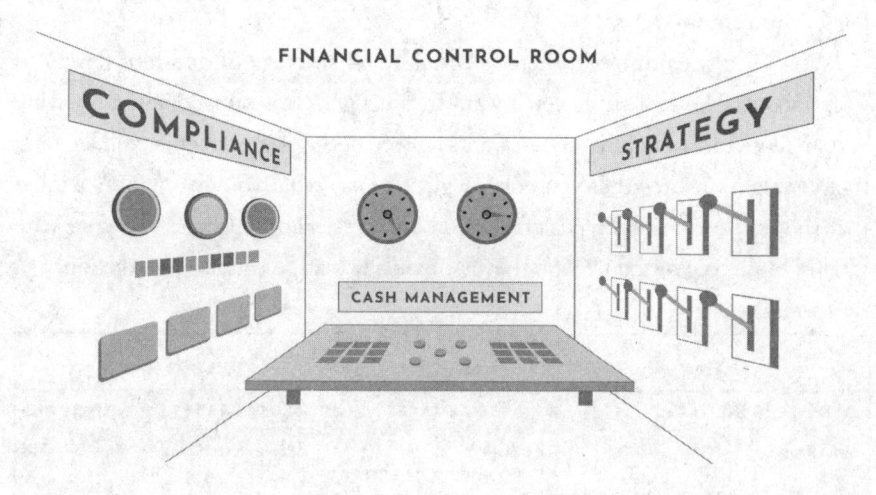

FINANCIAL CONTROL ROOM

COMPLIANCE — CASH MANAGEMENT — STRATEGY

As the control room operator, what exactly can Joseph (and you!) do to keep all of the financial duties running smoothly? Let's dive deeper into all of those switches, gauges, and levers to understand how they relate to the Big Three financial duties.

Compliance

When you walk into your Financial Control Room, to the right you see a series of safety switches on the wall. Some are green, while others are blinking yellow or red. The lights represent your Compliance financial duties, including federal, state, and local tax obligations, regulatory requirements, and other necessary filings. They're the safeguards that keep your business running legally and securely, warning you when something needs immediate attention to avoid penalties or issues. Your job as the business owner is to make sure these switches stay green, so your business stays in good standing and you can focus on growth without having to worry about compliance issues sneaking up on you.

Compliance duties are the first of the Big Three financial duties. They are incredibly important because neglecting them can get you into hot water *fast*. If we don't make compliance a priority when we start our business, we almost always end up learning those lessons the hard way.

The first step in making sure no alarms go off? Understanding your tax and legal requirements.

When it comes to taxes, there is certainly no shortage of different flavors to worry about. The first thing you'll want to do is get clear on *who* you are paying certain taxes to. Every jurisdiction wants a piece of the proverbial pie, and keeping them straight ensures that you don't neglect to pay what you owe. Here's a table that shows the common types of taxes on businesses and business owners in the United States organized by who they are typically paid to (the tax jurisdiction).

TAXES IN THE US

FEDERAL TAXES	STATE TAXES	LOCAL TAXES (COUNTY, CITY, ETC.)
Income Taxes	Income Taxes (some states have no state income tax)	Sales & Use Taxes
Payroll Taxes (i.e., self employment tax)	Sales & Use Taxes (product-based businesses)	Various Other Business Taxes (Real estate, personal property, etc. Less common)
Excise Taxes (not common)	Excise or Other Business Taxes (varies by state)	

For most business owners, federal income taxes and payroll taxes represent the largest chunk of change you need to pay to the government. When you prepare your personal tax return (Form 1040), you are calculating the combined federal income taxes and payroll taxes that you are required to pay and comparing that amount to what you've already paid (via withholding from paychecks or paying estimated taxes). Any difference must be paid by April 15 (if you owe more) or is paid to you as a refund (if you overpaid).

Federal income taxes are generally paid on *all* sources of income, including both earned and unearned income. While federal payroll taxes work a little differently, they are also calculated on your Form 1040. Payroll taxes go toward Social Security and Medicare, collectively known as FICA, as they were established under the Federal Insurance Contributions Act. When you work for someone else as an employee, you are responsible for paying half of the payroll tax (7.65%) and the employer pays for the other half. However, when you are self-employed, you are responsible for paying *both* the employee and employer sides of the tax (15.3% total). Unlike income taxes, these taxes kick in *immediately* from the first dollar in profit you make when you are self-employed. For that reason, self-employed individuals typically have to file a tax return, even if they didn't make much money in a given year. Bit of a bummer, right?

Indeed, it may be frustrating to have to pay both halves of payroll tax when you are self-employed, but remember, as a business owner you can deduct your business expenses to arrive at the total income that is subject to tax. This is a perk that those who work as an employee don't get. Your entity structure can also impact the amount of self-employment tax you have to pay, which I'll talk more about in chapter 16.

Moving on to state taxes, the income tax rate imposed by states varies widely. Where you have to pay income tax is generally based upon where you performed the work. Typically, this is your state of residence, but you may have to file in other states if you performed significant work on-site there. States vary in their filing requirements, so it's best to check with any state where you earned income. Some states have no income tax, while others have a high income tax rate. That said, states with low or no income tax are more apt to make up the difference with other taxes, such as higher sales taxes, property taxes, or excise taxes on businesses. Understanding the tax landscape of the state you live in is important.

Speaking of sales tax, this tax is collected from customers who purchase your products and is then paid by you to your state and county or city. Typically, you'll have to register to pay sales tax to any state you have a sales tax "nexus" in. You generally always have a nexus in a state where you have a physical presence, which typically includes the state in which you live and any states where you might have significant operations, such as a local office.

Service-based businesses are typically not subject to sales taxes (phew!), though there can be exceptions if your service includes a physical product (for example, a photographer who provides clients with a physical photo album may need to collect and pay sales tax). As sales tax is paid by the purchaser to the seller and then remitted to the state and local taxing authorities, they shouldn't have a net impact on your P&L. That doesn't mean they aren't a total pain, though, especially since the rules on when you need to collect sales tax and to whom you need to pay it are all over the map.

To make matters worse, if you sell physical products to customers in various states (such as online sales), you may also have a sales tax nexus in states you don't live in, meaning that you would be subject to collecting sales taxes on sales shipped to customers in those states. Luckily, most states have nexus thresholds that exempt you from sales tax if you don't sell much in the state and don't have a physical presence there.

Wondering how to keep up with it all? Thankfully, there's an app for that (several, in fact). For my recommended tools to help you with sales tax, check out my resources at HiddenProfitTheBook.com.

You might also have to pay federal or state excise tax based on where you live and work and what industry you are in. Businesses that are often levied additional excise taxes include sellers of alcohol, tobacco, firearms, fuel, and luxury goods (sometimes referred to as "sin taxes").

And just for funsies, there are also random state and local taxes that certain jurisdictions decided to require for businesses based there. Often, we don't even realize these taxes exist until we get a nasty-gram in the mail about our payment being overdue. Make sure to be on the lookout for scams, since it's not hard to convince people that there is a tax they didn't pay (scammers gonna scam, after all).

If you're unsure, one place to check is your state's Department of Revenue website, which should have specifics about any business taxes that may be relevant to you. When in doubt, you can always give them a call.

If you're wondering how you are supposed to keep this all straight *and* run a business, that's a great question. Like we discussed in chapter 4, getting help is a game changer. While those safety switches are super important and need a good deal of supervision to prevent expensive system failures, *you* don't have to be the one always flipping the switches. Instead, you can hire someone to do the detailed tasks and monitoring, while you play the role of oversight manager. Compliance is the first task most business owners outsource to help them free up their time so they can focus on the tasks that only they can do.

Cash Management

Now that your safety switches are no longer blinking yellow or red, you can turn your attention to the motherboard in the middle of the room covered in knobs and gauges (think: the control panel in my favorite Disney movie, *Inside Out*). This control panel relates to the second of the Big Three financial duties: cash management. The large gauge in the middle shows your current cash balance. The other gauges show your upcoming bills and expected revenue from recent sales. The knobs allow you to adjust the timing of those payments or collections. In the middle is a big red button labeled "debt," which allows you to borrow money to pay your bills. Your primary job as the control room operator is to make sure your cash balance stays positive, preferably without hitting the "debt" button. But how?

Unless it's nearing April 15 and you're in tax-time scramble mode, my guess is that most of your day-to-day attention goes toward cash management. This panel is in the middle of your control room because these duties are the hardest to ignore. Without cash management as a central function to make sure revenue is coming in and bills are being paid, a business can't survive.

However, as we saw with Joseph, just because an owner spends their time on cash management doesn't mean that it's being done effectively. It's common for cash management to feel like a shell game, constantly moving money from one place to another. For many, the extent of their activities around this duty include logging into their bank account, checking their balance, and figuring out which bills they can (and can't) afford to pay. Then doing the same thing tomorrow, crossing their fingers that there will miraculously be more money there.

In the next chapter, I'll dive into specific strategies to help improve your cash flow and avoid the feast-or-famine cycle of cash.

72 Hidden Profit

For now, just know that when it comes to cash management, having a system to *forecast* your cash flow is critical. The gauges in your Financial Control Room can help you create this forecast. It's important to get into the habit of predicting your future cash inflows and outflows. While there are software systems that will charge you a pretty penny to use their (often wildly inaccurate) algorithms to project your cash flow, most small-business owners can do this effectively in a more analog (and much cheaper) way. Personally, I use a spreadsheet (no shocker there, I'm sure). I start with my beginning cash balance and then enter expected incoming cash (cash receipts) and outgoing cash (cash payments) over the next few days/weeks/months and recalculate my ending cash balance to see if I have any cash shortfalls coming up.

Here's an example of what cash flow forecasting looks like for me:

CASH FLOW FORECAST

WEEKLY	WEEK 1	WEEK 2	WEEK 3	WEEK 4	WEEK 5
BEGINNING WEEKLY CASH BALANCE	$ 5,000	$ 4,300	$ 6,200	$ 2,150	$ 650
CASH RECIEPTS					
Cash from Sales	1,500	2,500	2,000	2,500	4,000
Other Cash Receipts	-	-	500	-	-
Total Cash Receipts	$ 1,500	$ 2,500	$ 2,500	$ 2,500	$ 4,000
CASH PAYMENTS					
Raw Materials / Inventory Purchases	-	-	500	-	-
Insurance	-	600	-	-	-
Licenses / Permits	250	-	-	-	-
Office Supplies	50	-	50	-	50
Salaries	-	-	4,000	-	5,000
Office Rent	700	-	-	-	-
Subcontractors	700	-	-	-	-
Utilities	500	-	-	-	-
Credit Card Payment	-	-	-	4,000	-
Total Cash Payments	$ 2,200	$ 600	$ 4,550	$ 4,000	$ 5,050
Owner's Draw	-	-	2,000	-	-
CHANGE IN CASH (Cash Receipts - Cash Payments - Owner's Draw)	$ (700)	$ 1,900	$ (4,050)	$ (1,500)	$ (1,050)
ENDING CASH BALANCE (Cash on Hand + Change in Cash)	$ 4,300	$ 6,200	$ 2,150	$ 650	$ (400)

Importantly, when projecting cash flow, you want to include the cash inflows and outflows in the weeks they will actually come into or go out of your bank account, which may or may not correspond to when you receive or pay them. If you use a credit card, for example, you'll show the credit card payment as outflow in the week it is due to be paid, instead of tracking the date of each individual expense.

Looking at the table above, you can see that I'm projecting a shortfall in cash in Week 5 of this forecast. To solve this, I'll try to see if I can bring more income forward, reduce or delay some expenses, or perhaps (as a last resort) reduce the owner's draw I planned to give myself in Week 3. The key is that by looking ahead, I give myself the chance to evaluate my options *before* a problem arises. Without taking the time to forecast my cash flow, I'd reach Week 5 with a shortfall and far fewer choices for how to handle it, and perhaps end up relying on debt to plug the cash flow holes (more on this in chapter 8).

You'll notice that the forecast above shows cash movements by week; however, you could look at daily or monthly shifts instead. How detailed your cash forecast needs to be depends on how much your balances tend to swing from one day to the next. For example, businesses with high transaction volumes, such as retail stores and restaurants, often experience big daily shifts in cash balances and may benefit from setting up their forecast to track daily balances. On the other hand, a business with a more predictable, stable cash flow, such as a professional service firm with a few monthly invoices, might find that forecasting cash inflows and outflows for a full month is sufficient. I tend to lean toward forecasting my cash movements on a weekly basis, as it feels like the Goldilocks "just right" approach for my business. I'll typically look several weeks ahead (at least one full quarter) to see if there are any possible cash shortfalls and determine how much money I can take out of my business as an owner's draw to pay myself. I also use cash flow forecasting to help me decide when I should pay particular bills. Importantly, the purpose of cash flow forecasting isn't to predict your future cash balance "exactly right." Remember, it doesn't have to be perfect to be useful. Getting comfortable using estimates and looking at the big picture is incredibly freeing and keeps you from getting stuck in the weeds.

Regardless of how detailed your cash flow forecast is, I do recommend revising the forecast at least a few times a month. I start each week with "Money

Monday," when I spend five to ten minutes updating my cash balance and reviewing upcoming cash receipts and payments. Getting into a weekly cadence of reviewing my cash flow in this way has been a game changer for me and ensures that I rarely have unpleasant surprises when it comes to my cash flow.

I recommend cash flow forecasting to every business owner because this simple task can remove so much of the guesswork (and stress!) that comes with managing your finances. If you love templates as much as I do, make sure to grab your Cash Flow Forecasting Template at HiddenProfitTheBook.com.

Strategy

Now picture another wall full of levers in your Financial Control Room. This is your Strategy Wall. This is where you get to have a little fun!

It's likely no shocker that strategy is my favorite of the Big Three financial duties (I am a profit *strategist*, after all). Strategy is what creates all the moneymaking magic. While you can hustle your way to short-term success, sustaining your business or growing it past a certain point always requires a clear financial strategy.

I've found that most business owners encounter a financial "hump" at some point. Usually, this is after the initial period of putting in the hard work to start a business, hone their offerings, and build a client or customer base. The "hump" often shows up when a solopreneur wants to expand, but their time (and money) are already maxed out. Typically, I see this happen between $50,000 and $250,000 in revenue annually. The entrepreneur feels as though they have nowhere to go.

After talking with thousands of business owners, I can spot "the hump" quite quickly when I hear it—for example, when someone says something to the effect of "I'm totally burned out, but I can't afford to hire [more] help." If that's you, don't worry, my friend, there is a way over that hump. In fact, this book could probably have been subtitled "Getting over the Hump." This is my specialty.

As I'm sure you've guessed, the answer is financial strategy. That means using data to make informed, intentional decisions for your business. How you price your products and services, how you spend your money in your business, and even how and when you hire help are all related to financial strategy.

TRAINING YOUR BRAIN TO BE A CFO

Stepping into the role of CFO and embracing financial strategy can feel uncomfortable and bumpy at first. You may overthink things and wonder if you're doing it "right." That's totally normal. But with enough focus, you can actually train your brain to think like a CFO, and it's not as hard as it sounds!

Your reticular activating system (RAS) is the part of your brain that filters information and helps you focus on what is important. Our RAS determines what we notice. It's constantly working to filter out noise. For example, when you're driving down the street, you probably aren't actively noticing things such as the make, model, and color of the car two lanes over. Instead, your brain is trained to focus on what matters, including brake lights in front of you and traffic lights ahead.

But consider what happens when you're in the market to buy a new car. All of a sudden, you see that car *everywhere*. Did everyone on earth suddenly decide to buy a Honda Odyssey? Nope. All those minivans were on the road the whole time. The only difference is that now your RAS is primed to notice every Honda Odyssey because you've assigned a level of importance to that make and model of car. Our brain previously marked those details as "unimportant" and largely ignored them, until we told it that they are now relevant to us.[1]

Turns out we can use that same brain-training superpower to help us become a boss CFO. In fact, the simple act of reading this book will help you tell your RAS which financial details are important. All of a sudden, you'll start to see opportunities to improve cash flow, increase profitability, and invest back into your business that you may otherwise have missed.

The more you intentionally focus on your finances, the more you tell your brain that these things matter. While it may feel like a lot of conscious effort right now, before you know it, making savvy financial decisions will be second nature.

In part III of this book, I'm going to dive deeper into the levers on the Financial Control Room wall (Profit Levers), which will help you take control of your own profitability and craft a financial strategy. Until then, consider how you've made financial decisions thus far in your business. What has felt easy, and what has felt more difficult? If you feel as though you're currently struggling to get over "the hump," what is getting in your way right now? If you got over the hump, how did you do it?

Unfortunately, most businesses will go over more than one hump. "New levels, new devils," as they say. While that may sound depressing to some, the good news is that every hump you overcome is a learning experience that will make the next one easier to surmount. Overcoming hurdles will help you build not only a stronger business but also a more resilient *you*.

Remember Joseph, our skin care entrepreneur who was spending all his time dealing with tax notices and daily cash struggles? He finally decided it was time to outsource some of the more mundane financial tasks so he could focus on the ones that were more important. He instituted a weekly cash flow forecasting task that enabled him to look a full three months into the future and plan for any projected cash flow shortfalls. Looking forward helped him address potential cash flow issues before they became code red alarm bells, which led to his spending significantly less time panicking about having enough money in the bank. Because his compliance safety switches were all green and his cash management gauges were positive and healthy, he finally had time to direct his attention to the Strategy Wall of his Financial Control Room. He then used his Profit Levers to more than double his profit in under a year.

In part III, you'll learn more about the Profit Levers and how to use them to maximize your profit in your business, as Joseph did. But before we get there, you need to make sure the rest of your Financial Control Room is running smoothly. The rest of this section will discuss the various management duties you have in your business and how to make sure you aren't neglecting any foundational financial tasks.

Your Monthly Money To-Do List

In order to make sure that you are compliant, managing your cash, and spending adequate time on strategy, I suggest creating a monthly money to-do list. This should include:

- Making any relevant tax filings (federal, state, local)
- Reviewing your financial statements
- Forecasting cash flow (month by month, week by week, or day by day)
- Figuring out your next money move

Bonus points if you spend part of your time implementing advice from this book!

CHAPTER SIX
Manage Your Cash Flow

Of the Big Three financial duties we discussed in the last chapter (compliance, cash management, and strategy), the one that often feels most urgent on a day-to-day basis is cash management.

After all, cash is the engine of our business. Cash is what we need to make payroll, pay our operating expenses, and pay ourselves. Without cash, we can't run our business, at least not for long. Yet cash flow issues are incredibly prevalent in small businesses. A 2023 study by Xero showed that approximately half of all business owners reported having struggled with cash flow shortfalls in the past twelve months.[1]

Not only are cash flow issues incredibly common; they can also spell the end of a business. A widely cited U.S. Bank study that looked at small-business closures found that 82 percent of those surveyed cited cash flow problems as a primary reason.[2]

While those numbers are high, they don't paint the whole picture. Cash flow issues are most often merely a symptom of a greater problem within the business. There are innumerable possible causes of cash flow shortages, and often the culprit isn't one single thing. Sales declines, improper pricing, increases in labor and other operating costs, and unexpected expenses can all contribute to cash flow problems. Sometimes, what we perceive to be cash flow issues are really *profitability* issues. In those instances, by increasing profitability, we can also improve our cash flow. I'll address these causes further in parts III and IV of this book.

But sometimes even businesses that are profitable on paper don't have money in the bank. In this chapter, I'll talk about how this is possible and provide you with some tangible action steps to help you improve your cash flow almost overnight.

But first let's look at some of the reasons a profitable business can struggle with having enough cash on hand.

Accounting Funny Business

Let's revisit the simple formula I gave you earlier for calculating profit:

Revenue (money you made) − Expenses (money you spent) = Profit (or loss)

Easy, right?

In this example, you'd think that profit would match the amount of cash you made. If revenue is the cash that came in and expenses are the cash that went out, shouldn't they align?

That's where "accounting funny business" comes in to complicate things. In general, accounting rules dictate *when* certain cash transactions should be "recognized" on the P&L. Sometimes, the timing of this recognition differs from when the cash was actually spent. This causes a mismatch in when a cash transaction appears on the bank statement versus when (or if) the transaction shows up on the P&L.

You'll remember that in chapter 2 we walked through the accounting entries related to an inventory purchase Nancy made for her print shop. Recall that even though cash was spent, that inventory purchase was not immediately recorded as an expense on her P&L. Instead, it sat on the Balance Sheet until that inventory was eventually sold (or otherwise disposed of). This is an example of a timing issue that can cause a mismatch between accounting profit and cold, hard, usable cash, especially in the short term. In the month Nancy purchased inventory, her profit might still have showed as positive, but her cash balance was likely lower than her profit because the inventory expense hadn't yet appeared on the P&L. With most timing issues like this, profit and cash will typically align over the long term but may vary significantly in any individual period.

Why make things so complicated? You may think that accountants are bored or just trying to justify their jobs. But in reality, accounting and tax rules exist to smooth out results and prevent manipulation. Accounting rules are based on the "matching principle," which means that expenses should be recognized on the P&L around the same time the associated revenue is recorded. Since revenue isn't recorded on the P&L until the inventory is sold and cash is collected, the matching principle would say that the underlying cost of the inventory should be recognized at that point in time (even if it was bought months or even years earlier).

The same matching principle applies for buying long-term assets, such as machinery and equipment. If you purchase a large piece of machinery with cash, that will be recorded on the Balance Sheet just as inventory is. However, unlike inventory, that machinery is intended to be used over time in the business and not sold. So when will that asset purchase show up as an expense on the P&L?

This is where the concept of *depreciation* comes in. Depreciation is a way of spreading out the cost of an asset over its "useful life," or the number of years you'll use it. The IRS has guidelines for how long different types of assets can be depreciated. For example, let's say you are a seller of handmade goods making custom clothing and decide to buy an industrial sewing machine for $7,000. (Go, you!) According to the IRS, the estimated useful life of that sewing machine is seven years.

There are different tax options for depreciating equipment, but for simplicity's sake, let's assume you choose to depreciate the asset equally over the seven years. Each year, you'd record $1,000 of depreciation as an expense on your P&L. This gradual expense recognition reflects that you'll use the machine to generate revenue for many years, not just the year you bought it. In other words, depreciation helps match the timing of the expense with the time you're using the asset to make money. Little by little, you're moving the cost of the machine from the Balance Sheet to the P&L as you use it, giving a clearer picture of your business's true profit over time. At the end of seven years, the machine will be fully depreciated and show a zero value on the Balance Sheet. However, over that seven-year time period, you'll have a mismatch between paper profit and cash in the bank.

> ### MAKING RULES JUST TO BREAK THEM
>
> While this chapter talks about general accounting principles for things such as inventory and asset purchases, it's important to note that there are lots of caveats and exceptions that I can't cover fully in the confines of this book (and quoting IRS code sections would likely put you to sleep). For example, for certain asset purchases, you may have the ability to deduct most or all of the purchase in the year you acquired the asset rather than depreciating it over time. Additionally, some small-business owners who don't hold inventory for long periods of time may be able to deduct their inventory when purchased rather than when sold.
>
> This is where a qualified tax accountant can help you understand your options and make the best decisions for your business. Remember to consider the long-term impact as well. While deducting things up front may save you taxes today, it could increase your tax bill in future years. I recommend talking to an accountant before you make any large purchases to make sure you understand the tax implications.

To give you an overall view, here is a list of the main culprits that can cause profit and cash flow misalignment in any given period—and sometimes lead to cash flow crunches.

- **Inventory purchases:** As discussed above, inventory is generally recorded on the Balance Sheet as an asset (thing you own) until sold or otherwise disposed of, causing a mismatch between cash and profit.

- **Asset purchases such as machinery and equipment:** As discussed above, asset purchases are generally recorded on the Balance Sheet and depreciated to the P&L over time.

- **Debt:** When the cash from debt comes in, it is recorded as an increase in cash and a corresponding liability (thing you owe) on the Balance Sheet, instead of revenue on your P&L. (That means you don't pay taxes on cash from debt—yay!)

- **Debt payments:** The principal portion of debt payments reduces the Balance Sheet liability but does not impact the P&L. Only the interest portion of the payment is recorded as an expense on the P&L when paid. Since you didn't pay taxes on the cash when you took out the debt, you don't get a deduction when you pay back the principal balance.

- **Owner's draws:** As discussed in chapter 2, owner's draws reduce cash and equity on the Balance Sheet but don't have a P&L impact.

- **Using the accrual method of accounting instead of the cash method:** The accrual method isn't typical for most small businesses, but if you do use it for your tax filings, revenues and expenses are recorded when earned or incurred, not when cash is exchanged. For example, an accrual method taxpayer might record revenue on the P&L when an invoice for work performed is sent, instead of waiting to record the revenue when the cash is eventually collected (as would be the normal course for a cash basis taxpayer).

- **Timing of cash collection:** Even if you know your products or services are sufficiently profitable, cash flow crunches can arise if you have to pay your expenses *before* the related revenue comes in. This can often be remedied by making changes to your billing and payment processes. (More on this below.)

- **Business growth:** If your business is consistently growing, it may mean that you are reinvesting your cash back into the business to support the growth as fast as it comes in. More on this conundrum (and how to fix it) in part IV.

You may have picked up on the fact that most of these differences come down to one thing: timing. Some of this, such as depreciation, is outside your control. However, there are things you can do to improve your cash situation and avoid the dreaded cash flow crunch. The rest of this chapter details the practical steps you can take today to give your bank account a bit more breathing room.

Billing

Several years ago, Melissa started a music therapy business by herself, traveling to each of her clients' homes to perform weekly therapy sessions and music lessons. Fast-forward a few years, and Melissa's waitlist was growing. She decided it was time to hire another music teacher to meet the increased demand for her services. Around the time she began working with me, she brought on her first employee.

Quickly, Melissa realized that even though she had doubled her client capacity by hiring her first employee, she wouldn't have enough cash in the bank to pay her new teacher, even *after* I worked with her to increase her prices. If something didn't change, she was going to have to dig into her personal savings to pay her new employee—but how could that be? When I looked deeper into her data, I realized that her problem wasn't profitability; her margins were great, and her overhead costs were low. So why did she struggle to pay her new employee *and* herself? The problem was her billing process.

At the end of each month, Melissa would invoice her customers for that month's lessons. Her clients would then sometimes take three weeks or more to pay the invoices. While that hadn't been a big issue when it had been just Melissa giving the lessons, the cash flow crunch ramped up when she hired her first employee. She paid her employee every two weeks for the lessons he had taught in the previous two weeks, long before she invoiced the client for those sessions, meaning that she was typically paying her employee for the lessons the employee gave *before* she collected the revenue for those lessons from her customers.

Since Melissa's company was growing, it exacerbated the problem. It felt as though the more clients she got, the less money she had. She was profitable on paper but never seemed to have the cash she needed, and every dollar that came in went right out the door to pay her employee.

Melissa needed to make changes—and fast. The first step was looking at timing: When did money come into her business as revenue, and when did it go out to cover payroll and bills? The culprit was obvious: There was a significant lag of two to four weeks between when Melissa paid herself and her employee (through payroll) and when clients paid her. I advised Melissa that rather than invoicing *after* the services had been performed, she should bill customers on the first of every month and set up automated drafts from her clients' accounts (with permission, of course).

That meant that revenue would come in *before* she had to pay herself and her employee for work performed. The new billing cycle would also create a reliable payment schedule—and an accurate cash forecast!—while eliminating the time and energy spent chasing payments from customers. Though she knew it was the right decision for her business, Melissa was worried about what her customers would think about the new process. However, when she rolled out the changes, most customers were happy that they would no longer have to remember to pay their bills manually. It was a win-win for everyone!

Depending on your business model, making some tweaks to your billing process might be just what you need to stop the cash crunch cycle. Later in this chapter, I'll give you more ideas on how to evaluate and improve your processes for collecting payments from customers.

Inventory

A similar cash flow crunch was happening with another of my students, Susie. As an optometrist, Susie offered eye exams as well as sold eyeglasses and contacts. Though her business was doing well on paper—her clientele and revenue grew month after month—she struggled with having cash on hand. In her cash crunch dilemma, inventory was the culprit. There was a mismatch between when she purchased inventory and when it was sold.

This isn't just Susie's problem; I see it with many entrepreneurs who sell products. (And when your business is growing, knowing how and when to buy inventory can be an even bigger challenge.) The cycle often goes like this: You purchase inventory for $10,000 that you plan to sell. Over the next few months, you sell the inventory for $20,000, representing a 50% profit margin (yay!). As that inventory was sold, demand continued to grow (yay again!). To meet the expanding needs of your customers, you purchase more inventory than before, investing the full $20,000 into the next round. Since your P&L

includes only the cost of the inventory once it is sold (hence the line "cost of goods sold"), you look super profitable . . . on paper. But most of the time, there is little to no cash in the bank left to show for it (boo!). It can feel like a vicious cycle that is hard to escape.

For this reason, some product-based businesses have moved to a just-in-time or drop-ship fulfillment model, where they need to keep only limited or no physical inventory in-house. This helps keep costs down and ensures that you never have to deal with the financial ramifications of overstocking inventory. For some businesses, such as stores and boutiques to which customers go to purchase physical products, this may not be feasible. If you must stock physical inventory, tight control of that inventory is crucial to avoiding the dreaded cash flow crunch. This includes monitoring your inventory turnover ratio, which is the measure of how fast your inventory is typically sold.

> **PRO TIP:**
>
> For most physical product businesses that stock inventory, the inventory turnover ratio is a critical KPI to track.

When going through my program, Susie realized that she wasn't monitoring her inventory as closely as she should be. She ordered some products in a variety of colors to make sure she had plenty of options, but some sat on the shelves unsold. To fix that, she started monitoring her inventory more closely to understand client demand and adjusted her ordering process accordingly. Finding the right balance between overstocking and understocking took some time and attention (and a good tracking system!), but ultimately it made a massive difference when it came to Susie's available cash.

When it comes to inventory, you'll want to weigh any discounts on bulk purchases you may receive against the cash flow implications of large purchases. You want to make sure you aren't sacrificing your company's financial stability (and your ability to pay yourself) for the sake of growth. In part IV, I'll talk about how to set up a PROFFIT Plan that will enable you to pay yourself, pay your obligations, and grow your business. Setting up a PROFFIT Plan is also a great way to help you set money aside for additional inventory you may want to buy above and beyond your normal stock without negatively impacting your bottom line.

Get Creative: Quick Ways to Improve Your Cash Flow

As we've discussed, cash flow issues typically come down to timing. If having enough cash on hand is a struggle, start by asking yourself these questions.

1. How can I *move up* the timing of cash receipts?
2. How can I *delay* the timing of cash payments?

A simple change in Melissa's billing process transformed her cash flow situation. Because she was now collecting payment up front, her business growth no longer put a strain on her cash flow. She no longer had to front the money to pay her employees or spend time chasing overdue bill payments.

> ### HOW COULD THIS WORK FOR YOU?
>
> The great thing about cash flow is that small tweaks can make a world of difference, especially when your business is growing. That said, I understand that changing the way you charge customers or pay your bills can be nerve-racking. That's entirely normal; it's natural to stand by what we know and the way things were previously done. Moreover, this level of change often requires us to release preconceived notions about "how the industry works."
>
> I encourage you to get creative. Instead of coming up with reasons why changing things *won't* work, try reading the tips in this chapter considering how they *could* work for you. While some of the changes I suggest may require a bit of heavy lifting to institute, the effort is typically well rewarded by extra cash flow (and a lot more financial breathing room).

Now it's your turn. Here are some ideas to help get your mind moving. Feel free to start by picking one or two changes to try out first, then assessing your results.

To collect cash more quickly:

- **Require prepayment or a deposit up front** for your services.
- **Automate payments** by using payment processors that enable automatic recurring ACH or credit card payments with client permission.
- **Bill more frequently.** Rather than billing once per month, look at a weekly or biweekly billing cycle to get the cash faster.
- **Shorten invoice terms.** If you typically give thirty days for payment (i.e., "net 30"), consider reducing this to net 10 or 15.

CHIEF FINANCIAL OPINION:
Reduce the Payment Friction

One of the most impactful things you can do when it comes to your business finances is to streamline your payment process. Not only will this bring in cash faster; it will also result in more sales and more happy customers.

Yes, allowing people to use credit cards or certain payment processors to pay you will mean incurring fees. But the quickest way to lose sales is by making your customers jump through hoops to pay you. We live in a modern age, and even the slightest bit of difficulty in the buying process can (and does) contribute to losing sales.

Even something as simple as requiring customers to log in to place an order—and then failing to remember their password—can make them walk away. Surprise fees that aren't mentioned until checkout (such as shipping or convenience fees) can also cause shoppers to abandon ship (and their carts).

According to research compiled by Baymard Institute, the average shopping cart abandonment rate is around 70 percent. While

- **Assess penalties for late payment.** In general, 1% to 2% interest would not be unreasonable, but check your state for any caps on interest charges (called "usury laws").

- **Send payment reminders.** For payments that can't be automated, set up regular payment reminders (often available through invoicing services).

- **Monitor and follow up on unpaid invoices.** For customers who continue not to pay outstanding invoices, have a policy to halt services until payment is made to avoid performing more work for uncollectible accounts.

- **Make payment easy.** Provide various ways for customers to pay you conveniently, including electronic options such as credit cards and ACH.

> some of this can be attributed to browsers who weren't ready to buy, a whopping 48 percent of respondents said they had recently abandoned a cart due to extra fees they hadn't anticipated. Not only that, one in five would-be buyers stated that they had recently abandoned a purchase because the checkout process was too long or complicated.[3] Reducing difficulty for buyers should be paramount, and not only for e-commerce businesses.
>
> Rather than adding fees for customers who want to pay you by their chosen method, you could offer a discount to incentivize people to pay the way you'd prefer. The end result is the same (being paid via your preferred method), but customers generally respond to this option better. Psychologically, humans generally feel penalized by extra fees but love perks and incentives. For example, offering a discount to pay by ACH is typically better received than imposing a credit card surcharge.
>
> To understand what your customers experience, I recommend that you go through the purchasing process yourself to make sure that buying is as seamless and easy as possible.

To delay expenses:

- **Don't pay your bills early.** Pay bills on or just before the due date, unless there is a discount for early payment.

- **Delay supply or inventory orders.** Order materials only when needed to prevent excess inventory and negative cash flow impact. Consider if you can institute a just-in-time inventory model or use drop shipping to fulfill your orders.

- **Negotiate payment terms with your suppliers.** See if your suppliers will extend your time to pay. Depending on your relationship with your suppliers, this may be an accommodation they would make. You may also be able to negotiate a discount if you pay the way they prefer.

- **Pay employees in arrears** (i.e., after the work has been performed). For example, pay employees on January 30 for work performed from January 1 to 15. This is typical in many industries and gives you more time to log and approve payroll, especially for hourly workers.

- **Pay employees less often.** Where practical, paying employees every two weeks or twice monthly instead of every week may help your cash flow. (Be sure to check state employment laws.)

Take some time to consider where you may have opportunities to improve your cash flow. How would it change things if you didn't feel as though every dollar that came in the door would immediately go back out? Let that picture drive you to make change, starting today. It's not always easy, but it's always worth it.

CHAPTER SEVEN
Manage Your Budget

When it comes to financial management duties, I get a lot of questions about how much should be spent on various areas of business. How much should you spend on marketing? How about payroll? How much should you pay for rent?

Expense management is challenging for any business, but it's especially challenging for small businesses that don't have gobs of money to work with. It's understandable that small-business owners want to make sure they're doing it right.

In your Financial Control Room, expense management functions are one of the master controls that influence all financial operations. Every decision you make about spending—what to spend money on, how much, and when—needs to align with your business goals and available resources. Because each spending choice can affect all of the Big Three financial duties (compliance, cash management, and strategy), keeping a steady hand on expense management helps ensure that every part of your financial system will run both smoothly and efficiently.

Does that mean you need to watch every penny carefully? How can you make expense management easier?

Before we get into it, let's play a little word association game. What thoughts or emotions come to mind when you hear the word *budget*? My guess is that it doesn't spark joy. Some of you may even have a visceral response to the word. Honestly, I'm right there with you. As much as I love numbers, I *don't* love spending a painstaking amount of time watching every dollar that comes in and goes out. By nature, many of us who started businesses aren't the type to take "no" for an answer. While that defiance has likely served us well in many areas of life, it also means that we resist limitations and constraints, sometimes even when they are for our own good.

Now, there may be a few of you out there who absolutely *live* for budgeting. For you rare, budget-loving unicorns, this chapter may simply be informative. If you have a budgeting system that works well for your business, feel free to carry on. I recommend that you stick around for this chapter, though, because you might find an *even better* way to do it.

You Don't Need a Budget

Those of us (ahem, most of us) who don't love budgeting likely view it as a joy-sucking hassle, forcing us to live on rice and beans, count pennies, and clip endless streams of coupons. Yeah, no thanks. We likely started our businesses to achieve more freedom and flexibility in our lives and business, and a budget is the ultimate buzzkill.

Most of us budget (understandably) only when we feel we absolutely must—what I call "reactionary budgeting." It typically looks like this: We feel stressed because we know we've let things get a little loosey-goosey moneywise, so our knee-jerk reaction is to go into strict budgeting mode. We subscribe to new budgeting software, slash expenses dramatically, and meticulously categorize every transaction. Often, we do manage to maintain the new regimen for a while. But a reactionary budget rarely lasts. Once the immediate problem subsides, the motivation we had in the beginning also wanes. Old habits resurface, we find ourselves making excuses, and we stop budgeting altogether. Eventually we find ourselves struggling with expenses again and beat ourselves up over our lack of commitment. Then we try once again, vowing that *this* will finally be the time it sticks. And the cycle repeats itself.

If this sounds like you, I've got some good news: It's time to *stop budgeting* for your business—at least in the reactionary sense. To clarify, creating a budget in our personal life can be useful and important. That's because with the very limited exception of real estate, most money we spend in our personal life isn't expected to yield a return on investment. We buy things to consume and to enjoy. When we buy a new pair of jeans, we're not going to get any kind of meaningful return on them in the form of money. Even if we try to sell them when we're done with them, we're probably going to get pennies on the dollar on a buy-sell-trade site.

But business spending is decidedly different, whether we realize it or not. Unlike in our personal lives, the purpose of spending money in a business is to turn it into *more* money. We hire employees to free up time and capacity to serve more customers, which leads to more money. We use software to make our processes more efficient and scalable, which leads to more money. We buy audiovisual equipment to increase the quality of our audio and video production, which leads to more money. We invest in marketing and advertising to bring more awareness to our business and more customers in the door, which leads to more money.

You might be wondering "Okay, Jamie, but does that mean I can spend whatever I want?" Actually, yes. It's your business; you can always spend what you want. But in order for the no-budget approach to work well, you'll need to use the expense management master control in your Financial Control Room to do four things:

1. Calculate your profit margins

2. Determine your "run rate" (the baseline indirect costs to run your business)

3. Create a system for monitoring your profit margins and expenses

4. Evaluate your Return on Investment (ROI)

Calculate Your Profit Margins

As much as I love the energy of a new year, I've never been a resolution-making type of gal. That's probably because I know that eventually my motivation will wane and I'll end up feeling guilty about my lack of follow-through. However, in place of specific (and often overzealous) resolutions that likely won't make it past the Super Bowl, I've begun selecting a new "word of the year" upon the dawning of each year. This word of the year is a guiding principle that I can return to again and again. It helps remind me to be intentional about my decisions, while allowing flexibility for what those choices look like. I love this approach to annual intention setting, and it seems that others do as well! You've probably seen others declare their "word of the year" to friends and on social media.

In January 2020, after coming off of a particularly grueling year of building my business, I decided that my word for 2020 would be *margin*. Even though I'm an accountant, I wasn't just talking about profit margins (though that was part of it). Instead, I wanted to build more margin into all facets of my life and business.

In a general sense, margin represents *space*, having room to breathe. In a world in which it feels as though there is never a shortage of to-dos, more breathing room was just what I needed at the time. I set an intention for the year to create more space for myself. At that time, I made the decision to drastically reduce my client load and focus on developing and delivering my educational programs instead. For a short period of time, I felt as though I had succeeded in creating at least some of the margin I was looking for.

Then came March 2020. Almost overnight, the world shut down. I remember talking with the other neighborhood moms about the "inconvenience" and assuming that our kids would be back in school after spring break. Little did I know that it would be eighteen months before my kids would walk back into a school building. I also had no idea how much the pandemic would throw my word of the year for a loop.

Early on in the covid pandemic, I did have more time margin. Since I had off-loaded most of my clients and had just wrapped up delivering my first digital program, work was purposefully slower. We took walks and had family game nights every evening. I made homeschool lesson plans and tried new recipes. I even ordered organizing supplies with the goal of going all Home Edit on every room of my house. The world felt stressful, but I did my best to focus on what I could control. Maybe it was meant to be a time of slow days and quiet solitude?

But on the same day that the organizing supplies showed up on my doorstep, Congress decided to pass the first major pandemic relief bill, which created several programs to aid small businesses. Suddenly I got an influx of questions from my audience, many of whom were desperately seeking help to keep their businesses afloat. In those early days, there were no experts in the programs, and things were changing rapidly. The margin I had created for myself allowed me to step up to the call. I read hundreds of pages of legislation and worked alongside other talented CPAs to understand and interpret the rules. I did daily live streams on social media and YouTube to guide business owners and self-employed individuals on how to get the aid they so badly needed. I dedicated myself to helping as many people as possible for free, with hundreds of thousands of business owners turning to my content for guidance. The organizing supplies I had ordered sat idle by the door.

I tell this story here because I want you to think differently when you hear the word *margin*. Yes, we're going to talk about the different types of profit margins and how to calculate them in this section. But I want you to remember that margin is not just a calculation; it's also a *feeling*.

Creating a profit margin in our business can grant us much-needed breathing room. We can remove ourselves from the cycles of fear and anxiety that keep us from feeling secure. Profit margin in our business can also help us create time margin in our lives because we're no longer hustling just to make ends meet.

When I set out to create more margin for myself in 2020, I had no idea that by doing so, I was creating the space I would need to help others through a collectively difficult time. By June 2020, I decided to adapt my word of the year to something that more fully represented how I wanted to show up in the moment. My word of the year became *serve*.

Creating more margin in your business is what will enable you to better serve others, including your customers, your employees, and your community. Let me show you how to create some.

How to Calculate Your Profit Margins

Your profit margins are an indicator of how much "space" you have in your business finances. It's important to understand the inputs to the equation so you can interpret what the resulting calculation tells you.

In general, the formula for calculating your profit margin percentage is:

$$\text{Profit Margin} = \frac{\text{Revenue} - \text{Particular Costs}}{\text{Revenue}} \times 100$$

In this equation, "Particular Costs" will change depending on what type of profit margin you are attempting to calculate. There are many different ways to look at your profit margins, depending on what decisions you are trying to make. Are you trying to compare your profit margins on various products and services to see which is most profitable? Are you looking to get an overall understanding of your profitability, considering all of the costs to run your business? Depending on your goal and what you hope to garner from this data, you may calculate different types of profit margins to serve different purposes.

A popular profit margin to calculate, especially when evaluating the profitability of individual products and services, is gross profit margin. To determine your gross profit margin, you would subtract only your direct costs (the costs to create the product or deliver the service).

$$\text{Gross Profit Margin} = \frac{\text{Revenue} - \text{Direct Costs}}{\text{Revenue}} \times 100$$

Direct costs are closely tied to the actual product or service you are selling and don't include overhead costs such as rent, administrative staff, and so on. In part III, we'll dive into direct versus indirect costs and learn why it can be helpful to look at them separately. (Hint: it has to do with pricing!)

Another popular profit margin is called the operating profit margin. This shows how much is left of your revenue once you subtract *all* of the costs used to operate your business, including direct and indirect costs.

$$\text{Operating Profit Margin} = \frac{\text{Revenue} - (\text{Direct Costs} + \text{Indirect Costs})}{\text{Revenue}} \times 100$$

In this case, indirect costs include all the other costs related to running your business that don't directly relate to a specific product or service.

While gross profit margin and operating profit margin aren't the only margins that you can calculate for your business, they are generally the most useful to small-business owners. For example, larger corporations typically also calculate their net profit margin, which includes nonoperating costs such as interest and taxes paid along with operating costs.

When it comes to profit margins, clarity is key. The next time someone asks you about your profit margins (or your accountant references them), make sure to double-check exactly what ones they mean. What costs are they including in the calculation? Context is incredibly important here and is why you should exercise caution when googling (or asking AI) "What should my profit margins be in an XYZ business?" It's very easy to end up comparing apples and oranges when it comes to these calculations. When in doubt, clarify!

How to Use Your Profit Margins

As with all data, you'll use your profit margin calculations to make observations that identify gaps and opportunities for improvement.

For instance, gross profit margins help us analyze how specific products and services compare to one another. Because you include only costs directly related to providing the product or service in the calculation, overhead costs that are hard to allocate to specific products can't muddy the water by distorting the results. In chapter 12, I'll discuss how calculating a gross profit margin for each product or service you offer can help ensure that you're pricing them profitably enough.

Conversely, calculating your operating profit margin will tell you how much of every dollar you earned made it to the bottom line, giving you insight into how efficiently your business is running. To illustrate, let's imagine that this is your high-level Profit and Loss Statement for last year:

ANNUAL P&L STATEMENT

	ANNUAL P&L	PROFIT MARGINS
Total Revenue	$ 250,000	
Total Direct Costs	90,000	
Total Gross Profit	160,000	64%
Total Indirect Costs	65,000	
Total Operating Profit	$ 95,000	38%

In the case above, your operating profit margin is 38% ($95,000/$250,000). This means that of each dollar earned, $0.38 was left after paying expenses (other than paying yourself). You can compare this figure month over month or year over year to see how your profit margins are trending.

Perhaps you calculate your operating profit margin and determine that it is 12%, so only $0.12 on the dollar is making its way to your bottom line. This means that to be able to pay yourself $95,000 in draws from your business, you'd need to make close to $1 million in sales. Conversely, if your profit margin was 38%, as in the above example, you could pay yourself $95,000 on only $250,000 in total revenue. This is why profit margins are so critical. If we don't understand them and manage them, we'll be forced to work harder for the same (or worse) result. Paying attention to your margins and constantly looking for ways to improve them will help you make the same, or even more, money with less hustle.

In part III, we'll use profit margin calculations to help us make important strategic decisions in our business and also create more time margin in our lives. However, an important step that you can take right now is designing a process to monitor and manage your profit margins.

Determine Your "Run Rate"

As I discussed in part I, while you don't need to count every nickel or dime, you *do* want to keep a pulse on your baseline monthly expenses. In addition to understanding your profit margins, you want to know the approximate monthly/quarterly/annual cost to run your business (i.e., recurring indirect expenses).

Note that I say "approximate." This is about having a 30,000-foot understanding of what is going on financially in the business; it *isn't* about being able to cite your exact profit figure on command. Rounding and estimating are a CFO's best friends. As I've already said, your calculations don't have to be perfect to be useful.

Now it's time for me to put you on the spot: How much revenue did you make last month? How about last year?

If you're like most entrepreneurs I work with, you likely have a reasonable estimate of the money that came into your business. Business owners typically set goals based on revenue, especially because it's the easiest metric to track. But as we've discussed, profitability is really the end goal. It's possible to be making boatloads of revenue yet not make a profit. That's why knowing how much it generally *costs* to run our business is also key.

Now let's try this one: Do you know what your average monthly expenses are? How about annually?

If your expenses vary significantly from month to month, it's okay to average this out for the sake of determining the average cost to run your business each month (known as your expense "run rate"). Note, I'm talking *only* about core costs here. These are your regular indirect expenses, which are typically recurring in nature. Don't worry about one-offs right now. I'll talk about how to handle those in part IV.

Figure out this number and commit it to memory. When you review your P&L each month, compare your actual income and expenses to what your expectations are. Was revenue higher or lower than usual? Why? How about expenses? If you don't know the explanation for the variations from your expectations offhand, take some time to dig into it (or have your bookkeeper or accountant help you). Below, we'll talk about how to use your expense run rate to monitor your expenses without the need to create a painstaking line-by-line budget.

CHIEF FINANCIAL OPINION:
Beware of "Industry Standards"

It can be tempting to look at your industry for examples on how to run your business, including how you spend money. The problem is, a childcare center in rural Iowa has a completely different P&L than a similar center in Manhattan does. Not only that, most industry standards are derived by looking at the financial statements of large public companies. Your homemade jewelry business has virtually nothing in common with a company such as Pandora, so looking to it to understand what your margins should be is a fruitless task.

When you ask how much you "should" be spending on a particular cost, you ignore the nuances of your specific situation. Of course, it can be helpful to benchmark ourselves against similar businesses, but at the end of the day, you don't want to put too much stock in what Google says your margins should be.

So how can we make a plan for spending if looking at industry standards doesn't help? We strive to run our core business as profitably as possible, we monitor our KPIs regularly, and we use Profit Levers (which we'll discuss in part III) to find hidden profit. Remember: You are unique, and so is your business!

Create a System for Monitoring Your Profit Margins and Expenses

Thankfully, monitoring costs doesn't have to mean placing hard limits on your expenditures (whew!). Rather, you simply need to understand the overall spending picture of your business and keep an eye on where your money is going. I call this your *spend review*.

When you review your P&L each month, you'll want to calculate your gross profit margin and operating profit margin and compare them to both prior periods and your expectations. Additionally, you'll want to compare your typical run rate expenses to your actual expenses that month. If you notice that margins are declining or costs are creeping up from what you typically expect, it's time to pinpoint the cause. Sometimes it's just a timing variation (perhaps you made an insurance payment that goes through once a year), while other times it could indicate that you've gotten a little too laissez-faire with your business spending. Figure out the culprit, and use that data to make any necessary adjustments to stay on track for your financial goals.

The great thing about allowing for flexibility in your budget is that it gives you the agency to make decisions that are best for your business, rather than miss important opportunities in order to stick to a strict budget. If you have good reason to expect that you'll get a worthy return on investment on additional money spent, it may not make sense to place arbitrary limits on your spending (unless you find them helpful). In part III, we'll dive deeper into how to evaluate your potential return on investment.

However, if you determine in your spending review that you simply went over a bit with the credit card this month, it's time to pause and reevaluate—not from a place of shame, mind you, just to recalibrate and course correct to meet your financial goals. Put on your CFO hat, determine the cause, and decide how to get back on track.

The more often you review your profit margins and compare your costs to your usual run rate, the more comfortable you'll feel. When you know your business and costs well, there's no need to budget every dollar or set arbitrary limits on expenditures. You can be financially responsible and still have tremendous freedom.

It's helpful to do your monthly spending review around the same time you do your cash flow forecasting (discussed in chapter 5), especially if your baseline expenses tend to vary month to month. This will help you see how close your cash flow forecasts came to your actual cash. If you missed a few costs in your cash flow forecast that you expect to continue, this is a good time to adjust your cash flow forecast to include them going forward.

What about the one-off expenses that are out of the ordinary course of business? How do we know what we can afford if it is above and beyond our typical run rate? In part IV, I'll teach you how to set up an Opportunity Fund to earmark cash for business reinvestment opportunities.

Evaluate Your Return on Investment (ROI)

I'm not sure about you, but for me, the term *ROI* used to conjure up images of Wall Street brokers and crypto bros making conversation at the dinner party from Hell. Recently, I learned that an acquaintance of mine had purchased a boat that he had named *ROI*. I have to admit, I chuckled and rolled my eyes at the same time.

But ROI isn't just an overused buzzword; it's actually a pretty helpful concept to understand, especially for a small business. When we spend money in our business, particularly on indirect costs, the goal is for the investment to yield more money than we spent. If we invest in hiring an employee, for example, but the employee ends up costing us more than they generate or save us (in dollars or time), that hire probably wasn't a good investment. In that case, they didn't generate a return on our investment. When making decisions about where to spend your money in your business, it makes sense to prioritize the expenses you expect to have the highest ROI.

Return on Investment is calculated using a simple formula:

$$ROI = \frac{\text{Gross Profit - Investment}}{\text{Investment}} \times 100$$

In this case, your investment is the amount of money you originally spent. The gross profit is the total amount of money you made on the investment after any direct costs (such as cost of goods sold for a product business).

The easiest way to illustrate how to measure ROI and use it to guide business decisions is to look at an advertising campaign. Let's say Jim decides to run ads on social media for his e-commerce shoe business. He invested $5,000 into the campaign and made $15,000 in gross profit directly from sales his ads generated. What was Jim's ROI on that ad campaign? Let's plug the numbers into the above formula:

$$ROI = \frac{(15{,}000 - 5{,}000)}{5{,}000} \times 100$$

Which means:

$$ROI = 200\%$$

Not bad! Jim was able to triple his money within a month with that advertising campaign.

If you were Jim, how much would you spend on advertising in this case? Would you set a strict budget or even a percentage of sales? Personally, I wouldn't. If I knew a campaign was working, I would slowly scale it up and watch the numbers. If at any point I stopped seeing a return, I would discontinue running the campaign. But until then, I would put as much available cash as I could into it!

ROI helps us decide not only how to strategically reinvest in our business but also whether it makes sense to hire employees. For example, let's say Judy owns a graphic design agency. She rocks at what she does and has a waiting list of clients, so she decides to take on another graphic designer to help with the extra demand. She pays her staff a great hourly rate but bills her clients on a per project basis. If she pays her staff $8,000 in one month and bills her clients $16,000, that's a 100% return on investment, as illustrated below.

$$ROI = \frac{(16{,}000 - 8{,}000)}{8{,}000} \times 100 = 100\%$$

IT PAYS TO BE A BUSINESS OWNER

One massive advantage that business owners have over the general public is that we can invest our money into our business and make returns that far exceed anything you could get by investing in stocks and bonds. If you invested in the stock market for a long period of time, you might see a 10% average annual return if you're lucky. With a return of 10% per year, you'd double your money every seven years. Because of compounding, that means a $10,000 investment could become $100,000 in around twenty-five years. Not bad for a totally passive investment!

But could you imagine buying a stock that regularly gave you a 200% return? After making sure it wasn't run by Bernie Madoff, I'd probably scrounge up every penny I could to invest in it. But alas, opportunities for those kinds of returns are rare—unless, of course, you run a business.

As business owners, the money we *reinvest* into our business has the potential to provide a return that blows any other investment out

Clearly, hiring an extra team member was worth the investment for Judy. As demand for graphic design work grows, Judy plans to continue to expand her team while monitoring her ROI. As long as demand continues to support more hiring and she pays attention to her margins, she can expect to earn around a 100% return on each new team member she hires.

In these examples, we've had access to clear data that made it easier to calculate our ROI. Importantly, ROI isn't always this easy to calculate. For example, if you hire administrative support staff, the real ROI may be the time you free up to do activities that will generate more revenue. It can also be hard to measure the ROI of expenditures in more indirect investments, such as education or employee satisfaction. In these cases, monitoring metrics such as employee productivity or turnover can help you determine if you're getting an adequate return on your efforts. While you may not always be able to assign a specific monetary value to of the water—if we're smart about it. Let's say Jim took the $10,000 in profit he made from his first month running ads and reinvested it into more ads, which generated the same 2× return. He then took that whole $20,000 and put it back into ads, which generated him $40,000, and so on. In this example, by the end of just *one* year, he would generate $20,000,000 in gross profit as a result of his ads—even though he started with just $5,000.

Wait, *what?*

Yup.

While this is admittedly an oversimplification, getting a 200% (or greater!) return on your money in one month (or a few months) is very possible in a business. Of course, in reality, there is usually a point where your ROI starts to decline, so your business isn't necessarily an endless slot machine doubling your money. Nevertheless, this example illustrates the outsized ROI opportunity that business owners have. The key is to make sure you're tracking your ROI (even casually) and capitalizing on the opportunities in front of you.

your ROI, you'll likely be able to gauge whether the investment has been worthwhile on the whole.

Monitoring ROI isn't about getting it perfect or exact; it's about understanding what moves the needle in your business and what doesn't. In chapter 15, we'll talk more about how to evaluate investments and prioritize where you spend your money (and your time!).

You can probably see now how being hyperfocused on budgeting can get into the way of your business growth, especially if you are routinely missing great ROI opportunities. While of course it's important to be disciplined with money, we also don't want to be so rigid that we hinder our ability to scale up.

If this all feels a little too nebulous and unstructured, don't worry. In part IV, I'll talk about how you can set up systems that will support you and your financial goals and responsibilities without your having to spend hours every month reconciling a budget.

CHAPTER EIGHT
Manage Your Risk

As the CFO of your own business, you run the show when it comes to decisions that involve financial risk. In the context of business finances, risk management can include responsibilities such as mitigating the risk of being audited and making decisions about when to take on debt and how much.

As you might have guessed, risk management is another master control (along with expense management) in your Financial Control Room. It underpins each of the Big Three financial duties. Every decision you make at the controls should account for the relative risk involved and be influenced by your general risk tolerance level.

In working with small-business owners, I've seen just about every attitude imaginable when it comes to risk. It didn't take me long to realize how much people's individual psychology influences their overall risk tolerance.

In this chapter, I'll talk about what you're responsible for when it comes to risk management decisions such as tax deductions, debt, and business partnerships and how to mitigate some of these inherent risks of business ownership.

Know Your Risk Tolerance

Every expert out there loves to tell you that theirs is the *only* way to success and that if you give them XYZ amount of dollars, they'll share their imperial wisdom with you.

Oh, please.

You may have noticed by now that I am *not* a fan of one-size-fits-all advice. That's because you are an individual with your own talents, dreams, and way of processing information. We are not all the same, and that's especially true for risk tolerance. What you're comfortable doing may keep me up at night or vice versa.

Based on my work with thousands of entrepreneurs, I've created a rough spectrum of the attitudes I see toward risk in business. Keep in mind that the five descriptions below may not feel exactly like you. (Or your tolerance for risk may differ based on what you're doing. I know many people who are conservative with their business finances but wild out in other areas of their lives.) This scale is simply meant to get you thinking about how you handle risk in everyday life. As I've noted before, one-size-fits-all solutions are rarely effective and don't take differences among people into account. Even when it comes to financial decisions such as tax deductions and debt, there aren't always clear "right" and "wrong" answers. That's why knowing your risk tolerance is important when making financial decisions in your business.

RISK TOLERANCE SCALE

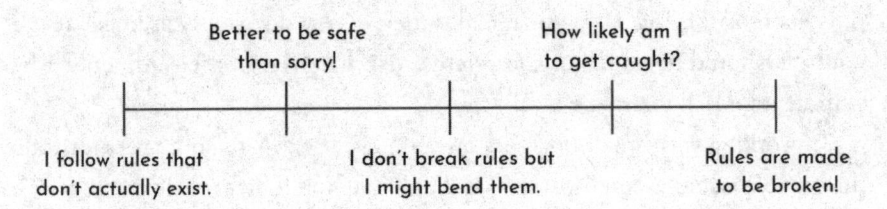

| I follow rules that don't actually exist. | Better to be safe than sorry! | I don't break rules but I might bend them. | How likely am I to get caught? | Rules are made to be broken! |

We make lots of decisions every day that involve our risk tolerance, but in this chapter, I'm going to focus on the two that involve both our money and our business, specifically, paying taxes and taking on debt.

Let's Talk About Taxes

Earlier in the book, I talked about how deductions are business expenses that lower your tax bill by reducing the profit you pay taxes on. Though I don't advocate writing off a Range Rover when your business doesn't need a gigantic SUV, you technically *can* deduct whatever you want. Say you are on the "rules are meant to be broken" side of risk tolerance and decide to deduct every trip you make to the grocery store and the local watering hole that has the best margaritas. No alarm bells will immediately go off when you file your taxes. But if you deduct a ton of personal expenses, such as the margs and the groceries, there's always a chance you could end up with a ton of back taxes and fines if you are audited.

In an extreme case, you might go to jail for tax fraud.

Or . . . you might never be audited at all.

That's why write-offs and deductions are, at least in part, about your personal risk tolerance. As a CPA, I can't advocate for writing off expenses that are clearly personal in nature (that's outright fraud). However, there is a wide range of gray area, especially when it comes to small businesses.

If the fear of letters from the IRS keeps you up at night, you should probably be more conservative about what you deduct. However, if you're more of an "ask for forgiveness instead of permission" type, you may decide to take a more, shall we say, relaxed approach to your deductions. Wherever you land on that continuum, you'll want to be aware of it and make sure any service professional you engage is aligned with your views. Accountants, just like anyone else, have varying degrees of risk tolerance and interpretations of tax law.

Want to test where you stand on the risk tolerance scale? Say these words out loud:

IRS audit.

Did your heart just start pounding? Mine did, and I knew that I was creating the test! The mere thought of a tax audit strikes fear into the hearts of many. You may even picture a full task force appearing unannounced at your house, ready to repossess your belongings *Schitt's Creek* style. But in actuality, audits are decidedly less dramatic than that. Most of the time an audit is a nuisance, not the end of the world (or your business). In fact, it's likely that you'd never actually meet or even talk to an agent during your audit (whew!). Most investigation is done by mail, asking for additional support for certain line items on your tax return, such as business deductions.

Still. We want to avoid audits when we can.

CHIEF FINANCIAL OPINION:
You Are Ultimately Responsible for Your Finances

Enlisting support to manage your finances—from bookkeepers to tax strategists—is a move I wholeheartedly endorse. But of course, not all financial professionals are created equal. I've heard countless horror stories that involve misplaced trust leading to unmet expectations or even financial mishandling. Heck, I've learned this lesson the hard way myself.

Sometimes the root of these problems is a lack of clear communication or misaligned expectations. Sometimes it's more egregious, resulting from the actions of an incompetent or unscrupulous actor. Regardless of the reason, the bitter pill we need to swallow is that the responsibility ultimately lies with us. Long story short: Just because an accountant "lets" you deduct something doesn't mean you are off the hook with the tax authorities.

Did your accountant neglect to file a state return you thought they filed? Maybe your tax pro overlooked your estimated tax payments? Perhaps your bookkeeper didn't log all of your income? The taxing authorities don't care *who* is to blame; you'll be the one on the hook for the penalties and interest. Although seeking restitution from the service provider is possible, it often entails a costly and lengthy legal process that isn't worth it.

The key takeaway? While you don't have to memorize 70,000 pages of tax code, having a foundational understanding of your obligations under federal and local tax laws is essential. It's wise to review your financial statements and tax filings critically and ask questions of your service providers. Keep close tabs on your finances, even if you've delegated the day-to-day tasks to other people. Ultimately, the responsibility rests on your shoulders.

That's why it's important to make sure our deductions hold up if and when an IRS agent decides to look closer. So how do you know if the IRS will allow your deductions under an audit? Unfortunately, there is no exhaustive list of things you can deduct versus not deduct in IRS guidance (if only!). While certain things have specific rules about their deductibility (interest, mileage, certain taxes, research and development, etc.), beyond these, the water gets murky. The same deduction allowed for one business might not fly for another. That's because the tax laws focus less on what the expense *is* and more on how it is *used* to determine deductibility. The IRS's guiding principle? Your deductions must be both "ordinary" and "necessary" within the context of your industry.

Okay, so what do these terms really mean?

According to the IRS, an "ordinary" expense is common and generally accepted in your industry. If others with similar businesses wouldn't raise an eyebrow at your expense, it's likely ordinary. However, the IRS also requires that an expense be "necessary" to be an allowable deduction. You might assume that means the expense must be *required* to run your business, but thankfully that isn't the case. In IRS-speak, a "necessary" cost is defined as one that is helpful and appropriate for your business. If that cost helps you run your business or make more money, it would likely be considered necessary.

A quick example to drive this home: David Rose owns an apothecary shop on his quaint town square that sells various artisan items. Would purchasing skin care products count as a "write-off" for the business? It depends! If he's purchasing them to test them and possibly sell them in the store, it would likely meet the requirements for a business deduction (if documented, of course—save those receipts!).

However, if he's purchasing them to use on himself because he's "the face of the business," that rationale likely wouldn't pass muster. Ultimately, the IRS isn't a big fan of people getting a little too cute with their deductions.

You may wonder how to show the IRS that an expense is both ordinary and necessary for your business. The key is to document, document, document (and then document some more). Make sure to note the business purpose of the expense, especially if it isn't immediately clear. Chances are you don't have a superhuman memory, which means you won't remember much in the way of specifics about a certain charge years from now. The IRS has three to six years to audit you, so by the time it comes knocking, your brain will probably have replaced all of that important information with more pressing facts, such as the minute details of the latest Netflix dating show.

You can jot down the details anywhere that works for you! On the receipt, in your accounting software, or even in a file saved in a special folder on your computer labeled "Important Stuff." It doesn't need to be official, and it certainly doesn't need a notary signature. The key is to put it somewhere you'll be able to find it later. Think of it as doing your future self a solid.

The purpose of keeping detailed expense records is twofold:

1. To show you made the payment you are claiming a deduction for

2. To support the business purpose of the charge

Some business owners decide to rely on bank and credit card statements rather than keep receipts, which can substantiate that the payment was made. However, whether you keep your receipts or not, you'll still need some way to prove the *nature* of the expense. Just having proof you paid for something doesn't guarantee that the IRS will agree it is an allowable deduction, especially if the business purpose is unclear. That box of receipts under your bed isn't going to do you any good if you don't have the details documented.

On the plus side, as technology advances, that box of receipts is becoming less and less relevant. There are many receipt capture tools that you can use from your phone, allowing you to scan your receipts, categorize your expenses, and include further details related to your charges electronically. If you use an accounting software, see if it has this functionality. It could save you lots of time and headaches chasing receipts!

To Overpay or Underpay?

Speaking of taxes, how (and when) we pay our taxes is also a matter of individual preference and risk tolerance. When you are self-employed, you are responsible for making sure you adequately estimate and make payments toward your tax liability. Ideally, this is done throughout the year via salary wage deductions (for corporations) and/or estimated tax payments. When you eventually file your taxes, your total tax liability as calculated on your return is compared to the amount you already paid to the taxing authority for that tax year.

If the amount due is higher than what you already paid (underpayment), you must make an additional tax payment for the difference.

If the amount due is lower than what you've already paid (overpayment), you'll get a refund.

Given all the factors involved in calculating your effective tax rate, it's nearly impossible to hit this number on the nose, especially for a business with less predictable earnings. Objectively, whether you underpaid or overpaid throughout the year, your total tax liability due is the same. Underpaying may have financial advantages, such as your being able to reinvest the money into your business or have more liquid cash in the bank, rather than tying up that money in taxes. But overpaying just feels fun, at least in the end. Psychologically, most individuals prefer getting a tax refund. A study published in *Psychology Today* found that even though 80 percent of households were expecting a refund for that tax year, only 19 percent planned to adjust their withholding the following year to withhold less.[1] Receiving money as a refund feels as though we've received a windfall gain, even when it was our money in the first place.

As entrepreneurs, we get to choose: If the chance of an unexpectedly large tax bill popping up scares you, you may opt to overpay your tax estimate as a kind of "forced savings." Alternatively, those who are more risk tolerant may look to pay the smallest amount possible throughout the year, waiting to "settle up" until their tax return is due.

In the middle might be the person who meets regularly with their tax accountant and tries to get as close as possible to the actual amount of taxes due, attempting to minimize the risk of both overpayment and underpayment. None of these approaches is wrong. The key is to know yourself and your risk tolerance and make a choice about the best path for you.

Let's Talk About Debt, Baby

Any decision related to debt should be made with your relative risk tolerance (or lack thereof) in mind. When we enter into any debt arrangement, there is risk involved. Whether it's a business loan, a line of credit, or a business credit card, we now owe something or someone money that must be paid back with interest. If we don't make good on our end of the bargain, there will likely be penalties and interest charges. For some, that risk may be worthwhile; for others, it could be psychologically crippling. When it comes to debt—and so many other money matters—a good choice for one person is not necessarily a good choice for another. (I'll talk more about debt and strategies to pay it down in chapter 17.)

Wherever you land on the issue of debt, there are ways to reduce your risk exposure while still getting the money you need for your business.

1. **Shop around.** Get quotes from big banks, local credit unions, and online banks. Ask fellow business owners what banks they recommend. Compare interest rates and repayment terms. Don't be afraid to negotiate; the worst thing they can do is say no.

2. **Get your documents in order.** Getting a business loan often requires proof of past earnings (such as tax returns) and future forecasts. You'll want to show that your business will be able to repay the loan without a problem. Hiring someone to help you create or refine a business plan and forecasts could be beneficial.

3. **Understand the terms of the loan.** Does the loan require collateral? What about personal guarantees? What will happen if you close the business? Know what will happen in a worst-case scenario so you can enter into the agreement with eyes wide open.

4. **Know your options.** Looking to solve a short-term cash flow need? Instead of carrying credit card balances, consider taking out a business line of credit that you can tap into if and when you need it. These are generally easier to get than fixed-rate business loans and have a shorter repayment period, but you'll pay interest only on what you borrow. Plus, you'll avoid the sky-high interest rates associated with carrying credit card balances.

Remember, though, that any time you enter into a debt arrangement, you are essentially borrowing from your future self, who will have to pay the debt back with interest. You are using tomorrow's money to fund today's expenses. If you are more risk averse, you'll likely be better served by using yesterday's money, not tomorrow's money, to grow your business. That means reinvesting a portion of the profit you've already made back into your business to grow it, rather than borrowing cash that must be paid back with interest at a later date.

We'll dive more into this concept when we talk about my PROFFIT Planning™ system later in this book. Organic growth like this may be slower, but it also comes with significantly less risk.

Risk Management and Partnerships

Risk management can get even stickier when you are in partnership with someone who has a different risk tolerance than you do. From that perspective, business partnerships aren't that much different from romantic partnerships. If you're in a committed relationship with someone who has a very different money philosophy, you know it can be a source of significant tension. When my husband and I got married, we learned this lesson very quickly. I saved half my lunch money every day from the time I was eight and started investing at the age of seventeen. He opened six credit cards his freshman year of college to get free T-shirts and once overdrafted his bank account buying Wendy's chicken nuggets. (Delicious? Yes. Worth it? No.) Needless to say, we didn't always see eye to eye when it came to money and risk.

While I'm no marriage counselor, I do know that communication has been the key to working through these differences. Talking about how each of us sees money has allowed us to move toward the middle a bit and even learn from each other. He now enjoys saving and investing, and I allow myself the occasional almond milk caramel macchiato without a shred of guilt (or fear of overdraft). A business partnership is no different; it's important to find common ground.

Going into a business partnership often seems less risky than starting a business on our own, but it comes with its own set of risks and frustrations. Leadership clashes, unequal commitment, and even dishonesty with money can create strife. Not only that, but a partnership is easy to start but often hard to unwind. Before structuring your business as a partnership, consider whether a different structure may be a better fit in the long term. There are other structures that allow for collaboration without both parties having an ownership stake in the entity.

For example, it may make sense for one person to own the business while another is an employee of the business. Alternatively, each individual can create their own business and work together in a strategic alliance or joint venture. This can make it much easier to separate down the line (and with fewer hard feelings).

Finances can be tough to manage on your own but become even more complicated when you introduce other people with totally different backgrounds, goals, and perspectives. If you do decide to move forward with a business partnership (or are already in one), aligning early and often on financial matters will make things go much smoother. From a financial perspective, a business partnership really isn't much different from a romantic partnership; open communication, values alignment, and trust are incredibly important to long-lasting success.

Take Action

Regardless of where you fall on the risk spectrum, there are seven important steps you can take to manage risk in your business:

1. **Document the business purpose of your deductions.** If you are under audit, having a receipt won't help you if you can't adequately explain why something was a business purchase. Put a process into place to document the business reason(s) for your purchases (perhaps in your accounting software, on a spreadsheet, or in a separate file on your computer—just make sure to back it up!).

2. **Have a separate bank account to save specifically for taxes.** Keeping money in a separate account will keep you from accidentally (or on purpose) borrowing from what you need to pay for taxes. I love surprises, just not when it comes tax time.

3. **Before entering into new debt, make sure you have a clear purpose and payoff plan.** How will you use the debt to get a return on your borrowed money greater than the loan interest? How will you leverage the debt for business growth? Do you want to repay the debt early, and if so, how and when will you make extra payments?

4. **If you enter into a business partnership, have an operating agreement and an exit strategy.** An operating agreement lays out important things such as who is responsible for what and how the profits (and losses!) will be split between the owners. It should also include an exit strategy. Functioning much like a prenup in a marriage, an exit strategy will outline what happens in case the partnership breaks up. If you're already in a partnership, it's not too late to create (or update) an operating agreement. Working with a lawyer to help mediate can reduce the tension and make sure you have all your ducks in a row.

5. **Determine how much of your own money you are comfortable investing into the business.** This is especially important at the beginning of a business, when extra capital might be needed to

get things moving. Having a limit on the personal equity you'll put into your business can help prevent you from putting your financial stability in jeopardy trying to kick-start a business that may turn out to be unprofitable.

6. **Determine how you will manage your money on an ongoing basis.** How much money will you take out of the business and when? How much will you set aside for reinvestment or emergencies? How will you give back? Creating a PROFFIT Plan (which I'll discuss in part IV) can greatly simplify decision-making and put your finances on autopilot.

In addition to the risk-related business decisions we've discussed in this chapter, other financial risks include employee fraud, economic risk, regulatory risk, credit risk, and more.

At the end of the day, all risks (and rewards!) will land on your shoulders as the business owner. Avoid the temptation to put blinders on, and, instead, tackle risk head-on. Your future self will be glad you did!

CHAPTER NINE
Manage Yourself

There's no shortage of tactical financial management duties in a small business. Your Financial Control Room is filled with all kinds of knobs, switches, and gauges to monitor and adjust the numbers in your business. But there's more to taking control of your finances than the numbers. In fact, the success of your other management activities will hinge on your awareness of one thing: yourself.

When I first started teaching entrepreneurs, I focused *only* on imparting my knowledge and tactics for managing money and optimizing profit. It didn't take long for me to realize that there was *so much more* to being financially successful than robust tactics. Yes, we need the practical advice, the templates, and the tools. As you can see, I've got loads of that. But if that's all I give you in this book, I'll be leaving out an incredibly essential component of success. And this one's not easy to track or calculate on a spreadsheet.

I'm talking about understanding yourself, including your motivations, beliefs, habits, and desires when it comes to money. When you understand yourself, you can better tap into your unique strengths and be more aware of potential pitfalls.

Once I started to incorporate this type of self-reflection into some of my financial programs, I saw my students' success rates drastically improve. Even if you're tempted to skip this chapter and get back to the meat-and-potatoes financial strategies, I hope you stick around. You just might benefit the most from this section.

Your Money Personality

Once I recognized how much of our success with money hinges on understanding ourselves, I went digging for resources to help my students with some self-reflection. I knew there must be brilliant thought leaders who had already done some amazing work in this area that we could benefit from.

While sleuthing through the internet one day, I happened upon Kendall SummerHawk and her eight Sacred Money Archetypes® and instantly saw how useful those insights would be for the entrepreneurs I taught. I became a certified coach of the Sacred Money Archetypes®, and I have now integrated her resources into my teachings.

For some of you reading, the term *sacred money archetype* might feel a little bit too "woo." Or perhaps you're stoked that we're talking about archetypes in a book on finance. When it comes down to it, an archetype is just a way of looking at a shared human experience. While we are wholly unique as human beings, we aren't alone in how we operate in the world.

Partly for the benefit of my non-woo friends, in this book I'll refer to these archetypes as your "money personality types." As with any other personality test, the goal is to help you understand yourself more fully and gain insights into how you make decisions and operate in the world, and ultimately implement a financial strategy that will leverage your unique strengths as a business owner.

Think of your money personality as the personal operating system in your Financial Control Room. These are your "factory settings," the built-in programming that shapes how you interact with each knob, switch, and gauge. Your money personality influences every decision you make in the control room, from how much risk you're comfortable taking to how closely you monitor your cash flow. But remember, while these "factory settings" are part of your financial DNA, they're also influenced by external factors, such as how you were raised and what you learned (or didn't learn) about money. Just as you can update software, you can adjust your financial "operating system" as you grow in self-awareness, which will help you make more intentional choices in your business.

Rest assured, there are no "bad" or "good" money personalities. Each has strengths and gifts, as well as challenges. Additionally, it's common to have several different money personality types influencing your decisions. The goal of understanding your primary money personality types is not to change them; instead, it is to help you lean in to your strengths and away from your weaknesses when it comes to money and finances. Learning about your money personalities can also help you design a unique money management system that will actually work *for* you, rather than forcing you to be someone you're not.

I recommend pausing a moment and taking the Money Personality Quiz at HiddenProfitTheBook.com. Take note of your top three personality types, and consider whether they resonate with you. All of the money personalities influence you in some way; however, your top three are typically the most prevalent in your day-to-day life (and can sometimes be in conflict, as we'll discuss).

CHIEF FINANCIAL OPINION:
That Expert May Not Be *Your* Expert

If you've tried to follow a program by an "expert" to help you improve your money habits but it hasn't stuck, that's probably because it wasn't built for someone with your money personality. In fact, many financial programs are created for and by people who are inherently motivated by fear to save (and sometimes hoard) their money.

But what if that's *not* you? Does it mean you are destined to live from paycheck to paycheck forever? Thankfully, the answer to that is a big fat *no*. Read on to find out why.

The Eight Money Personalities

Within Sacred Money Archetypes®, there are eight distinct personalities, each with its own beliefs about and approach to money. Below is a list of some of the core beliefs these personality types tend to have. While you may identify with several (or even all) of these beliefs on some level, your top three personality types will likely point to which beliefs are most deeply held and prevalent in your decision-making.

The Accumulator: You believe that your money could run out or disappear at any moment, and you need to be prepared.

The Alchemist: You believe that there are lots of creative ways you can make money, even if they are unconventional.

The Celebrity: You believe that money is a tool to achieve status and recognition.

The Connector: You believe that personal connections are more important than money and somehow you'll always be taken care of financially.

The Maverick: You believe that making money is a game, and you play to win.

The Nurturer: You believe that helping others often means sacrificing yourself and your financial resources.

The Romantic: You believe that money is to be enjoyed in the moment. YOLO!

The Ruler: You believe that the more you hustle today, the more happiness you'll have in the future.

As I mentioned before, each personality has strengths and superpowers that help you make (and keep) more money. Each also has obstacles and challenges that can hinder you from doing so. As with anything else in life, achieving self-awareness is the first step to making positive changes.

Manage Yourself 123

MONEY PERSONALITIES

	UNIQUE GIFTS	COMMON OBSTACLES
ACCUMULATOR (THE BANKER)	You are incredible at finding the best deals, and your saving habits help you reach financial independence.	You may struggle to be generous or invest in yourself or your business out of fear.
ALCHEMIST (THE IDEALIST)	You visualize endless moneymaking possibilities and idea generation never stops. You attract money in unconventional ways.	You may rebel against creating strict money habits and goals.
CELEBRITY (THE BIG SHOT)	You are a magnetic leader who makes a big impression, attracting money and opportunities.	You may spend compulsively and put status above financial security.
CONNECTOR (THE RELATIONSHIP CREATOR)	Your genuine nature makes it easy for people to trust you and want to buy from you.	You may avoid facing your money situation, hoping it will improve by leaning on others.
MAVERICK (THE REBEL WITH A CAUSE)	You have a knack for financial complexity and aren't afraid to forge new paths to get things done.	You may take big risks or dive headfirst into get-rich-quick opportunities that don't pan out.
NURTURER (THE SPONSOR)	You always overdeliver and give amazing value to people, leading to great customer reviews and repeat buyers.	You may find it difficult to set financial boundaries and can be taken advantage of.
ROMANTIC (THE HEDONIST)	You aren't intimidated by money and appreciate it for the abundance it brings to life.	Your "live in the moment" attitude might compromise your future financial security.
RULER (THE EMPIRE BUILDER)	You are a visionary leader with the power to innovate new and exciting ways of doing business and making money.	You never feel satisfied that you've done enough and are constantly moving the goalposts for yourself.

As you can see, every personality type has some amazing qualities that can be used to help you be financially successful. The key is to work with yourself and your own natural motivations and strengths, rather than trying to change them.

Now let's bring these money personalities to life and see how they can show up in our business and influence our decisions. Pay attention to whether you identify with any of these business owners and their thought patterns or actions.

As the owner of a small local coffee shop, Cynthia loves talking with interesting people and forming relationships with her regulars. Though she can handle even the pickiest coffee order with a smile, she gets overwhelmed quickly when it comes to managing her business's money. She struggles to build wealth for herself, but her optimistic outlook helps her keep faith that everything will be okay.

Cynthia's primary money personality type is Connector. Connectors value relationships and exude faith and optimism. They generally don't overly stress about money. Sometimes this leads to a lack of financial knowledge and independence or blindly trusting others with financial decisions. In business, a Connector often outsources as much of the finances as possible, including deferring to others on important financial decisions whenever they can. Cynthia is the embodiment of a Connector.

Contrast her with June, who owns an online education business that appears to be very successful. She stockpiles money "just in case" and avoids anything she perceives as risky. She keeps up with her books and prides herself on her financial responsibility. June is on track to retire early. Her primary money personality is Accumulator.

Accumulators are super comfortable with money and prefer to save. Outwardly, they are often envied for their fiscal responsibility and independence. Internally, they can find it difficult to be generous to others out of fear. Accumulators chase security and believe that money will make them feel safe, yet they never get to the point where they feel like they have enough. In business, an Accumulator is often hesitant to invest in their business and may struggle to hire help and grow because of the risk involved. While they can appear from the outside as if they have it all together, inside they worry that they could lose it all at any moment.

Lee owns a personal organizing business, and she's absolutely amazing at it. She could organize Marie Kondo's closet. She has some good financial habits and isn't particularly prone to overspending. But she struggles to charge what her work is worth and finds herself offering discounts to just about everyone. She has trouble setting boundaries and often says yes to too much, which at times causes her income to suffer. Lee is a bona fide Nurturer.

Reading these stories, do you identify with any of them? Do you envy any of them? Feel judgment toward any of them?

Think back to some recent financial decisions you've made, big or small. Can you see how those choices may have been influenced by your money personality? Whether you are a Maverick who fell for another get-rich-quick scheme that didn't pan out or a Nurturer who gave a friends and family discount to the mailman, your money personality types probably play a role in your business decisions.

The Power of Three

Depending on your quiz results, you may notice that you have one dominant money personality type that takes the lead in making most decisions. Or if your scores for several types are fairly close, it could mean that you have several personality types regularly in play. Your personality types don't cancel one another out, but they can sometimes create internal tension. Having multiple money personalities may make you feel overwhelmed and conflicted, but in reality, their internal checks and balances serve an important purpose.

When I work with my students, I always want to know their top three money personalities. Why? Because different money personalities can come out at different times. I'm often told that business owners tend to have one dominant personality type that shows up in their personal financial life and another one that typically shows up when making business decisions. That's totally normal. Overall, the more awareness you have of these patterns, the better!

For example, I'm an Accumulator-Maverick-Ruler.

Like June, my Accumulator always wants me to play it safe, while my Maverick pushes me to take risks. My Accumulator tells me it's frivolous to add guac to my burrito, whereas my Maverick encourages me to get every extra that Chipotle offers, even the hot sauce I'm not sure I can handle. At times, it can feel as though I have both a devil and an angel on my shoulders, whispering into my ear (I'll let you decide which you think is which). Then, out of nowhere, my Ruler joins the conversation and has me daydreaming about starting my own Chipotle franchise.

However, after learning about money personalities and my specific types, I realized that this conflict is actually productive and can help me make better decisions. For example, if I'm considering making a big investment into my business (perhaps hiring an employee or trying out a new marketing method), I can allow my three main archetypes to duke it out among themselves. My Maverick will be happy if I'm taking a risk, any risk; my Ruler will be satisfied once I have a really clear vision or plan, and my Accumulator just wants to see the cash flow analysis and how the decision will affect the business financially. Collectively, this creates a balance in my decision-making that I wouldn't otherwise have.

> **CHIEF FINANCIAL OPINION:**
> **We Can't All Be Accumulators**
>
> It's common for people to tell me that they wish they were an Accumulator. There's a general impression that this money personality is the best because it excels at budgeting and puts a priority on saving more than some of the other personalities do. (Like, cough, the Romantic or the Celebrity.) But in reality, Accumulators typically struggle with a lot of worry, even when they have stores of money that could make Scrooge McDuck jealous. Trust me, I know, because I am an Accumulator myself. For us, the fear of not having enough can be all-consuming. That scarcity mindset can creep into your business and cause you to penny pinch to a degree that isn't helpful or productive.
>
> I'll say it again: There isn't a "good" or a "bad" money personality. Even Accumulators have challenges. They just might not be yours.

Take Action

Knowing your main money personalities can help you design a money management plan that will work for who you are, what you value, and what motivates you. For example: Romantics and Celebrities will resist anything that takes a "beans and rice" approach to spending, while Nurturers and Connectors will have trouble sticking to a plan they believe puts money over people. Mavericks and Alchemists need to have room in their budget for innovation and exploring new ideas, while a Ruler needs to know they are building something of lasting value, and every Accumulator needs to feel as though a decision won't put them into financial jeopardy.

Let's go back to Cynthia, our coffee shop–owning Connector from earlier. Cynthia's top three types are Connector-Nurturer-Alchemist. With this combination of money personalities, it's likely that people love the community she has created at her shop. Her customers feel connected to her, and her employees are incredibly loyal. Any financial plan that would require her to cut salaries or benefits for her team or impact the quality of what she sells would likely be a nonstarter. Instead, knowing her money personalities, she taps into her Alchemist to come up with creative ways to make more money in her business, including capitalizing on her loyal following.

When she finally recognizes it's time to increase her prices because her costs have increased, she decides to institute a new loyalty and referral program to reward customers who come back often and bring their friends. With her business now running more profitably, she satisfies her Nurturer's need to give back by hosting monthly "coffee for a cause" events, where she partners with local organizations to donate a portion of that day's proceeds. Cynthia also knows that her Connector is inclined to hide from finances, so she hires a bookkeeper who will have regular meetings with her to make sure her finances stay up to date, and she stays informed about what's happening financially in her business.

This is just one example of how you can use all three of your primary money personality types to design a money management plan that will work best for you. If you're wondering how to institute this practically, I recommend going through a few steps to help you utilize your money personalities in a positive way.

1. **Identify your nonnegotiables.** What is most important to you when it comes to business? List one to three things. Don't compromise on these. Let them guide your decision-making.

2. **Find the financial management gaps in your business.** Where do you struggle? Do you find yourself overspending? Hoarding money? Undercharging? Ignoring your finances altogether? Don't be afraid to be honest with yourself and note these down.

3. **Consider how to put processes into place to help you bridge your financial gaps.** If you tend to overspend, consider automating your savings. If you hoard money, consider creating a savings fund for reinvestment purposes. If you undercharge, institute a formula for determining prices. If you ignore your finances, perhaps outsource your financial compliance and set up regular meetings with an adviser to go

over your results. In parts III and IV of this book, we'll dive into these systems and strategies in more detail.

4. **Reflect on your strengths.** Are you utilizing them effectively in your business? How could you lean more into your capabilities and gifts? Have fun brainstorming new moneymaking ideas and creating a plan of action.

Leaning in fully to who you are and what matters to you will be a gift that keeps on giving. Unlike what you may have been told, the key to financial success isn't reinventing yourself and becoming a whole new personality type. Instead, the money plans that actually create wealth are customized to fit your life and your personality. Work with what you have; I guarantee it's already enough.

Bonus: Treasure Hunting in Your Business

Use your money personalities to find some quick cash now! Here are a few ideas on where to look to find some quickly available hidden money, based on your primary money personality types.

The Accumulator: Your hidden money may be opportunity cost. Where could you be using your money to foster growth? What measured risks could you take to help you grow your money without hustling harder?

The Alchemist: Your hidden money might relate to a past path that you have moved on from. Are there costs you are still incurring for an old idea (software subscriptions, website hosting, etc.)? If you aren't ready to fully let go of them, see if you can pause your membership for free or a low cost for a while.

The Celebrity: Not all "luxe" experiences are actually luxurious. Review your recurring expenses with a focus on what return you receive. Do you get a lot out of your Soho House membership or flashy business credit card? Or would you rather spend that money on creating a luxe experience for your customer that will generate even more cash and profit later on?

The Connector: You've likely built a diverse and loyal network of people who have your back and want to help you succeed. Tap into that network to seek out referrals and collaborations. You're already doing the same for others, after all!

The Maverick: Where might you need to cut your losses? Review the ROI on past business investments and determine which types have been successful and which have not. Cutting your losses now could free up capital for your next big, calculated move. Consider pivoting to something new where the odds of success will be more in your favor.

The Nurturer: Where have you secretly felt resentful when it comes to money? It may be time to raise your prices, collect on your past due invoices, or ask friends and family to finally repay your "loans" to them.

The Romantic: Where might you be paying for experiences that you no longer value or enjoy? Remember, the more you save now, the more you will have available to spend in the future.

The Ruler: Time is the most valuable asset you have. Where could investing money help you free up time? Consider investing in systems to automate or delegate small tasks so you can focus on making more money.

In part IV, I'll dive deeper into how to create a customized plan for your business that satisfies the needs of your money personalities. For now, just know that the most successful financial path forward for you is one that works with your ingrained money personality traits, rather than fighting against them.

PART III

Find Your Hidden Profit

In part I, I covered the importance of knowing your numbers and understanding what they're telling you. Then in part II, you stepped into your Financial Control Room, learning how to take control of your business finances. You've begun to get familiar with the different switches and gauges, especially compliance and cash management.

Now it's time for the fun part—the Strategy Wall—where you put on your CFO hat and start uncovering hidden profit in your business. Believe it or not, there's untapped profit already hiding out in your business, just waiting for you to find it. And as in any game of hide-and-seek, success depends on knowing where to look.

In this section, I'll guide you through finding hidden profit with eight powerful financial strategies, or Profit Levers, that you can adjust to make strategic and calculated decisions. By the end of the section, you'll know *exactly* which actions to take to boost your profitability—and feel like the true BOSS that you are.

CHAPTER TEN
Become Profitable

For years, Beth had been loosey-goosey with her business finances. As a dog groomer, she wanted to raise her salary but also knew that taking on more clients would make her feel even more burned out. She felt stuck. Her business was making money, but she worried about being able to afford extra help. She believed that there had to be a way for her business to pay her well, be profitable, *and* give her some free time to spend with her family and friends and even her own dog!

Beth's situation is based on a common experience of many of the students I've worked with over the years, each facing similar concerns. Running a consistently profitable business can often feel like a pipe dream, especially during times of economic uncertainty or when your business relies heavily on high sales volumes. But we often have more control than we realize.

For a lot of business owners, constantly running after more sales seems like the best solution for many, many problems. And while it's true that a business can't exist without sales, generating more sales and revenue is not the only way to create profit.

> **CHIEF FINANCIAL OPINION:**
> **Ditch the Excuses**
>
> As with anything else in life, things in business don't always go as planned. But even then we have a choice: We can either stew on it, throw ourselves a pity party and blame our circumstances on everything (and everyone) else, or step up and take back control.
>
> Business owners who take ownership and accountability for their results are more resilient in the face of adversity, both mentally and financially. They know that challenging times aren't an "if" but a "when"—and they prepare for the unknown as best they can. They save up financial reserves and actively practice adaptability, remembering that the status quo is never guaranteed, especially in business. Resilient companies are more likely to have healthy Balance Sheets, encourage innovation, and focus on long-term sustainability. Developing psychological and financial resilience is a crucial skill for staying in business. In fact, research done by Accenture found that companies that were considered highly resilient could expect to grow their revenue 6% faster and have profit margins 8% higher on average than their peers.[1]
>
> This is what I want every entrepreneur to understand: Even when circumstances are beyond your control, you can still control your *response* to those circumstances. Don't wait for tough times to practice this mindset; start taking control now. By honing these skills during good times, you'll build resiliency you can tap into when times inevitably get tougher.

Introducing the Profit Levers

Remember the Strategy Wall filled with levers in your Financial Control Room? Picture yourself walking up to that wall. Each lever is labeled with a different aspect of your business that impacts your overall profitability. When you pull a lever, voilà, more profit.

Become Profitable

The primary Profit Levers in your business are:

1. **Volume:** The number of sales you make
2. **Price:** The amount you charge for each sale
3. **Mix:** The mixture of products and services you sell
4. **Average Transaction Value:** The average value of each sale
5. **Direct Costs:** Costs that directly relate to creating a product or providing a service
6. **Indirect Costs:** Overhead costs that can't easily be assigned to specific sales
7. **Taxes:** Federal and state income taxes and payroll/self-employment taxes
8. **Debt:** Your business's outstanding debt and interest

PROFIT LEVERS

VOLUME PRICE MIX AVERAGE TRANSACTION VALUE

DIRECT COSTS INDIRECT COSTS TAXES DEBT

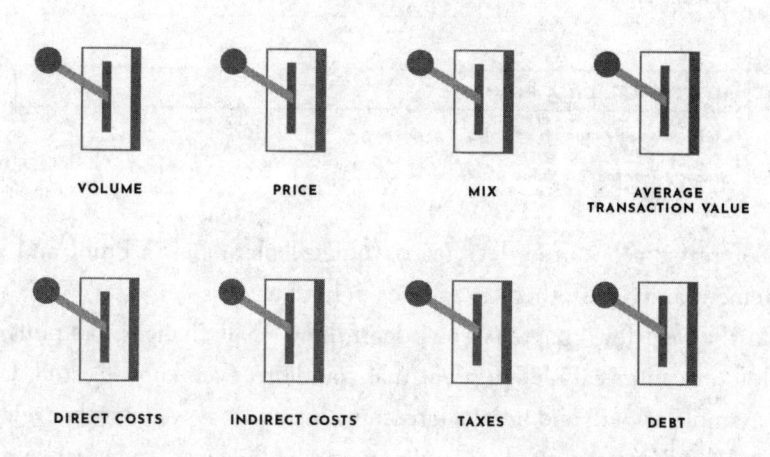

As the control room operator, you have the power to adjust any of these levers to make an impact on your business's bottom line. Tweaking any one of the levers will typically impact your profit in some way, and learning how to use them to your advantage is a skill you can hone.

136 Hidden Profit

This concept was born out of my experience in finance at a major Coca-Cola bottling company, where holding pity parties and doing nothing weren't options. If we were nearing the end of a quarter and not quite hitting our target profit numbers, the CFO would ask, "What lever should we pull?" We would look at the data and make a plan of action. Could we promote certain products? Increase prices? Make spending cuts? The answers varied based on the situation, but the point was always the same: *We* had control. And now so do you.

Learning about your Profit Levers will help you overcome any obstacle that comes your way. Feeling comfortable in your control room can take some time and effort, but I promise that you will succeed.

BETH'S ANNUAL P&L

	P&L	PROFIT MARGIN %
Revenue	$ 130,000	
Direct Costs	54,000	
Gross Profit	76,000	58%
Indirect Costs	46,000	
Operating Profit	$ 30,000	23%

ADDITIONAL DATA POINTS

Average weekly number of sales	50
Average Transaction Value (ATV) per sale	$50

Before we get started, let's take a quick look at Beth's Profit and Loss Statement and a few other key metrics in her business.

In the next few chapters, you'll learn how small changes, or "pulls," on each lever can reveal hidden profit that you didn't even know existed. Using the example of Beth and her dog-grooming business, as well as other relevant examples, I'll demonstrate how "pulling" each of the levers can create a ripple effect that will transform your finances and how you see your business— and ultimately help you feel more confident when times get challenging.

CHAPTER ELEVEN
Sell More

When I work with entrepreneurs, I start by listening. I want to hear, in their words, where they feel they are struggling in their business. What keeps them up at night? What feels hard? What feels easy? Typically, within the first five minutes, I know which Profit Lever would be most beneficial for them to pull first. That was the case for my client Julia.

Julia had an artisan soap business that was well known in her local area. She had recently overhauled her prices to ensure adequate profit margins and had hired some help to increase her production capacity. She was feeling the cash flow crunch of having an employee on payroll for the first time and was second-guessing if she had made the right decision.

Julia hired me to review her financials and point out opportunities for improvement. When we first chatted, she seemed to think that the answer to her profitability problem was to scale back her business to just her again. Her overall profit margins were higher without an employee on staff, and she knew she'd be able to pay herself more routinely if she didn't have payroll to worry about (even though what she'd be able to pay herself was meager compared to the amount of work she put in).

I quickly explained to Julia that eliminating her staff might help her feel more financially secure in the short term but could significantly limit her future earning potential. In fact, she was poised for growth, and she just needed to go for it. Since she had increased capacity and healthy profit margins, it was time for her to make a plan to increase her sales volume and thereby her profit. It was time for her to pull a lever.

The first and most obvious Profit Lever (and the one Julia needed to focus on) is **Volume**. Volume is the number of sales you make in a given time period. Sales volume is arguably the "default" lever in our business. When we aren't making as much money as we'd like, our first (and sometimes only) solution is that we need to *make more sales*. And a lot of us conflate *sales* with *marketing*. That's why teaching marketing to business owners is a multibillion-dollar industry. Whether they're learning the latest social media algorithm hacks, understanding how to get found on Google, or absorbing new email list–building strategies, entrepreneurs are thirsty for more marketing know-how.

Don't get me wrong; your marketing strategy is an incredibly important part of your business. But marketing isn't the only thing that matters. For example, it cannot fix a profitability problem. When you have a product or an offer that isn't profitable, adding more sales to your business is only going to make that problem more evident.

Let's go back to Dave and Chuck, our winery owners from chapter 3. Before I began working with them, they assumed that the answer to their financial woes was to sell more wine. But since they were unknowingly selling their chardonnay at an unprofitable price, increasing the amount they sold would have made matters worse. They'd be working harder for even *less* money and likely spending more on marketing campaigns at the same time. In my experience, focusing on marketing before your finances is one of the quickest ways to experience burnout and drain your cash reserves. While there are seasons when we do need to chase sales, we can't do it permanently.

So when is the right time to pull your business's Volume Lever? One important time to focus on volume is when you are first starting out in business. You want and need to bring in those first few sales to test your offer and make sure it is something that people actually want and will pay for. But once you have the first customers under your belt, it's likely time to move your focus away from volume—for now. Don't worry, we're not going to let that lever get too dusty. Instead, we're going to utilize the other Profit Levers first to make sure we maximize the profitability of each and every sale we make. Then, and only then, will it be time to come back and pull the Volume Lever again.

If you're a seasoned business owner, pull the Volume Lever when:

1. You've reviewed your cash collection and payment processes and made tweaks to maximize your cash flow, as detailed in chapter 6. Growing sales too quickly is a major cause of the dreaded cash flow crunch, so it's important to get ahead of it.

2. You know that your profit margins on all of your products and services are where they need to be to meet your profitability goals (we'll talk about this more in the next chapter).

3. You run a service-based business and have excess capacity, or you run a product-based business with lots of on-hand inventory. Assuming that your profit margins are healthy (see number 2 above), it's time to focus on bringing in more customers so you can sell that excess capacity.

My student and artisan soap maker, Julia, met all of these criteria. When we reviewed where she was making the most sales, the answer was clear: farmers' markets and craft expos. For her, pulling the Volume Lever looked like increasing the number of markets and expos she attended. And because she had recently hired help with the production side of the business, she had more free time to focus on sales growth.

It's worth noting that many business owners don't have extra capacity or a helping hand. If you feel totally overwhelmed and burned out by your business, as our dog groomer, Beth, did, bringing in more sales without making any other changes will likely cause more harm than good. If that's you, resist the urge to say yes to everything, even if that means turning down sales (yes, really).

Like many entrepreneurs, when I started my business, I assumed that I should say yes to anyone and everyone who wanted to work with me. Because of that mindset, I routinely modified my services to fit every prospective client's individual wants. Need someone to clean up your QuickBooks? Sure. File your tax return? You got it. Pick up your dry cleaning? Why not? (Okay, perhaps that last one is an exaggeration—but not by much!)

Late one evening, while sorting through years of receipts a client had literally left on my doorstep, I had an epiphany: I *hated* doing compliance work. Why had I said yes to this? To make matters even worse, when I did the math to estimate how much I was being paid per hour for something that I didn't want to do, it made my stomach sink even more. I had made more money waiting tables as a college student.

Staring at my kitchen island covered with years of my client's receipts, I vowed then and there that I wouldn't do that to myself again. As it turns out, it *is* possible to say "I'm sorry, that's not something I offer." When we do, we open the door to customers who want to buy the services that we love to provide.

I learned this lesson so you don't have to: *Not every sale is worth making*.

While it may be tough to say no to someone who wants to give us money, it's sometimes necessary. Remember, saying yes to something (or someone) means we're saying no to something else. The more we dial in to who we are and who we want to serve, the more good-fit opportunities will show up for us. As it turns out, being true to yourself is the quickest pathway to more (and better-aligned) sales.

This is especially important when it is time to pull the Volume Lever because hopefully your efforts will result in more leads coming your way, requiring more discernment about whom you want to work with as well as whom you will politely say no to. And while I don't pretend to be an expert in all things sales and marketing, I *do* know what has worked for me when growing my business. As much as we think sales is a game of luck (or going viral), I've found that going back to these tried-and-true strategies works every time.

Proven ways to increase sales include:

1. **Refine your message.** Have clarity about who you serve and how you serve them, and make sure your unique value-add comes across in your marketing. Consider your best customers. What makes them a perfect fit for you? Ask those customers why they picked your business. Use that information to hone your messaging and marketing strategy.

2. **Figure out what's working.** How did your current customers find you? Remember the Pareto principle: 80 percent of our results come from 20 percent of our actions. What is the 20 percent that is driving people to your business? Do more of that and cut out the rest.

3. **Build your marketing plan with longevity in mind.** Don't waste your time searching for a quick fix. If your business success depends on going (or staying) viral, that's not a great business plan. Trendiness is difficult, if not impossible, to sustain long term. Algorithms change, but understanding the psychology of how and why people buy is timeless.

4. **Ask for the sale.** Remember, sales and marketing are *not* the same thing. You can be an excellent marketer and abysmal at actually selling. Marketing is about creating awareness; sales is about converting that awareness into a purchase. Don't let fear of being "too salesy" keep you from asking people to buy, whether in person, via email, or on your website/social media. Remember, what you have to offer is valuable, and people need it. Brag about your business just as you would your favorite restaurant or clothing boutique.

5. **Focus on sustainable growth.** Growing before you have the systems in place to support that growth is a quick way to end up with unhappy customers and a marred reputation (not to mention a burned-out owner). Consider: Do I have the capacity to service more customers and still maintain quality and service levels? Will taking on more clients impact the overall customer experience of existing customers?

Start by aiming for just 2% volume growth, meaning that if you normally make 100 sales in a month, you should aim for 102. Once you hit that goal, aim for another 2%, and so on. It may seem slow, but remember that growth compounds. Starting slowly can give you the traction you need to move forward and will also ensure that your business doesn't grow faster than your systems can handle.

If you steadily grow your sales by just 2% per month, by the end of Year 1, you'll be making 27% more monthly sales than you were at the start of the year.

Powerful, right? If 2% per month of sales growth still feels overwhelming, start by targeting just 2% in *annual* growth, especially if your capacity is limited.

Remember our friend and pet groomer, Beth? She was already feeling maxed out on clients, so she decided to set a target of just 2% sales growth over the next year. But before that, she knew she had some work to do on the other Profit Levers to make sure that 2% growth would have the biggest possible impact to her bottom line. Which is exactly what we're going to talk about next.

CHAPTER TWELVE
Raise Your Prices

When Sarah started her business, she set her prices low, thinking affordability would help her attract more customers. She wanted to get her name out there and figured that lower prices would make her services more appealing. But even as she gained clients, she found herself struggling to make ends meet. Then she started seeing advice online:

"Charge what you're worth!"

"Raise your prices to reflect your value!"

"You're undercharging because you don't believe in yourself. Double your prices now!"

It seemed as though every business coach on social media was saying similar things. Inspired by that advice, she doubled her rates overnight. But instead of feeling more confident, she felt uncertain every time a client asked about her fees. She began second-guessing herself, even wondering if she should lower her prices again to keep business steady.

The truth is, "Charge what you're worth," while empowering in theory, isn't always helpful in practice. **Your worth as a human being is immeasurable**, and no price tag can capture that. Pricing isn't about your personal worth; it's about the value of what you're offering to your audience and the costs to deliver it.

If you've ever felt confused about pricing, wondering how to charge in a way that's both fair and profitable, you're not alone. Should your prices match those of a competitor? Should your prices account for every hour you work? And what about the clients who say they can find someone cheaper to do the same work?

Setting the right price can be challenging, but it doesn't have to be arbitrary. In this chapter, I'll walk you through a simple, data-driven formula that focuses on real value, so you can set prices confidently and with purpose. By the end, you'll know exactly how to price your products and services to reflect their true worth—and feel empowered doing it.

However, first I must talk about *wrong* ways to set prices. When I ask small-business owners how they determined the prices they charge for their products or services, these are three responses I typically get.

Mistake 1: Basing your prices on what competitors in your industry or local area charge for similar products or services

On its face, this approach seems reasonable, right? Of course we want to be competitive in the marketplace. If we have direct competition and price our services or products way higher than other businesses do, it stands to reason that we'll make fewer sales.

Similarly, if our goal is simply to make more sales, it makes sense to price lower than everyone else. But as we discussed in the last chapter, selling *a lot* of something without first making sure those sales will be sufficiently profitable is a recipe for burnout (and bankruptcy).

Additionally, when you base your prices on your competitors', you don't know what you are comparing yourself to. You have absolutely *no* idea what it costs your competitors to run their business or if they're even able to pay themselves. They could have tons of customers and still be **struggling** financially (and based on the average income figures of small-business owners I talked about earlier, it's more likely that they *aren't* rolling in dough).

Or your top competitors could be independently wealthy and not rely on their business to generate income. What other businesses charge for their products and services has little to do with what *you* need to charge to meet your income goals. Sometimes you need to resist the urge to look around and simply keep your eyes on your own paper.

CHIEF FINANCIAL OPINION:
There Is No Such Thing as Competition

I use the word *competitors* reluctantly, because I no longer believe in the idea of competition in business. A better term would be *industry peers*. Competition implies that there is a limited amount of business (and income) to go around, so we need to fight constantly for our share. After buying into this idea for far too long, I now completely reject it.

I know what you're thinking: "But Jamie, there really *is* a limited market for what I sell in my town." That may be true. I'm not saying that there is an endless supply of customers out there for every business. But I do believe that there are *enough*. Instead of focusing on how to compete with others, it's more productive (and less impostor syndrome inducing) to focus on making your product or service the best it can be.

And if you're a woman, as I am, you probably know firsthand how society tries to pit us against one another. Whether in Hollywood, in sports, or on social media, it seems as though women are expected, and sometimes encouraged, to be rivals. But as much as society tells us this competition is natural, I believe our true nature is one of care and collaboration.

My business really gained traction when I decided to get to know other people in my industry on a personal level, without any ulterior motive. When I made the first move to reach out, my network grew exponentially. People I had secretly envied from afar became trusted friends and confidants. Our conversations opened the door to shared initiatives that benefited everyone involved.

Business is *not* a zero-sum game. For you to win, others don't have to lose. There is tremendous power in numbers when we choose collaboration over competition.

Mistake 2: Basing your prices on feelings

As the owner of a small independent furniture company, Maria makes custom pieces such as dining tables, desks, and shelving units for her clients. Originally, she charged what "felt" like a good price. She attempted to anticipate what her customers would think was fair. If you do this, too, you're not alone. I've found that it's common practice for business owners to "eyeball it" when determining prices.

But that also turns setting prices into making emotional decisions rather than mathematical ones. And that's problematic because feelings can lead us astray, especially when money is involved. Our emotions and thought processes are heavily shaped by our history, our circumstances, and what we believe to be true.

Every time Maria was asked to provide a quote, she tried to predict how much that person would be willing to spend. She was scared to lose business by quoting prices higher than what customers might expect, so she often lowballed her work. On more than one occasion, that led to her feeling resentment over being underpaid for a job that she herself had set a price on!

While setting a lower price made her temporarily feel more confident and comfortable, the fear of rejection that went into creating that price in the first place contributed to her setting a price she regretted later. To avoid pricing regret and maximize profit, pricing must include a formula—in addition to feelings.

Don't get me wrong; emotion does have a place in pricing decisions. Some business owners may choose to charge less for their products and services because they want to be accessible to a market they are passionate about serving.

However, when you are running a for-profit business, it's important to know the math so you can ensure that your company will be able to support itself (and you) at the prices you plan to charge. If you charge so little that you can't afford to stay in business or can't grow, you won't be able to serve your customers at all. Knowing your numbers also means that you won't be tempted to give everyone and their barista a "friends and family" discount that will wipe out your profit (I'm looking at you, Nurturers!).

Mistake 3: Taking blanket pricing advice from people who don't know your business

Like Sarah, we can easily get swept up in pricing advice from coaches or social media experts who advocate blanket solutions such as "Just double your rates!" While these statements may sound empowering, they often miss the nuances of your specific business. Following advice that doesn't account for your unique costs, market, and goals can lead to your setting prices that don't work for you. And if you feel uneasy about your prices, that hesitation often shows to your clients.

The key is to set prices you understand, believe in, and can explain with confidence. When you take the time to calculate prices based on your underlying costs and the value you provide to your customers, you'll feel empowered to stand behind them.

How to Price Your Products and Services

Now that you know how *not* to price your products and services, what should you do instead? Use your data, of course!

There *is* a formula for coming up with appropriate prices (hurrah!). It will help you determine the *minimum* you need to charge to create sufficient profit, based on the costs associated with producing a product or service and your target gross profit margin, which we'll discuss below. The Pricing Formula is:

$$\frac{\text{Direct Costs}}{1 - \text{Target Gross Profit Margin \%}} = \text{Minimum price to charge}$$

Let's break this down step by step so you can calculate the minimum price to charge for each of your products and services.

Step 1: Determine your direct costs.

When setting prices in your business, the most important data point to consider is the costs to create the product or deliver the service, called direct costs. These are closely tied to the product or service you are selling and don't include overhead costs.

Direct costs are another of the Profit Levers, but because of their importance here as well, it can be helpful to analyze them in tandem with the Price Lever.

In some cases, such as retail sales, figuring the direct cost of a given product may be fairly straightforward. For example, if you are buying purses wholesale from a manufacturer to resell in your retail store, the direct cost is the price you paid the wholesaler for the purses.

However, for other types of businesses, especially service-based ones, estimating your direct costs can be more complex. In a service-based business, the primary direct cost is typically the labor involved in performing the work for the customer. It's important to note that only labor related to delivering the service paid for by the customer counts as a direct cost. For a service-based solopreneur, your time may be the primary direct cost—but how exactly do you value that? We'll tackle valuing owner labor for the purpose of calculating your prices later in this chapter.

Distinguishing between direct and indirect costs is crucial to accurate pricing. Including indirect costs along with direct costs in your pricing equation can distort your view of profitability because it's difficult, if not impossible, to allocate them accurately to each product or service. For example, if you try to allocate your business's utility bill to each product or service, how will you do it? Based on the number of sales? Total revenue? Total profit? You technically *could* allocate it any way you want, but that allocation wouldn't necessarily be helpful when it comes to assessing the profitability of each profit or service. Attempting to allocate indirect costs for the purpose of pricing makes for inconsistent gross profit margins and unnecessarily overcomplicates the computation process. That's not to say we don't want to consider indirect costs at all when setting prices (more on that in a bit); we just don't want to consider them in the numerator of the Pricing Formula.

As a further example, let's say you own a brick-and-mortar bookstore. In addition to purchasing the books you sell, you pay rent, utilities, marketing, and your store staff, among other costs. Which of these costs represent direct costs for your business? If you said only the books you purchase to resell, you'd be right. That's because all the other costs would not be easy to allocate to any specific sale. While your bookstore staff may help sell the books by providing recommendations, in most cases it would be difficult to allocate their pay to each individual sale. An exception to this would be if you pay your staff a sales commission based on the amount they sell. Their commission would be directly related to each sale and would be considered a direct cost. Because of that, you will also want to consider any commissions you pay on sales when you set your prices.

It might seem as though I'm irresponsibly casting indirect costs to the wayside, but I'll get to them very soon! Even though indirect costs aren't factored into your pricing analysis, they should be considered when setting your target gross profit margin percentage, which we'll discuss in the next step.

Step 2: Determine your target gross profit margin.

As you will recall from chapter 7, direct costs are also a key component of another formula: your gross profit margin. As a refresher, your gross profit margin is calculated as:

$$\text{Gross Profit Margin} = \frac{\text{Revenue} - \text{Direct Costs}}{\text{Revenue}} \times 100$$

While typical gross profit margins can vary widely by business or industry, I suggest aiming for a *minimum* target gross profit margin between 40% and 60% for *each* of your products or services.

How do you determine where in that range to aim? This is where indirect costs come in. If your business has significant overhead (indirect costs), I recommend aiming to make 60% gross profit (or more). This ensures that you will have enough gross profit to cover your indirect costs *and* pay yourself. Brick-and-mortar businesses and those with significant administrative staff (including contractors) may fall into the category of having significant overhead. If you have a low gross profit margin and high indirect costs, chances are you won't have much (if any) profit left over. Conversely, if your overhead is low, a 40% gross profit margin may suffice. This could apply to a solopreneur service provider who works from home.

Now you know everything you need to set your prices.

Step 3: Calculate your minimum price to charge.

Once you have determined your direct costs for a specific product or service and set a target gross profit margin, you can easily calculate the minimum price to charge for that product or service using the Pricing Formula:

$$\frac{\text{Direct Costs}}{1 - \text{Target Gross Profit Margin \%}} = \text{Minimum price to charge}$$

Importantly, the higher the gross profit margin, the better—provided you can make sales at that price! This calculation tells you the *minimum* price needed to run a sufficiently profitable business based on your costs. But it doesn't tell you whether that price is feasible for your market.

What happens if the Pricing Formula suggests a minimum price that you believe is too high for your market? That doesn't mean you should simply accept a lower profit margin to keep your prices low. Instead, it's an indicator that it's likely time to reexamine your direct costs and look for opportunities to reduce them. This could mean analyzing your cost of goods or the time it takes to perform the service. Reducing either of these will allow you to charge a lower price while maintaining a healthy gross profit margin.

To show how this works in practice, let's bring the formula to life with real-world examples.

Let's say Beth wants to target a 60% gross profit margin in her pet-grooming business. She knows that a regular cut for a large dog typically takes one hour.

In this example, we're going to assume that she has hired a head doggie stylist to help and pays them $22 per hour. Assuming that there are no other direct costs (aside from minimal ones such as the cost of a dollop of shampoo, which we can ignore), the calculation of what to charge would look like this:

$$\frac{\$22 \text{ (direct cost of the haircut)}}{1 - 60\% \text{ (target gross profit margin)}} = \$55 \text{ (minimum price to charge)}$$

Now let's look at a small-dog haircut, which typically takes only thirty minutes for Beth's head doggie stylist to do. If she's still aiming for at least a 60% gross profit margin, her minimum price should be:

$$\frac{\$11 \text{ (direct cost of the haircut)}}{1 - 60\% \text{ (target gross profit margin)}} = \$27.50 \text{ (minimum price to charge)}$$

Note that everything stayed the same in this equation except for the direct cost, since the labor time was only half of what was required in the first scenario.

Importantly, these calculations determine the *minimum* price to charge. Because Beth was already charging $30 for her small-dog haircuts and they were selling well, she decided to keep the price where it was rather than reducing it. If you are selling well at a higher margin, that's fantastic! The purpose of this exercise is to make sure your margins are *at or above* the recommended thresholds where possible.

I realize that these examples are fairly straightforward, which is not the case for every business. There is a variety of factors that can make direct costs harder to calculate, especially when it comes to labor. For example, staff may be paid a salary and split their time among different duties, making it difficult to quantify the direct labor involved in servicing each customer. Or perhaps your business serves numerous customers at once, so determining the cost of labor per sale is a challenge. Additionally, the value of owner labor can be hard to quantify, especially if you don't pay yourself a specific salary amount. The key here is to do the best you can at coming up with estimates without spiraling down a rabbit hole.

AVOIDING OVERANALYSIS PARALYSIS

Whenever I start discussing profit margin calculations with my students, I know that super specific questions about calculating direct costs will soon follow. These questions are almost always preceded by a confession that the questioner may be overanalyzing things. Most of the time, they're right.

Some of these questions include:

- Should I include payroll taxes?
- What about the envelopes I use to ship my products?
- Should I estimate the amount of shampoo I use on each dog?
- What if my time spent varies?

As someone with a college degree in overanalyzing numbers (ahem, Analytical Finance), I get it. While I commend the effort of those who spend the time to parse out every little cost, try not to get lost so far in the

---

If you run a product-based business, the same Pricing Formula applies. Ensure that you include all direct costs, such as ingredients, packaging, and any supplies used to create the product or service.

For businesses that purchase and resell finished goods, calculating direct costs is straightforward. However, for those producing handmade items, estimating the direct costs of each product can be more complex. In these cases, you'll need to consider the cost of materials and supplies used for each item. Additionally, include an estimate of the labor cost to create the product, factoring in your own labor.

By accurately accounting for these costs, you can set prices that will support paying yourself and any future employees, ensuring that your business will remain profitable and scalable.

trees that you can no longer see the forest. This is not about getting it right down to the penny; it's about getting reasonably close. When in doubt, averages are your friends. If a particular cost varies, you might choose to use the high end of the range for pricing purposes, ensuring that you will make your desired profit even if costs become higher than usual.

The goal of this exercise is to gain intentional insights into your business. Let go of the need to do it the "right" way. There are countless "right" ways to approach this work. The important part is that you do it. Consistency is key. If you include an estimate for payroll taxes in the labor cost of one service, do the same for others so your profit margins are comparable across services.

When you find yourself going down a rabbit hole, remind yourself that your calculations don't have to be perfect to be useful. I emphasize this because I want you to get into the habit of looking at the big picture as a true CFO does. Numbers are powerful, but it's easy to get lost in them or give up entirely when the task becomes overwhelming. Take a step back, breathe, and keep moving forward. Perfection is not the goal; usefulness is (thankfully!).

Valuing Owner Labor

As entrepreneurs, we often provide the actual work or service ourselves. But when the owner provides, for example, a haircut (or in Beth's case, cuts a poodle pouf into a fauxhawk), how do you account for that?

Let's start with price. Unless you as the owner have a significantly different level of proficiency than your team does, the price shouldn't be different. And even though Beth doesn't pay herself a salary—her business is not a Corporation—she can use the hourly rate of a staff member to estimate the value of her own labor for the Pricing Formula.

The same thing is true even if you don't have employees yet. You can approximate the direct cost of your owner labor for a given service by estimating what you would pay someone else if you were to hire them to perform the job instead. Don't forget, the labor cost you are calculating is related to what you would pay another person to serve the customer, *not* run the business. Importantly, it doesn't matter whether you actually *would* hire someone for that task or not; the point is that your labor has a market value, and we want to make sure to include that as a cost when calculating your optimal prices. If you build in the cost of labor, even when you're the one doing the bulk of the work, you'll be better prepared to hire help when you need it and still make a healthy profit from each sale.

CHIEF FINANCIAL OPINION:
Don't Forget to Pay Yourself

Unless you were lucky enough to snag some venture capital, there's a good chance you started your business as a solopreneur. Financially, this is typically the easiest way to start, as you don't have payroll to worry about. Instead, you pay yourself via owner draws from your business when and if you can afford to. Because of this, the cost of owner labor is often overlooked.

By incorporating what you pay yourself into your Pricing Formula as if you were your own employee, you ensure that your prices will support not only paying someone else to serve customers but also create enough margin to pay yourself as the owner. Being able to pay staff and still make a profit is key to scalability, and charging adequate prices is a crucial part of that.

Even when it's just you, make sure you aren't inadvertently ignoring the value of owner labor in your pricing. If you're maxed out in your business but feel that you "can't afford to hire," it probably means you haven't priced your products and services adequately.

Pricing for Businesses with Few Direct Costs

In certain situations, you may have few to no direct costs in your business. This situation is common for businesses that don't incur additional time or costs with each sale. For example, a digital product that you create once but sell repeatedly has minimal direct costs on a per sale basis.

If you don't have much in the way of direct costs, the standard Pricing Formula may not be very helpful. In this situation, set your price based on the estimated number of units you think that you could sell at various price points. For example:

ESTIMATED REVENUE BY PRICE POINT

POSSIBLE PRICE POINT	NUMBER OF EXPECTED SALES	TOTAL REVENUE (PRICE x VOLUME)
$ 100	100	$ 10,000
150	90	13,500
250	75	18,750
500	30	15,000

Note that the number of expected sales is less important than the relative change at each price point you are evaluating. For example, the above table assumes that if the price was increased from $100 to $150, 10 percent of would-be buyers would decide not to buy. Another 15 percent would drop off at the $250 rate, and at $500, only 30 percent of the original number of buyers would buy. Analyzing these relative changes helps you determine the most profitable price point for your product.

The table above illustrates that while pricing lower probably means you'll sell more, it doesn't mean you'll make more money. In the scenario above, the business owner would likely select the $250 pricing option, as it has the highest total projected revenue.

Of course, we can't see the future, but we can make educated assumptions based on past experience and what we know about our clientele.

Uncertainty is a part of business, and becoming comfortable with making data-driven decisions in light of that uncertainty is critically important to the success of our businesses.

Pricing for a Business with No Pricing Flexibility

In some highly regulated industries, you may not be able to set your prices. For example, doctors may not have much control over insurance company reimbursement rates, and independent sales consultants may not be able to set their commission structures. If that's you, I still recommend calculating your profit margins by product or service as key data points. While you may not be able to influence the prices, there are still important conclusions to be drawn from this data.

For example, a doctor may not be able to influence insurance reimbursement rates but can decide which insurances to accept based on a review of their profit margins. Additionally, independent sales consultants may not be able to influence the prices of the products they sell, but they can use profit margins to decide which products are worth promoting and which aren't. Even if you can't influence the prices you charge, determining your profit margins by product or service can provide important data that will help your business become more profitable.

For most businesses, it is essential to focus on the Price Lever. Ensuring that your pricing is optimal before pulling the Volume Lever means that you'll get more bang for your buck (or in this case, more buck for your bang!).

Pull the Price Lever (i.e., recalculate your prices) when:

- You have a steady stream of sales or a wait-list.

- You know in your gut that you have underpriced your products or services but have held off making changes because you're worried about how your customers might react.

- You'd love to hire someone to help you but can't afford it because you'd have to pay them more than what you pay yourself.

- Your costs (cost of goods sold, labor costs, etc.) have increased by more than a nominal amount since you last set your prices.

- You are regularly attracting budget shoppers, even though you provide a top-notch service or product.

- You sometimes feel resentful when you get new sales because you know how much extra work they mean for you.

If any of these is true, it's likely time to raise your prices. Start small or go big, but most important, be brave. Will you lose customers? It's possible. But remember, raising prices means that you can make the same amount of money with *fewer* customers, so it's totally okay if some of them decide to part ways with you. Let's be honest: They probably weren't the best fit for you anyway!

Proven strategies for raising prices (without the anxiety):

1. **Start small.** If you adjust by only a few percent, there's a good chance your clientele won't even notice or bat an eye. A 2% increase likely means very little to them but could have a major impact on your bottom line when applied across all of your sales.

2. **Begin by charging new customers more.** You don't have to adjust everyone's rates at the same time. Starting with new customers will show you whether they will buy at the new prices and give you more confidence when it's time to adjust prices across the board.

3. **Tell people why you are increasing your prices.** If your operating costs have gone up due to a cause such as inflation, or if you haven't increased your prices in years, letting your customers know that you need to adjust prices to keep your business running sustainably is something most of them will understand and support.

4. **Institute a price increase with your most demanding clients, and don't hold back.** If they accept the increase—great! You're finally being compensated for the extra work you're already doing.

If they balk at the increase, this is a great time to wish them well and create more capacity to serve for right-fit clients who will value what you do.

Let's return to our friend Beth, the dog groomer. We know that she has been feeling pretty maxed out with the clients of her dog-grooming business and doesn't feel that she's making the income she deserves. She has a steady stream of clients but feels as though she can't afford to hire more help. It's a safe bet to assume that she isn't charging enough. After looking at her numbers and using the Pricing Formula, she decides that she has underpriced her large-dog grooming.

But she's super-duper nervous about instituting a big price change. So she starts with just 2%. What was a $50 large-pup groom is now $51, and she does the same for the rest of her offerings. Her clients barely even blink, and immediately Beth is making $50 more each week ($1 extra per sale × 50 sales per week), which seems small but gives her over $200 more of profit every month. Pretty soon she realizes that she has a cool choice: she can increase her take-home pay by over $2,500 this year—or close her business for a week and take a vacation. Possibly both—all while working the *exact same* number of hours as she did before. Beth is proof that even small price increases (just $1 per customer in her case!) can add up to real money.

CHAPTER THIRTEEN
Mix It Up

When I worked for a major Coca-Cola bottling company, we measured our sales in "unit cases," which meant twenty-four servings of eight ounces each. That was the standard measure, whether we were selling sparkling beverages (our fancy term for soft drinks such as Coke and Diet Coke), water, juice, or energy drinks.

As you can imagine, sparkling beverages typically made up the majority of our sales. However, during the nearly ten years that I worked there, there was a shift in the marketplace away from soft drinks toward beverages that were perceived as healthier, such as bottled water.

While more customers switching from soda to water may seem like a big problem for a brand such as Coca-Cola, it actually had a positive effect on the company's bottom line. Because products such as specialty water have higher profit margins than sugary beverages do, the company's profit *grew* because a larger portion of total sales came from those higher-profit-margin products.

Put another way, if you know which of your business's products, services, or packages have the highest profit margins, you can use that data to increase your bottom line. If you aren't sure, you won't know which products or services to focus on, meaning that you'll work harder than necessary to reach your financial goals.

Most business owners I know focus a lot on sales and prices. The *mixture* of the goods and services that they sell tends to fly under the radar. Your "mix" will be easiest to understand if you visualize a pie graph.

The total number of sales you make is 100% (i.e., the whole pie); each product, service, or package that you sell makes up a percentage of that pie. Note that that mix is the *number* of sales you make, not the total cash collected from each sale. Your mix is the volume of sales you make broken down into specific categories.

I highly recommend keeping a breakdown of your sales mix and revisiting it regularly—preferably monthly. This is especially true if you have more than a few products or services or if those products and services vary widely in profitability. Note, however, that your mix doesn't just reflect the sales split among various types of products; in fact, you can stratify your data in various ways to gain useful insights.

As a real-life example, at the bottling company, we looked at our mix from a few different perspectives:

1. **Product mix:** How much of each product (or service) we sold. For us, that meant tracking subcategories such as sparkling flavors, juices, and waters.

2. **Package mix:** How much of each package type we sold. We looked to see what percentage of sales were in cans, plastic bottles, and glass.

3. **Channel mix:** How much volume we sold by location type. Specifically, we looked at "home" and "cold" channels. For us, the home channel was grocery stores that sold multipacks for home consumption, whereas the cold channel was convenience stores where single bottles were sold for immediate consumption.

There are lots of different ways to look at mix data. The key is to figure out what is most helpful for you to know when it comes to making business decisions. In the next section, we'll talk about different ways to stratify your data to help inform your financial decisions.

Understand Your Mix

Product, package, and channel mix are the most common ways to look at your mix data. Not every business will have all three types of mix, but many do.

Even service-based businesses have mix data. For a service-based business, each service you sell constitutes a different "product" for the purpose of understanding your mix.

For example, here's how Beth could break down her sales to review the mix of what she is selling.

1. **Product mix:** How many full-service grooms does she sell versus baths versus nail trims? Small-dog haircuts versus big-dog haircuts?
2. **Package mix:** How many grooms are sold via one-off service versus how many are sold as part of a multiservice package deal?
3. **Channel mix:** How many mobile groomings does her business do versus groomings done at her store?

Consider all the different ways you can stratify your data that would be helpful for you to see regularly. Once you know what you want to see, you may need to make changes to your bookkeeping to ensure that you can easily view relevant mix data in real time. For example, if you are using a bookkeeping software, many offer class and location tracking or allow you to add tags to certain transactions so you can easily pull reports with the data you need. As we talked about in part I, having access to well-organized, accurate data is key to being able to make good financial decisions. Without easy access to this info, you won't be able to use it to pull the Mix Lever when you're ready.

Increase Your Profitability with Mix Data

When you pull the Mix Lever, you shift sales from one product, service, or bundle to another with a higher profit margin. Keep in mind that the goal isn't for every customer to say yes. Instead, you simply need a few customers to opt for the products or services with the higher profit margins. Over time, that will result in higher profit for you and your business.

Remember, your highest-profit-margin products or services are not always the ones that are priced the highest. Instead, you want to look for the products that bring in the most profit after adjusting for the direct costs associated with the product or service (including your time!).

Timely Promotions

While it's true that we can't force customers to buy one product rather than another, mix data is valuable in helping you decide *what* to promote and *when*. The goal is to strategically promote higher-profit-margin items when it makes sense, whether that's based on seasonal demand, customer trends, or market opportunities. For example, during peak demand for certain products, you might focus your marketing efforts on promoting the higher-margin options within that category. In a storefront, you might place higher-margin products in prominent, easy-to-see locations or add "Staff recommendation" signs to encourage customers to choose those products. For digital sales, you could feature high-margin items prominently on your website to draw more attention to them. The goal is to make your higher-margin products and services as attractive to your customers as possible to increase the likelihood that they will choose them over your lower-margin products or services.

Hone Your Offerings

When reviewing your mix data, you may also identify opportunities to phase out or reduce your focus on lower-margin offerings that don't contribute as much to your bottom line. Sometimes, it may even be strategic to bundle them with higher-margin items to improve your average profit. By understanding your product mix, you can better allocate resources to promoting the most profitable items, leading to a more optimized sales strategy overall.

Does it ever make sense to promote a lower-margin product? It can be a strategic move to promote a "loss leader"—a product or service with a low profit margin or even a loss—to attract customers. The goal is to convert these customers to higher-margin products or services. For example, e-readers such as Kindles are sometimes discounted below the cost to make them, meaning that the company is losing money on each device sale. However, the company bets on making a profit from e-book sales, which carry a high profit margin. Grocery stores also use this strategy by reducing or eliminating their profit margins on certain staples (such as meat or milk) to draw in buyers, with the expectation that those buyers will buy other products in the store with higher margins.

While this strategy can be effective, it is also risky, especially for smaller businesses. If you decide to use this approach, track your conversion metrics to ensure that it's working as intended. Monitoring your average Customer Lifetime Value (CLV) as a Key Performance Indicator (KPI) can help ensure that your strategy will be successful. If you decide to sell products or services with a low or no profit margin, it's important that this be intentional and strategic as opposed to accidental.

Mixing It Up in Action

Beth began reviewing her product mix by examining how many sales she made of each service.

Next, she went through a profit margin analysis and realized that her large-dog haircuts were running at a respectable 56% gross profit margin, yielding her $28 in gross profit per sale ($50 price less $22 cost). Her small-dog haircuts were priced at $30

BETH'S MIX (BY NUMBER OF SALES)
- FULL-SERVICE GROOM 20%
- SMALL-DOG HAIRCUTS 40%
- LARGE-DOG HAIRCUTS 40%

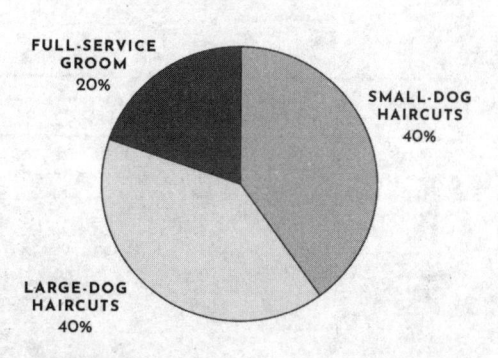

and had direct costs of $11, so her gross profit margin for that offering was $19 (63%). When she evaluated her Pampered Paws full-service grooms, she realized that they were yielding her a stellar 64% profit margin and $57 in profit per sale ($90 price less $33 cost). That data helped her realize that she should incentivize her customers to opt for the full groom over just a haircut. So she made some changes to her marketing materials to highlight what a

164 Hidden Profit

great deal the full groom was compared to paying for each component separately. She also asked each customer if they'd like to upgrade and touted the health benefits of regular baths and nail trims.

As noted earlier, Beth currently makes around 50 sales per week, averaging between 200 and 230 sales per month. Based on the chart above, she knows that her large-dog haircuts and small-dog haircuts each amount to 40% of her sales (approximately 90 per month each), with the full-service grooms making up 20% (approximately 45 per month). But what if she could shift just 2% of the sales from each of the haircuts to the full-service groom?

Here's a monthly view of the impact it would have if she were to shift one in every forty-five buyers from a haircut to a full-service groom:

2% SHIFTS

BEFORE

	GROSS PROFIT PER SALE	MONTHLY SALES	GROSS PROFIT
Small-Dog Grooms	$19	90	$1,710
Large-Dog Grooms	29	90	2,610
Full Service	57	45	2,565
Total		225	$6,885

AFTER

	GROSS PROFIT PER SALE	MONTHLY SALES	GROSS PROFIT	CHANGE IN GROSS PROFIT
Small-Dog Grooms	$19	88	$1,672	$(38)
Large-Dog Grooms	29	88	2,552	(58)
Full Service	57	49	2,793	228
Total		225	$7,017	$132 Monthly Increase
				$1,584 Annual Increase
				5% Annual Profit Increase

While a $132 monthly increase in gross profit may not seem like much, it's actually pretty significant. Since Beth's total operating profit was $30,000 before she pulled any levers, this represents an increase in her profit of over 5%. Not bad for a few small tweaks!

But what if Beth decides she can do better than 2% shifts? Maybe she thinks she can convert one out of every nine (11%) of her haircut customers. Let's see how that effort would pan out for her.

10% SHIFTS

BEFORE

	GROSS PROFIT PER SALE	MONTHLY SALES	GROSS PROFIT
Small-Dog Grooms	$ 19	90	$ 1,710
Large-Dog Grooms	29	90	2,610
Full Service	57	45	2,565
Total		225	$ 6,885

AFTER

	GROSS PROFIT PER SALE	MONTHLY SALES	GROSS PROFIT	CHANGE IN GROSS PROFIT
Small-Dog Grooms	$ 19	81	$ 1,539	$ (171)
Large-Dog Grooms	29	81	2,349	(261)
Full Service	57	63	3,591	1,026
Total		225	$ 7,479	$ 594 Monthly Increase
				$ 7,128 Annual Increase
				24% Annual Profit Increase

That's right, she could actually increase her profit by over 24% simply by shifting one in every nine customers to her full-service groom (from $30,000 profit to $37,128 profit after pulling the Mix Lever). That's over $7,000 extra profit for the *exact same* number of clients. For Beth, that's the equivalent of nearly three months' worth of extra profit! It may be time for Beth to take that vacation she's been planning for years!

Thus is the beauty of mix shifts: They enable you to make more money without needing to hustle for more sales.

Mix shifts are powerful because they generally don't require much, if any, additional effort or cost to deliver, enabling you to get more profit out of the work you (or your team) perform. That said, as with the other Profit Levers, you want to make sure you pull the Mix Lever at the right time.

MEMOIRS OF A SUBPAR SERVER

What do mix shifts look like in the real world? As a consumer, you may not pick up on it, but many businesses regularly utilize strategies to push you toward certain purchases and away from others.

Long before working in finance for Coca-Cola, I spent a few summers as a server at a local restaurant during my college days. The manager would frequently run contests among the waitstaff to see who could sell the most of a particular featured appetizer or dessert that night, awarding the winner a $50 prize. Looking back, it's obvious to me that the restaurant was looking to clear out inventory and push sales of higher-margin items. The restaurant manager was most certainly pulling the Mix Lever with those incentives, and boy, did it work.

While I was not an asset to the food service industry (apologies to all of my patrons whose meals I forgot to send to the kitchen), my competitive nature *lived* for these contests. I'm pretty sure I still hold the restaurant record of most spinach and artichoke dip appetizers sold in a single dinner rush (twenty-two, if you are curious). It turned out that while waiting tables wasn't a skill of mine, marketing definitely was!

For you as a business owner, getting creative with strategies that gently lead consumers toward specific offerings can make a big difference on your bottom line!

Pull the Mix Lever when:

- You realize that the majority of your sales comes from products and services that have lower profit margins.
- Your products and services have seasonal demand. In this case, you will want to evaluate your offering mix regularly to make sure you're meeting consumer needs at the right time.

- Industry trends are changing, and you want to stay ahead of the curve. Keeping an eye on changing customer wants and needs is paramount. Regularly talking to customers and tracking your sales data can give you insights into where demand is headed.

- You have a product business with excess inventory that is selling more slowly than expected. It may be time to use strategic promotions to clear out stale inventory.

- Business growth seems to have plateaued. It may be time to look at your offerings and evaluate the products and services you offer.

In the next chapter, we'll take the concept of mix shifts up a notch by looking at other ways to increase the average value of each and every sale you make.

CHAPTER FOURTEEN
Generate More Value

As someone obsessed with having a physical planner to help me organize my life, I went through at least ten different planners before discovering the amazing company called Plum Paper. On its website, I could completely customize my planner. It was a paper planner lover's dream come true.

I was able to pick the size, cover design, binding, start month, page layout, tab colors, and holidays and even add extra pages to the back (yes to extra to-do lists and notes pages!). Some customizations were included, while others came with an additional fee.

After adding my custom planner to the cart, I was presented with a list of tempting add-ons tailored specifically to me. Free shipping kicked in only over a particular dollar amount, slightly above the cost of one planner, which incentivized me not to be stingy with the add-ons. When I purchased my planner, there was even an accessory bundle deal offering a discount for buying three or more items.

When I first visited Plum Paper, did I spend *double* what I normally would on a planner? Yep. Would I do it again? Absolutely. (And I have!)

I *adore* my planner because it was made specifically for me, and I may never go back to another "off-the-shelf" version again. The way that Plum Paper's website led me through the customization process is a perfect example of increasing the value per transaction. And while I don't know the company's financials, my guess is that its profit margins are pretty freaking fabulous. Its website is designed to encourage customers to willingly and happily increase their transaction value at every turn. This strategy not only boosts profit but can also enhance customer satisfaction when done well!

Plum Paper is a great example of utilizing the power of the **Average Transaction Value Lever**, which calculates the amount of revenue you make from each sale. To determine average transaction value, simply follow this easy formula:

Average Transaction Value = Total Revenue/Total Number of Sales

Typically, a transaction (or sale) occurs each time you charge a customer for a product or service you sell. If you offer a monthly service that charges the customer on a particular day each month, each monthly charge would be considered a separate sale or transaction for the purpose of figuring your average transaction value. By adding an add-on or "upsell" to a portion of your sales, you can increase the average amount of money you make from each transaction.

Consider how every grocery store you've ever been to is likely set up. When you go to check out, you probably see a cooler with cold drinks, some candy and gum, and gossip or recipe magazines. This placement isn't accidental. The store knows that if it puts those displays there for shoppers to look at while waiting in line, at least *some* percentage of customers will snag a little extra something for themselves (or, if you're like me, to placate their unruly kids who are chanting for a king-size Reese's). Even if only one in ten shoppers adds something extra, it adds up to big bucks given the large number of people who shop there in a given week.

If the idea of "upselling" leaves a bad taste in your mouth, you might have some underlying negative associations with selling in general. This is especially likely if Nurturer or Connector is one of your top money personalities and you worry that being too "salesy" can harm your relationships or make people feel uncomfortable. It makes sense to have these feelings—after all, we have all felt pressured to buy something we didn't need or been nickeled and dimed half to death. No one wants to feel "sold to," but we *do* want to buy things!

The truth is that selling (and upselling!) can be helpful to both you *and* your customer if done right. It's not about annoying your customers with extra fees they didn't expect or putting pressure on them to buy more. The key is to look at what they are currently buying from you and why and then consider what could *complement* it and add *even more* value for your customer. Remember, people want what you have to offer; otherwise they wouldn't have come to you in the first place!

Ways to Increase Average Transaction Value

How this works in practice will vary based on your business model, but a few ideas include the following.

- **Order bumps for retail sales.** This could be done in person (as in checkout displays) or online ("People who purchased this also like" recommendations). Just be sure that whatever you add as an order bump or add-on is complementary to the product or service the customer is already considering and buying. For example, adding a one-on-one coaching call to a group coaching program is a great order bump, whereas offering gardening tools to someone buying office supplies may not fare as well.

- **Free shipping for sales over a particular dollar amount.** Typically, the dollar amount to qualify is slightly above the average price of one item. Who hasn't bought something extra just to avoid pesky shipping costs?

- **Package bundles or subscription plans.** Offer a way to buy several items at a slightly discounted price to encourage customers to purchase more (e.g., "Buy three and save!"). You could also convert one-off customers to subscription-based customers, which helps you build a dependable monthly recurring revenue base.

- **Premium or VIP upgrades.** For example, a fitness studio could offer priority booking or exclusive classes for VIP members only. This is a great way to cater to your Celebrity money personality clientele!

- **Customizable options.** Customers will often pay more to customize their purchase exactly to their needs or wants. I'm an avid customizer, so this one always gets me.

Remember, you aren't *forcing* anyone to opt for an upgrade, buy more, or customize; you're just giving them options and incentives that they can take advantage of *if* they choose. They are already buying something from you because you have something they want. What else might they want or need that you could provide?

Play the Long Game

It's worth noting that increasing the average transaction value is an effective way to boost your **Customer Lifetime Value**, the total amount a customer will spend with you over the duration of their relationship with your business. While we'd love for customers to keep coming back forever, there is generally an average length of time we can expect to retain them. Businesses such as restaurants, retail shops, and service providers often have a longer average customer life, as customers return regularly for ongoing needs. In contrast, more transactional purchases such as luxury items, wedding dresses, or travel-related purchases naturally have a shorter customer lifetime value, as these tend to be one-time or infrequent purchases.

For businesses with a naturally shorter Customer Lifetime Value due to the nature of their products or services, increasing the average transaction value is essential, since it may be the only time you interact with that specific customer. However, if your business does have repeat or ongoing customers, you can look to increase your Customer Lifetime Value by lengthening your average customer retention.

Having data to tell you how long customers generally stay customers and how often buyers make repeat purchases can serve as useful KPIs. If you are struggling to retain customers as long as you'd like, there is likely an opportunity to improve. If customers don't come back because they weren't happy or satisfied with your offerings, you may have some customer service or quality issues to sort out. However, if they aren't coming back because they simply don't realize you have something more that they might be interested in, it may just be a matter of communicating with past customers about what else you have to offer. People can't buy what they don't know exists! Remember, it is much easier (and cheaper!) to sell to an existing customer than it is to find and sell to new customers. Make sure you don't accidentally neglect your current (or former) customers as you search for new ones!

Increasing customer retention can be done in a number of ways, but here are a few ideas.

- **Happy customers = return customers.** Product or service quality and good customer service are essential to scoring repeat business.
- **Regular communication.** Make sure your customers know what you're offering and how it could benefit them!
- **Loyalty programs.** Give customers perks or discounts for return purchases. A well-designed loyalty program can ensure that customers choose your business over and over again.
- **Easy shopping.** Offer subscriptions or make booking or purchasing super simple.
- **Surprise and delight.** Show your customers that they are a priority. Look for opportunities to go above and beyond when you can, and you'll make customers for life.

Average Transaction Value in Action

Let's consider how our friend Beth could use the Average Transaction Value Lever in her dog-grooming business. As we discussed in the last chapter, she offers both a regular groom and a full-service groom that includes a bath and nail trim (her Pampered Paws package). Let's say her current average transaction value across all her services is $50, but she'd love for that to be higher without having to change the price of her services (because she recently adjusted her Price Lever).

To increase her average transaction value, Beth could also offer several à la carte options that could be added to any package, such as ear cleanings, tooth brushing, or even doggy-safe fur dyeing (because the only thing more adorable than a shih tzu is a shih tzu with a pink mohawk). If she wanted to take it a step further and get super creative, she could even consider adding photography services, where she'd dress up and pose your pup for a "Glamour Paws" session after their groom. The key to increasing customer transaction value is to offer something that feels like a natural complement to what the customer is *already* buying—without significantly adding to your business's direct and indirect costs. Remember our discussion of mix and profit margin: you want to make sure that any add-ons are high margin and worth your time and resources.

Even if only one in ten customers opts for a $10 add-on, Beth's average customer transaction value will increase by 2%. That's nearly another $2,500 a year—with the *same number* of sales as before. If one of every five opts for a $15 upgrade? That's another 6% increase in sales, or $7,500. The best part? Beth didn't have to raise her base price or hustle to find a bunch of new customers to make more money.

That said, if you do focus on this lever, you'll want to make sure it's done well and with your customers' overall satisfaction in mind. Apply it the wrong way, and customers will feel nickeled and dimed into oblivion (I'm looking at you, airline industry).

The goal is not to squeeze every possible dime out of every transaction, especially if it leaves your customers feeling frustrated. Annoyed customers might walk away from a transaction entirely or make one purchase but never return. Importantly, you don't just want to increase a customer's transaction value *one* time; you also want to be mindful of your customer retention rate. You don't want to sacrifice that in favor of increasing your average transaction value. When in doubt, try out some new offerings and see how your customers respond. As with our example of Beth and her new "pink barkhawk" offering, don't be afraid to have a little fun with it!

Pull the Average Transaction Value Lever when:

- Your customer base is strong, but it feels as though growth has plateaued.

- You don't currently have opportunities for your customers to customize or add extra value to their purchases.

- You already have opportunities for your customers to add extra value to their purchase, but they may not be aware of them because you aren't actively promoting them.

- You have a relatively high customer retention rate for your industry (meaning that your customers regularly come back). Loyal customers are more likely to trust your upgrade recommendations.

If you decide to pull this lever, make an initial goal of increasing your average customer transaction value by 2% via add-ons, bundles, or other extras. Start with one or two strategies that feel aligned with you, your brand, and your business model, and monitor their effectiveness as well as the overall reception by your customers. Getting more customer complaints or abandoned carts? It may be time to go back to the drawing board and try something else. Continue to tweak as needed until you find a winning strategy.

Remember, the goal is not to have 100% of customers opt for upgrades. However, if even a small portion of your customer base decides your upgrades are right for them, they can make a *big* difference to your business's bottom line.

CHAPTER FIFTEEN
Cut (Unnecessary) Costs

Mark was stumped. His business offering sales coaching to fellow entrepreneurs had grown by leaps and bounds, and he was consistently making high-ticket sales. He had grown a team to help support him. He had even implemented some great strategies for increasing customer transaction value that were already paying off.

It seemed as though his business should be booming (and from the outside, many people assumed it was). He had been chasing the prestigious goal of $1 million in annual sales, and it finally looked as though this was the year he would reach it. Yet month after month he found himself barely being able to pull enough out of his business to pay his personal bills. Where had all that money *gone*?

Mark made the classic mistake so many business owners do as they grow: He assumed that as long as there was ample money coming into the business, he must be doing well. For Mark, revenue was a marker of success. He wanted to have a "million-dollar business." He assumed that once he reached that goal, all his worries would be gone.

Mark was a rock star at sales. He could sell a raincoat to a mermaid. Heck, that was why he had become a sales coach! Unfortunately for Mark, he was about to realize that there is more to having a financially successful business than its top-line revenue number.

You may have noticed that the Profit Levers I've discussed so far have focused on increasing the amount of cash coming *into* your business (your revenue). But there's another element of the profit equation we can't ignore (and neither can Mark): **Expenses.**

If we don't keep a watchful eye on our business's overall expenses, our costs can balloon even as we increase our revenue. When this happens, we're bringing more money into our business, but the bottom line doesn't budge.

As I discussed previously, expenses can be either direct or indirect. In this section, we'll dive a little deeper into each of these Profit Levers to see how we can find more hidden profit.

Direct Costs as a Profit Lever

Direct costs relate specifically to the product or service you are offering and generally increase or decrease directly with sales. Direct costs include the cost of materials, inventory purchased, or labor related to creating the product or rendering the service.

Typically, you'll look at the Price Lever and Direct Costs Lever together, because both can help you increase your gross profit. Said another way, *if you are looking to increase your gross profit margins, you can do so by either increasing your prices or reducing your direct costs (or both!).*

When raising your prices would kill your sales or you don't have the ability to increase your prices because of regulatory or other restrictions, it's probably time to look at your Direct Costs Lever to increase your bottom line—specifically, reducing those costs as much as possible.

Proven Strategies for Reducing Direct Costs

A scalable company is one that focuses on constantly improving its systems and processes to get the work done more effectively and efficiently. Without this, a business will struggle to scale up past a certain point. Being mindful of direct costs, including hidden owner labor costs, is critical to building a business with limitless potential. Here are a few strategies that can reduce your direct costs and therefore increase your overall profit margin:

1. **Streamline your processes.** Review your process for delivering a finished product from start to finish. Are there steps you can eliminate? Processes that cause blockages or delays? The goal is to reduce the amount of time it takes to perform your client service duties. How can you streamline your processes so your business runs more efficiently?

2. **Create Standard Operating Procedures (SOPs).** Put SOPs into place to help your staff get tasks done more efficiently and with fewer errors. Thankfully, there are software systems these days that let you effortlessly document your processes as you perform them, including step-by-step screenshots and videos. This will also be beneficial to have on hand if key staff members take vacations or you have employee turnover.

3. **Invest in time-saving technology** to help you leverage your and your staff's time more effectively and cut down on time-sucking manual work. If you are selling handmade items, investing in technology can help reduce the time it takes to make each item.

4. **Delegate or outsource tasks.** This is a huge time saver and one that entrepreneurs are the least likely to leverage! Look at all the tasks you perform, and determine which are the most impactful to your business results. What can only *you* do? The list is likely shorter than you think. Focus on the most meaningful tasks, and delegate or outsource the rest (that is, if you can't eliminate them entirely). While it may seem counterintuitive that outsourcing can save you money, that's actually the entire philosophy behind scaling up a business. The more time you have to focus on what matters, the more likely you are to achieve exponential growth. Tip for deciding what to outsource: Determine a pay rate for yourself. When

you are doing your most important work, how much can you make per hour? $50? $250? $1,000? Guesstimate if you need to, and remember that rate. If there are tasks you could hire someone else to do for *less* than your own rate, do it! (Note: The same principle can apply in your personal life!)

5. **Buy wholesale, and make sure you compare suppliers.** Don't look just at price; also consider minimum purchase requirements, payment terms, and lead times for getting your products.

6. **Take advantage of bulk pricing discounts.** If your cash flow situation allows and you deem it prudent, buying in bulk is a great way to reduce recurring costs, especially for inventory you know you'll be able to sell.

7. **Negotiate deals with existing suppliers.** If applicable, use the goodwill you've built by being a long-term customer to negotiate better rates.

8. **Switch suppliers.** If suppliers won't negotiate, it may be time to look at other options for sourcing your products or materials to make sure you are getting a good deal.

9. **Use cheaper comparable materials.** What alternate materials could you use without sacrificing quality? For example, if you run a product-based business, you might switch from expensive branded packaging to generic high-quality packaging that will serve the same purpose at a lower cost. Another example is using sustainable or recycled materials, which are often less expensive but can still be durable and appealing to customers. You can find new options by researching industry suppliers, testing samples, and seeking recommendations from industry peers.

10. **Focus on improving your inventory management and reducing waste.** As I discussed in chapter 4, inventory turnover is a critical metric for product-based businesses. Even if you have stellar profit margins, your costs will skyrocket if you overbuy inventory or regularly

dispose of products or components that don't get sold or used. Tracking your inventory turnover data can help make sure you stay in the "Goldilocks zone" when it comes to balancing too little inventory and too much waste.

If you're looking to improve your company's systems but aren't sure if the cost of additional software, personnel, and so on will be worth it, consider the ROI calculation that we discussed in chapter 7. While investments in efficiency and effectiveness can take some time to see a return, they're often worth it in the long run. This is especially true when you utilize those time savings to perform more meaningful business tasks that only you can do. Remember the pay rate for your most important work that you estimated above? If you estimate that a new system would cost you $120 per month but save you three hours per week on client work, that equates to around $10 an hour ($120 cost divided by twelve hours of time savings per month). If the pay rate you came up with for yourself is more than $10 (and I certainly hope it is!), that means it's likely a worthwhile investment that will provide a return in the long run.

Once you've reviewed your direct costs and hopefully found some opportunities to lower them, you'll want to run through the Pricing Formula again (see chapter 12) to determine a minimum price to charge. If you reduce your direct costs, your minimum price will also be reduced since you will have fewer direct costs to cover. That said, you don't *have* to decrease your prices if you are selling well at your existing prices. In that case, the money you save on lowering your direct costs will simply increase your gross profit (and likely your bottom-line profit as well). Plus, higher profit margins means you can afford to offer specials and discounts while still remaining profitable.

In some locations or industries (for example, a small town with limited customer potential or an industry such as childcare or grocery stores), even when you are super mindful of your direct costs, it may not be practical to reach the recommended 40% to 60% gross profit margin. If that's the case for you, you'll want to put a heavy focus on the next lever I'm going to cover, the Indirect Costs Lever.

Indirect Costs as a Profit Lever

If you have healthy gross profit margins but very little profit left over at the end of the month, the culprit is likely your indirect costs.

Indirect costs are sometimes called "overhead" costs, and they generally don't move in direct relationship to sales. For example, while you may need to rent a bigger warehouse if you have more sales, your warehouse rent costs don't fluctuate on a sale-by-sale basis. In fact, you could make zero sales in a month and still need to pay your warehouse rent. Similarly, administrative staff who don't service clients or make products are considered indirect costs, as are things such as insurance, taxes, legal fees, marketing costs, training costs, and most business software fees. Some indirect costs will be recurring, while others will be only occasional.

Indirect costs are also the area of the Profit and Loss Statement that can quickly get out of hand if you aren't paying close attention to them. This is especially true in the age of credit cards, autopay, subscriptions, and one-click checkout carts. There is such a thing as *too* easy when it comes to indirect expenses.

Picture trying to fill a bucket with a big hole in the bottom. You're filling the bucket with water (representing cash that comes into your business), but it's flowing through the hole in the bottom (representing your expenses) as quickly as it comes in. Turning the water pressure up (i.e., increasing sales) won't help, as the water will eventually drain out through the hole. You may be able to hold some of the water a little while longer, but as soon as sales start to slow even a bit, you'll have an empty bucket once again. In order to fill the bucket, you have to patch the cash leaks *first*.

For our sales coach Mark, indirect costs were *killing* his bottom line. He was so focused on sales and revenue that he neglected to pay much attention to where his money was going.

Now, before you start slashing costs right and left in your business to increase your short-term profit margins, I want to give you a word of caution: Not all cuts you make to your expenses are created equal, and some can actually backfire on you. So how do you know which costs to cut when pulling the Indirect Costs Lever? Let's walk through it step by step.

Step 1: Determine if a cost is an expense or an investment.

The key to understanding which types of expenses to get rid of completely, which to reduce, and which to keep is answering one simple question for each cost in your business: Is this an expense or an investment?

Let's build on the conversation we started in chapter 7 about investments and ROI. Importantly, the words *investment* and *expense* take on slightly different meanings in the context of our CFO strategy. (Hint: These concepts have nothing to do with the accounting in your financial statements.) Determining whether an indirect cost is an investment or an expense is all about whether the cost will help you reach your business goals. Here's how I'll define investment and expense for the purpose of this chapter.

Investment: Money you spend in your business on indirect costs that you expect to create a return *greater* than what you initially spent. This return is usually in the form of money, but the cost could also save you time and/or energy that would be better used elsewhere.

Expense: Money you spend in your business on indirect costs without a clear or definable return. These costs don't identifiably contribute to business growth in any meaningful way.

Here are a few examples of business costs that *could* be investments.

Hiring staff	Networking
Buying an asset	Software to improve efficiency
Expanding to a new location	Advertising and marketing
Education and training	Inventory

I say "could" because one person's investment is another person's expense. For example, the purchase of inventory could be an investment if you sell more as a result, but if the goods sit unsold for long periods of time or need to be written off as unsalable, it is an expense. Buying an educational program or going to an industry conference can be an investment or an expense, depending on how you *act* on what you learn (or whom you meet there). Investing in software can be an investment if it will save you time or money, or it can be an expense if you don't put it to good use. As you can see, it's not the *type of cost* that determines whether something is an investment or an expense; rather, it's *how you use it*.

Importantly, money isn't the only thing you can invest in your business to grow it; you can also invest *time*. In fact, when we first start a business, the time we put in is often the biggest investment we make. That's because time is often more abundant than money in the early stages. Our time also feels like a less risky thing to invest as we grow a business through trial and error. Sure, we may lose time when things don't pan out, but at least we don't have a debt collector knocking on our door.

However, there comes a point when we *do* need to invest money into our business in order to grow it. That's partly because we can't do everything ourselves (despite what we might think) and partly because our time is finite. Unlike money, which is totally renewable and replenishable, often through sales, we don't have endless hours to spend on our business.

I speak from experience. When I worked one to one in my business, I had to coordinate meeting schedules with my clients. Most of it was done via email back-and-forth to find the right time, set up a Zoom meeting, and send follow-up reminders. It was a massive time suck for me, but it never seemed worth trying to fix, so I let it go.

After one particularly exhausting back-and-forth, I discovered the magic of scheduling software. For a mere $12 a month, I streamlined the process from start to finish. Clients could choose their time slots, Zoom calls were automatically scheduled, and I even collected essential information up front. What a game changer!

However, during one of my cost-cutting sprees, I had the fabulous idea of canceling the software to "save money." And boy, did it backfire. I estimate that in that first month, I wasted close to six hours on scheduling tasks, including setting up virtual meetings, sending reminders, and handling reschedules. That meant I was essentially valuing my time at under $2 an hour (the $12 monthly software cost divided by six hours of my time). The opportunity cost was staggering; I could've used that time to take on another client or simply enjoy a well-deserved break. What I've learned since then is that creating time for yourself—not just to work but to rest, have fun, and enjoy life—provides a return on investment that can't be beat.

So if you are past the initial "bootstrapping" phase of your business but are still using your own time as your main investment to grow your business, it's probably time to change your strategy. Start letting the money your business makes work *for* you. Embrace the idea of spending wisely to free up your time, because *you* are the ultimate resource in your business. Take it from me: You don't have to be exhausted to be successful. As with everything else in this book, you can start small.

Dust off that P&L or log in to your business bank account and make a list of your business's recurring expenses, as well as the typical amount you pay per month. Next to each one, write whether it is an expense or an investment. Be honest with yourself. In the long run, will you make more money back than the amount you spent on each item? How direct is the return? How long will it take? Start by making some informed assessments using your gut and what you know about your business. You don't need to be able to assign an exact dollar amount to each one, but you do want to have a general idea of what's paying off and what isn't.

In the real world, calculating your Return on Investment isn't straightforward. In some cases (such as online ad spend), the return might be easy to measure and track; in others (such as employee training or benefits), the return will be harder to quantify. For example, if you spend money on employee training and development, you likely won't be able to attribute a specific dollar amount in sales to the effort. In those instances, you can turn to other metrics to evaluate the return on an investment. You can use metrics such as employee turnover, customer satisfaction, or increased output to monitor progression. If the related metrics improve and meet or beat targets, it's likely that your investment is paying off.

Step 2: Decide which expenses you want (or need) to keep.

The goal of identifying something as an expense is *not* to shame you for your choices or to cut them all (that's likely not even possible). Instead, identifying costs as expenses instead of investments can help you be more intentional about your spending decisions.

Remember the customized planner I talked about in chapter 14? If I'm honest with myself, I know that as spectacular as my planner is, it is an expense for my business and not an investment. Having an awesome planner doesn't have a clear relationship to the amount of money I make in my business. Sure, it keeps me organized, but I could achieve that in cheaper (or even free) ways. Does that keep me from buying it? Nope! Instead, I recognize that it is an expense and intentionally decide that it is worth purchasing anyway. That's the great thing about being your own boss: *You* get to make those decisions.

You can be responsible with your business finances and still get to splurge a bit on the things that matter to you. There's no guilt and no need to trick yourself into justifying an expenditure. Want that oat milk latte while you network? Have a penchant for pretty pens? Go for it. If you are intentional about your spending decisions and aren't making them willy-nilly, the occasional discretionary indulgence won't create a big hole in your bucket. Cash flow leaks are most likely to occur when you aren't paying attention, so just make sure you're making an active decision to spend.

Sometimes business expenses can't be avoided. For example, hopefully, you'll never see a Return on Investment for, say, your business insurance. In fact, it's best if you never have to use it at all. Even though insurance is likely to be an expense, it could still be well worth it for the protections it affords in case something goes wrong. Costs related to registering your business and staying compliant with laws and regulations are likely to be expenses as well, but they are still necessary.

Resist the urge to justify every penny you spend as an investment. The more real you can be, the better off your business finances will be. It's worth saying again: Eliminating all expenses is *not* the goal. Determining your non-negotiables first will help you with the next step of the process.

Step 3: Implement the 80/20 rule of indirect costs.

I recommend that at least 80% of your indirect costs go toward investments, which means that no more than 20% of your indirect costs should be spent on expenses (both necessary and discretionary).

When thinking about how to leverage the Indirect Costs Lever, start by analyzing your recurring costs, since reducing those will have the biggest impact on your business's long-term profitability. Evaluate whether you're getting a return on those investments. Are you still utilizing everything you are paying for? Could you downgrade or pause your subscriptions? Recurring subscriptions that aren't fully utilized are one of the biggest money leaks in your bucket, so make sure to assess them regularly.

I make it a practice to review my indirect costs at least quarterly and make adjustments as needed. I've found that the longer I go without diving into where my money is going, the more money ends up being wasted.

> **PRO TIP:**
>
> Make it a practice to set up calendar reminders a few days before subscriptions are set to renew or free trials expire to give yourself a chance to assess whether you'll continue. Making this a habit can help keep those cost leaks at bay!

Mark quickly realized that running a million-dollar business didn't automatically make him as wealthy as he had hoped. Determined to fix his leaky bucket, he dived headfirst into his indirect costs and made some critical discoveries. When he ran the detailed numbers, he realized that his marketing costs were through the roof. In fact, for every $100 in marketing that he was spending, he was averaging only $105 in additional sales. While it seemed as though he was getting a return, that wasn't the full picture. When he factored in the Ad Strategist he paid monthly to run his ads, he realized that his marketing efforts were actually *costing* him money (which is unfortunately all too common, especially among online entrepreneurs).

Additionally, Mark was using his money to invest in high-ticket programs and masterminds but wasn't acting on anything he learned from them (or even showing up regularly).

So what did Mark decide to do once he spotted the biggest holes in his indirect costs bucket? Did he stop marketing altogether and leave every program he was part of? Nope! Instead, he started by having a conversation with his Ad Strategist. When they dived into the numbers, he realized that the ads for one of his offerings were performing super well but those for another offering weren't. They decided to discontinue those ads while they worked on a strategy that would better convert to sales. Mark also decided to drop an expensive mastermind he had joined so he could focus on another program that was relevant to his business. He vowed to put in the effort to make sure he saw a return on that program and made a plan for how to make it a priority.

All told, Mark was able to increase his profit margins by a full 20% with these moves alone. Indirect costs are the most likely to creep up until they're out of control, but thankfully they are also the easiest to reduce for a quick boost to your bottom line.

Proven Strategies for Reducing Indirect Costs

To use this Profit Lever in your business, start by identifying at least 2% of the monthly costs you can reduce or cut, focusing on expenses that aren't providing a reliable return. Go for the low-hanging fruit first, and give yourself a quick win to keep yourself motivated. Then, when you have more time, do a deeper dive into the rest of your costs.

The Indirect Costs Lever is even more important if you have thinner than recommended gross profit margins (i.e., under 40% to 60%). If that's the case, keeping your indirect costs low is the key to eking out as much profit as you can.

Don't have a ton of costs in your business and can't find 2% to cut? You probably have some Accumulator in you! It may be time for you to look at investing *more* into your business. Businesses with super-low expenditures often struggle to scale up, as they typically rely heavily on the owner's time, which is a finite resource, to drive the business. Remember, money is fuel for your business to grow. If you aren't feeding your business properly, it will likely stay stagnant.

CHAPTER SIXTEEN
Pay Less Taxes

When your business is profitable, you have to pay taxes. Though it doesn't always feel like it, owing taxes is a sign that you are doing something right! It means that you made money! And as long as you are prepared to pay taxes, including paying estimated taxes or setting aside cash during the year to make sure you can pay the bill when it comes, taxes shouldn't be something you spend too much time worrying about. Remember: It's important to shift your focus *away from* trying to find a tax-erasing magic bullet and *toward* time-tested strategies to keep you from overpaying.

However, like any other savvy entrepreneur, you don't want to fork over more of your hard-earned cash than necessary. In this chapter, I offer four proven strategies that can reduce your tax bill by at least 2% (or more!).

Tax-Savvy Strategy 1: Don't Miss Out on Deductions

Business deductions (commonly referred to as "write-offs") reduce business profit and therefore the amount of income you are taxed on. Like we discussed in chapter 2, it's important to have a good tracking system for your business expenses so you don't miss anything.

> **CHIEF FINANCIAL OPINION:**
> **Stop Looking for Ways to Avoid Taxes**
>
> Take it from a CPA (me): It's not worth spending your precious time and energy on searching for obscure tax loopholes—or on frivolous expenses—to "save on taxes."
>
> The truth is, many of the favorable tax breaks that help the extremely wealthy, including offshore tax havens and luxury real estate loopholes, aren't accessible to or practical for the rest of us. Once you are making millions of dollars in profit annually, more advanced strategies will come into play. At that point, you'll be more likely to have the cash necessary to pay lawyers and accountants beaucoup bucks to set up and manage a complicated entity structure.
>
> Similarly, the worst way to reduce taxes is to spend more money than you otherwise would have spent on costs that *don't* yield a return. Does it work? Sure, but it also means that there is less profit available to you.

You might be thinking "But, Jamie, didn't you just say that deductions aren't a good tax reduction strategy?" And you would be right. However, I'm talking about taking deductions for money you've *already* spent. Very often, the reason that small-business owners pay more in taxes than they need to is that they miss taking legitimate tax deductions on money they already spent.

Commonly overlooked deductions include auto and home office expenses, and you may even be able to write off a portion of your cell phone and internet bills. These expenses are regularly missed because they're typically paid out of personal funds. However, the business can often take a tax deduction for the percentage of these costs that represent business use or reimburse the owner for those expenses tax free.

Additionally, you may be able to deduct travel expenses even when a portion of your trip is for personal reasons, so long as you are strategic in your planning. For example, if you have a day or two between working days when on a business trip, you can utilize the "sandwich day rule." According to the IRS, if a business trip includes nonworking days such as a weekend in between working days, the expenses for even the nonworking days can be considered part of the business trip for deduction purposes (as long as the trip is well documented!).

Of course, when in doubt, it's always a good idea to work with a professional. There are a few acceptable ways to calculate things such as auto and home office expenses, and the requirements for taking these deductions can vary by entity type. A qualified professional can help you maximize your deductions while staying within the IRS guidelines.

Tax-Savvy Strategy 2: Save for Retirement

Is this the sexiest way to save on taxes? Perhaps not. But putting money into a retirement account is one of the most effective tax-saving strategies out there. Not only that, but it's accessible to business owners at all income levels, not just millionaires and billionaires!

Depending on the type of retirement account(s) you use, the tax implications can vary. If you have a tax-deferred plan such as a SEP-IRA, 401(k), or Traditional IRA, any contributions you make during the year will not count toward taxable income this year, which reduces the total taxes you pay now. Sure, you will eventually be taxed on the money when you begin paying yourself from the account in retirement, but by that point the money will hopefully have grown significantly. When determining what type of retirement plan(s) you will utilize, pay attention to contribution limits as well. A Traditional IRA tends to have a lower contribution limit, whereas plans geared toward self-employed individuals, such as SEP-IRAs and Solo 401(k)s, can have much higher limits that are based on business profitability. In essence, the more profitable your business is, the more money you can put toward tax-deferred retirement, reducing the taxes you pay today.

Conversely, if you use a Roth IRA or Roth 401(k), there is no tax benefit today, but later you can draw from the account tax free. The Roth option is great for those who are young and expect their earnings to grow substantially between now and retirement and those who have a low effective tax bracket today but expect it to increase later as their earnings increase. Unfortunately, Roth IRAs do have income limits, which makes them harder to utilize as your income grows.

> **PRO TIP:**
>
> You don't need to choose just one retirement account. In fact, it may be optimal for you to have a few tax-deferred options, such as a Traditional IRA and a SEP or 401(k) as well as a Roth IRA. That can help you maximize how much you contribute and give you greater flexibility to use your retirement savings as an effective tax-planning tool. Whatever you choose, you'll want to be aware of how (or if) contribution limits on specific types of accounts overlap.

Of course, talking with a financial adviser about your options is always the way to go when making retirement plans and investment decisions. It's never too early to start planning for our retirement (you'll read more about that when I get to Tax-Savvy Strategy 4). Investing in retirement accounts not only helps with your tax bill; it's also a great way to let your money work *for* you (instead of having to always work for your money!). That's the dream after all, right?

Tax-Savvy Strategy 3: Optimize Your Entity Type

When it comes to taxes, entity type matters. Before we go too far, you're going to want to make sure you know what your entity type is from both a legal and a tax perspective. Often, your legal entity type and your tax entity type are conflated, which can lead to confusion and incorrect advice. When someone (such as an accountant or lawyer) asks what type of entity you are, you'll want to be able to fill in the blanks in this sentence:

I am a **[your legal entity type]** taxed as a **[your tax entity type]**.

For example, if you are the sole owner of an LLC who has not elected different tax treatment, you would say, "My business is a single-member LLC taxed as a sole proprietorship." If you have partners in your LLC and have elected S corp treatment, you would say, "My business is a multimember LLC taxed as an S corporation."

To be clear: Making a tax election *doesn't* change your legal entity.

Here's a handy table for reference. Note that while this isn't an exhaustive list, it does cover the most common legal and tax entity types of small, for-profit businesses.

BUSINESS ENTITIES

LEGAL ENTITY	DESCRIPTION	TAX ENTITY OPTIONS
SOLE PROPRIETORSHIP	Owned and operated by one person, without distinction between the owner and the business. No official entity has been created. No legal liability protection.	Sole proprietorship. File Schedule C as part of individual return (Form 1040).
PARTNERSHIP	A business operation between two or more individuals who share management and profits. A General Partnershop has no liability protection, but a Limited Partnership does.	Partnership. File Form 1065.
SINGLE-MEMBER LIMITED LIABILITY COMPANY (LLC)	A legal entity owned by one person that gives the liability protection of a corporation with the tax treatment of a sole proprietor, unless otherwise elected.	Default: Sole Proprietorship. File Schedule C as part of individual return (Form 1040). Election: S Corporation. File Form 1120-S. Election 2: C Corp. File Form 1120. (less common)
MULTIMEMBER LIMITED LIABILITY COMPANY (LLC)	A legal entity owned by more than one person that gives the liability protection of a corporation with the tax treatment of a sole proprietor, unless otherwise elected.	Default: Partnership. File Form 1065. Election: S Corporation. File Form 1120-S. Election 2: C Corp. File Form 1120. (less common)
CORPORATION	A legal entity separate from its owners, offering the most protection from personal liability.	Default: C Corporation. File Form 1120. Election: S Corporation. File Form 1120-S.

Importantly, it's the *tax entity* type that dictates how tax is calculated for a particular entity, not the *legal entity*. A sole proprietorship and a single-member LLC are taxed the same unless the LLC makes a different tax election. Your legal entity type impacts—you guessed it—your *legal* requirements and structure but not your tax liability. This is why it's important to know your entity type from both a legal and a tax perspective.

It's important to note that most small businesses pay their taxes personally—not at the business level. You pay taxes at the business level only if you are taxed as a C corp. That means that if your business is taxed as a sole proprietorship, LLC, partnership, or S corp, it is considered a "pass-through entity" because any profit is "passed through" to the owner's or owners' personal income tax return and is combined with any other sources of income you or your spouse may have. While you may still need to file a separate business tax return, you won't actually pay taxes at the business level. Instead, your business tax return determines how much business income you need to claim on your personal tax return. This is one reason it is difficult to determine how much of your tax bill relates to your business, since it is calculated by adding all sources of income together.

Sole proprietors and single-member LLCs that haven't elected to be taxed as an S corp file a Schedule C as part of their personal tax return. Certain pass-through entities may still need to file a business return (a Form 1120-S for an S corp or a Form 1065 for a partnership); however, no taxes are calculated or paid on this return. Instead, those forms calculate your share of the profit that needs to be claimed as income on your personal income tax return. This is also why it is due a month before your personal Form 1040, as you'll need the information on it to file a correct personal return.

You might be wondering what tax entity type will result in the lowest tax liability. As you may have guessed, the answer depends on your specific situation.

A normal progression for a small business is to start out as a sole proprietorship or general partnership (if there are partners) and then form an LLC for legal protection. When your business becomes an LLC (whether right away or later on), you can decide if you'd like it to be taxed as an S corporation.

While sole proprietorships are still the most common structure for businesses that don't have employees, nearly half of businesses with employees are taxed as S corporations.[1] That's because certain pass-through entities that elect to be taxed as an S corp can save on self-employment taxes, sometimes substantially.

How exactly can electing S corp status save on taxes? Let's go back to the discussion of the taxes you owe in chapter 5. If you're taxed as a sole proprietor, your entire profit is subject to both income tax and self-employment tax. Self-employment tax is akin to payroll taxes and goes to Social Security and Medicare. As I talked about, when you're taxed as a sole proprietor or partnership, the 15.3% self-employment tax will kick in on your first dollar of profit.

However, electing to be taxed as an S corp means that you'll essentially be able to divide your profit into two different categories. The first is the salary that you pay yourself for the work you do in your business (also called reasonable compensation). This portion is taxed just like profit for a sole proprietorship, meaning that it's subject to both income and self-employment taxes. However, any additional profit an S corp has above and beyond your reasonable salary is essentially considered compensation for being an investor and not an employee, and therefore you are exempt from self-employment tax on that portion.

Here's a very simplified example. Let's say you have a total of $100,000 in profit before paying yourself. You do an analysis and determine that your reasonable salary would be $60,000 if you were an S corp. Using a back-of-the-envelope calculation (something I don't advise in the real world; always consult with an expert, who will do a full analysis of your situation!), your potential tax savings if taxed as an S corp instead of a sole proprietor could be estimated as:

S CORP SAVINGS EXAMPLE

	LLC TAXED AS SOLE PROP	LLC TAXED AS S CORP
Total Profit Before Owner Wages	$ 100,000	$ 100,000
Owner W-2 Salary	-	60,000
Subject to Income Tax	100,000	100,000
Subject to Self-Employment Tax	100,000	60,000
Income Tax (Assuming 25% rate)	25,000	25,000
Self-Employment Tax (15.3%)	15,300	9,180
Estimated S Corp Savings		$ 6,120

Once you are consistently making $70,000 or more in profit, it's a good time to start assessing whether S corp status could be right for you (even if you don't have employees yet). Note that for many businesses, the tipping point might be significantly above that, which is why it is essential to have a *detailed* calculation done to support making a change in entity type. In the real world, tax calculations are much more complex than the example above and require more knowledge of your overall financial situation to estimate your potential tax savings.

DON'T JUST TAKE YOUR ACCOUNTANT'S WORD FOR IT

As I mentioned before, I'm a big fan of having a financial support team. But I'm also a believer in the importance of empowering yourself with financial knowledge, because, as the CFO and CEO of your own business, you are the one with the most at stake.

That doesn't mean you need to know everything a CPA does, but it does help to know the right questions to ask. Choosing an entity type is one area where business owners would benefit from some foundational knowledge and understanding.

I've heard countless stories of accountants who recommended that a small-business owner elect S corp tax treatment without much explanation or any kind of real analysis. Many times, they also don't educate the business owner about the additional requirements of being an S corp (payroll, additional tax filings, different expense deductibility rules, and so on), which leads to (sometimes costly) problems down the line.

Or they tell them about the extra requirements and increase their fees to accommodate the extra work, so any tax savings end up in the accountant's pocket instead of yours. I've even heard of accountants setting up a brand-new business as an S corp before the company made even $1 in sales. To me, that's irresponsible. It rarely makes sense for a brand-new business to elect S corp status straight out of the gate.

So: Before you change (or establish) your entity type, make sure you understand both the implications of that decision as well as why and how your adviser(s) got to it.

In short, you'll want to make it a habit to evaluate your business structure as your business grows. The more profit you make, the more avenues available to you for saving on taxes by getting strategic about your structure. But be sure to have a detailed analysis performed by a qualified professional before making a decision on changing your entity. If you change your business structure, you also want to make sure you are fully informed about the requirements of that structure, which can impact more than just your tax calculation. For valuable resources to help you determine what entity type is best for you, go to HiddenProfitTheBook.com.

Tax-Savvy Strategy 4: Hire Your Kids

As a mom of two kiddos, this is my absolute favorite strategy. Based on existing federal labor law exceptions, a child can be legally employed *at any age* by a sole proprietorship or LLC owned by one or both parents (with no other owners). Not only that, but there are significant tax and financial benefits for starting them working early.

As long as they are doing actual work in the business, you can pay them a reasonable amount and deduct it as a business expense, which reduces your taxable profit. On the child's side, they likely have a much lower (or even zero) tax rate because they're likely making less than you (and if they're not, you have a problem!). In essence, paying them helps you shift income from a higher tax bracket to a lower one. Income shifting is a common strategy used by millionaires and billionaires to legally save on taxes, and you can use this one too—legally!

In fact, it's possible for your child to pay no taxes at all if their employment is well structured. If your child's total income is under the standard deduction ($15,000 in 2025), they will have a 0% income tax rate. Additionally, there are IRS exemptions from payroll and unemployment taxes for minors under eighteen employed in a parent's business, which means that you could feasibly employ them totally tax free—and get a business deduction for it! Here's an example of how much this could save in taxes for each child.

CHILD EMPLOYMENT BENEFITS

	NOT EMPLOYING YOUR CHILD	EMPLOYING YOUR CHILD
Profit That Could Be Paid to Kids	$ 15,000	$ 15,000
Amount Paid to Kids for Work Performed	-	15,000
Subject to Income Tax	15,000	-
Subject to Self-Employment Tax	15,000	-
Income Tax (Assuming 25% Rate)	3,750	-
Self-Employment Tax (15.3%)	2,295	-
Total Taxes	$ 6,045	-

In this scenario, hiring your minor child and paying them $15,000 (the 2025 standard deduction limit) could save you more than $6,000 in taxes. Not bad, right?

What's your minor child going to do with that much money? You can pay their salary into a custodial account (controlled by you) and use the money for things you would be paying for anyway, such as summer camp registration fees, sports league fees, or even private school. What you pay them will contribute to their future.

While the best tax benefits exist for minors, there may still be benefits to paying your adult kids, especially if their effective tax rate is lower than yours. They'll still be subject to self-employment tax, but collectively you'll likely pay less income tax than you would if you kept the income in your business.

If there is one financial gift you can give your children, investing early into a Roth IRA is a fabulous choice. Roth IRAs are open only to people with earned income, and opening a Roth IRA means giving them the gift of tax-free compound interest. Time is the most powerful tool of all when it comes to investing, and investing in a tax-advantaged Roth IRA will help you set up their financial future from an early age.

Want to see what I mean? If you hire your nine-year-old and put $7,000 per year into their Roth IRA until they are eighteen (in this case they must have earned income of at least $7,000 per year), you will see the following retirement account growth.

EXAMPLE ROTH IRA GROWTH

Age they began working for you	9
Amount to Contribute to Custodial Roth	$ 7,000
Number of Years to Contribute	9
Total ROTH Contributions for Child	63,000
Expected rate of return*	9%
Value at age 65	$ 5,233,461

*Average Returns on the S&P over a 30+ year period are typically 8-10%

Yes, you read that right. A total contribution of $63,000 while your child is a minor is estimated to amount to over $5 *million* when they reach retirement age, without you or your child contributing another dollar into it after they turn eighteen. Sure, $5 million when they retire won't have the same purchasing power as it does now, but it will be worth a heck of a lot more than $63,000. Oh, and it will be totally *tax free* when they take funds out of it.

As their parent, you can also contribute to a custodial Roth IRA in the child's name. Essentially, as long as the child has earned income, the money going into the Roth IRA can come from the parents' funds, allowing the child to keep some or all of their earnings while still benefiting from the Roth IRA contributions. Best. Parent. Ever.

Employing your kids is not only great for taxes but also a wealth-building tool to set your children up for success. And in my experience, it's an awesome opportunity to bond with your kids and teach them how to be money smart from an early age.

Wondering what your child can do in your business? Believe it or not, there are tons of ways they can help out. Administrative and organizational duties, social media, graphic design—there are endless opportunities that will also help them build real-world skills that will serve them in the future. Even very young kids can be paid for photo or video shoots used on the business's social media accounts or other marketing materials. If you'd like help brainstorming, grab my free "101 Jobs Kids Can Do in Your Business" guide at HiddenProfitTheBook.com.

> **EDUCATION, NOT EXPLOITATION**
>
> I highly recommend allowing your minor child some autonomy to decide whether they want to work for you and, if so, when and how they will do so. Of course, you'll want to be mindful of appropriate working hours and safe working conditions. It's important that this be a positive experience for them that will also help them build skills and confidence. If you use your kids as models or actors, make sure to exercise judgment in determining what to show publicly. As they get older, it's a good idea to get their explicit permission to use their likeness.
>
> Most important, enjoy getting to spend some extra time with them, sharing what you do. As we know all too well, they grow up way too fast!

The Watchouts

As with any tax strategy, there is no shortage of "watchouts" when it comes to employing your kids. You'll need to make sure that the work is age appropriate and not hazardous and be aware of any state labor law requirements, such as work permits or hourly limitations. While most states follow the federal exemption for youth employment by family businesses, some states have more stringent rules and minimum ages, even when it's your own kid. Check with your state Department of Labor to confirm the specifics before hiring your child. While your child doesn't need to work regular hours, you will need to pay them reasonably for the work they actually do (for example, you likely couldn't justify paying a fourteen-year-old a $50,000 annual salary if they're working two hours per week). You'll need to keep detailed documentation of the work they've done to support the payments and deduct their wages as a business expense. For example, I keep a log of all the days my kids worked for me, what they did, how much I paid them, and how I paid them. I generally recommend putting them onto your payroll as you would anyone else, as it will strengthen your case that they truly are an employee of your business. Importantly, there are some added complexities to hiring your kids if your business is taxed as a Corporation (S corp or C corp) or has nonparent owners. For more resources to help you with hiring your kids (or grandkids), see HiddenProfitTheBook.com.

Pull the Taxes Lever When . . .

Since the Taxes Lever is largely independent of the other Profit Levers, you don't have to wait to pull it. It's smart to continually assess where you are on taxes and look for opportunities to save. However, because you pay taxes on your operating profit, pulling the Taxes Lever *won't* fix an unprofitable business. Additionally, the more profitable your business is, the greater the benefit you're likely to get from pulling this lever.

Proven ways to pull the Taxes Lever:

- Make sure you're taking all of the deductions you are eligible for.
- Consider putting your profit into a retirement plan such as a SEP-IRA.
- Optimize your entity type.
- Hire your kids.

I don't just talk about these tax strategies; I actively utilize all of them in my business. Even though I'm a CPA with years of experience in the world of corporate finance, I found small-business taxes intimidating when I first started working for myself. Now that I was no longer someone else's employee, it seemed as though there were endless taxes to worry about. I thought I had it under control—at least until my business's first big growth year. Like many entrepreneurs, I was taken aback by the amount of taxes I had to pay in that first "good" year of business. Thankfully I knew it was coming and had saved extra (something I'll talk about more in chapter 20), but that didn't mean I enjoyed making that big payment at the end of the year.

That was when I realized I needed to become a bit more strategic when it came to taxes. As an employee of someone else's business, there wasn't much I could do to impact my tax bill. As a business owner, though, there are more strategies available. While the health of my underlying business and profitability was of first and foremost importance to me, I still wanted to make sure I wasn't paying more in taxes than I needed to.

I start by being a stickler about taking all of my business deductions. I track my car mileage, plan personal time strategically during business trips so it can be deductible, and double-check my personal expenses to make sure I didn't miss anything that is truly related to business. Heck, I even check out separately at Target if I'm buying printer paper to ensure that I don't miss the deduction. I'm ruthless about making sure that every dollar I spend that is deductible is captured and documented as a business expense.

I also set up a SEP-IRA for myself in those early years of business so I could work toward my retirement goals and get tax benefits. Now that my business has grown, I have a 401(k) for myself and my employees. Even if you can't max out a retirement account, putting in whatever you can afford will set you on the right track to future financial security.

I also do an analysis every year to make sure I'm still electing the best tax entity type for my situation. As my business grows and changes, I evaluate what in my business structure may need to change.

I also began employing my kids when they were six and nine. While they work only limited hours and only when they want to, it's been an amazing learning experience for them. It has also enabled them to make their own money and learn how to manage it well at an early age. By the age of ten, my son was setting his own long- and short-term savings goals, investing in the stock market, and giving to charitable causes that matter to him. They both regularly come into my office to ask what work they can do for me (I keep a list of child-appropriate tasks on hand). Not only that, but both already have Roth IRAs that will have time to grow substantially, setting them up for financial stability and intergenerational wealth creation. While I know that as a parent I don't do everything right (as I'm sure they'd be happy to tell you!), setting them up for financial success in this way helps me feel like Super Mom.

Even after years in business, these tried-and-true tax strategies are still my favorites. Feel free to start small and pick one to focus on. If you don't have a great system for tracking your deductions, that's a great place to start. Simply being meticulous about tracking your business deductions, including things such as car mileage and travel expenses, can make a big difference on your tax bill.

I hope this chapter illustrates that you don't need to know the entire tax code to find tax-saving opportunities in your business and being tax savvy isn't about finding obscure loopholes or taking questionable deductions. While there are other strategies out there that may fit, depending on your type of business and financial situation, these are my favorites because they're widely applicable. You don't have to be making millions or billions of dollars to utilize these strategies. As your business grows, you may decide to work with an accountant who is well versed in tax strategy to help you find more opportunities to save. That said, remember always to prioritize being profitable over saving on taxes!

CHAPTER SEVENTEEN
Carry Less Debt

Meet Marianne, the owner of a popular local toy store specializing in educational toys and games for kids of all ages. By all external accounts, Marianne's business was booming. She had a great location and a steady stream of customers.

But behind the scenes, Marianne had accumulated a significant amount of business debt in the form of business loans, outstanding lines of credit, and credit card balances. At first, the debt she took on had seemed temporary. After all, her business was growing and doing so well. Surely, she assumed, any debt she took on would be quickly paid off by sales and profit.

Unfortunately, the opposite happened. Thanks to high interest rates, the payments on her debt grew to thousands of dollars every month. Marianne took out a merchant cash advance (MCA) from her payment processor to pay down a high-interest credit card. Though that eliminated the credit card debt, the loan payments were made by the payment processor she used taking a percentage of every sale she made. That meant Marianne received less money, which led to her taking on more debt to pay necessary expenses such as payroll for herself and her staff.

To make things worse, Marianne had been deeply in debt before. She felt ashamed that she hadn't learned the lesson of borrowing more than she could afford to pay back—so much so that she felt like an impostor every time a customer or friend remarked on her success.

If you can relate, you aren't alone. Nearly 70 percent of small businesses with employees carry debt, and the average small business owes nearly $200,000.[1]

When Marianne added up all of her business debt, it totaled over $150,000. She realized that she could use the Profit Levers and what you've already learned in this book to pay off the debt. She decided to start with chapter 1 and examine all of her numbers. She took the time to review every P&L for the past two years to figure out why she had needed to take on debt in the first place. She created a new KPI Dashboard that reflected the current state of her business, aligned to both her personal and professional goals.

By doing all of that, she recognized that the debt itself wasn't the problem but rather how she was managing her business's money. She reminded herself that she had gotten out of debt once and could do it again. This time, she had the Profit Levers to help.

Good Debt Versus Bad Debt

Debt can be a powerful tool, especially when it comes to business. It can also drag you into financial chaos. Luckily, it's easy to tell the difference between good debt and bad debt in a business: **Good debt** is for a specific purpose and facilitates growth; **bad debt** plugs holes.

Good Debt:

- Is used intentionally and responsibly
- Has a plan for its use and repayment
- Provides a return greater than the interest charged

An example of good debt is taking out a loan to buy new equipment that will increase your revenue.

Bad Debt:

- Is used to plug holes such as making payroll or paying bills without making a plan to pay it off

- Is used as a short-term solution to avoid addressing the root causes of financial issues

- Generally doesn't provide a return on investment in excess of the interest rate paid

An example of bad debt is using credit cards to pay for ongoing expenses without figuring out a repayment plan.

Essentially, good debt is about intentionality, expansion, and getting a return on investment, while bad debt is like stealing from tomorrow to pay yesterday's bills. Whether or not you choose to use debt to finance your business, it pays to be smart about it.

If you aren't sure what kind of debt you have, it's likely to be bad debt. Good, growth-oriented debt is carefully planned and closely monitored. Business owners who use debt strategically know their payback periods and can estimate their Return on Investment. They're intentional, using debt as a tool to reach specific goals. If you have no idea whether your debt is generating a return, chances are it isn't.

For my fellow sports fans (Go, Deacs!), think of good debt as playing offense and bad debt as playing defense. When you're on offense, you're playing to win. Good debt is strategic; it's about taking calculated risks you believe will drive your business forward. On offense, you're using leverage to score points, gain ground, and ultimately create opportunities for growth.

On the other hand, if you spend the whole game on defense, you're essentially just trying not to lose. Bad debt puts you into a position where you're focused on avoiding loss rather than achieving success. Instead of advancing, you're using resources to cover past mistakes or sustain a stagnant position, with no forward momentum. The goal is simply to run out the clock without falling behind, which doesn't put you into a position to win.

Make sure the debt you use keeps you on offense. Do research, ask questions, understand the debt terms, know how you will utilize the debt wisely, and make a payback plan. Resist the urge to paint an overly rosy picture of what will happen in the future, including sales projections and how fast you'll be able to pay off what you've borrowed. Remember in most cases, even if you close your business, you'll still be liable for business debt.

Evaluating Your Debt Options

Diving deeper, let's evaluate some of the pros and cons of various types of debt arrangements and what to watch out for.

Credit Card

- **Pros:** Easy access to funds; potential rewards and cash back; the ability to manage cash flow by making minimum payments when necessary.
- **Con:** High interest rates that can quickly lead to a cycle of debt if not managed properly.
- **CFO Tip:** Avoid carrying a balance at all costs. If you use credit cards, make sure you use only what you can pay off each month. Credit cards are great for things such as fraud protection and rewards, but their interest rates are high, making it difficult to dig your way out once you start running a balance.

Merchant Cash Advance (MCA)

- **What it is:** A merchant cash advance provides a business with a lump sum of capital in exchange for a percentage of future credit card sales or a fixed daily/weekly repayment.
- **Pro:** Fast access to cash through merchants you are already using (Stripe, PayPal, etc.).
- **Cons:** Very high cost of borrowing; typically a short repayment period. This can lead to cash flow problems if your sales drop unexpectedly. Merchant services generally use "factoring" instead of traditional interest-rate loans, which is expensive. For example, a factor rate of 1.5 would mean that a $10,000 advance could cost $15,000 to repay, which is the equivalent of 50% APR.

- **CFO Tip:** Merchant service providers make acquiring these loans too easy. They can end up costing you a lot and get you stuck in a cycle of borrowing, i.e., needing to borrow again to pay off the first advance. These companies take advantage of your need for cash now, but at a high cost. While very occasional use might not be as costly, for more sustained usage, a line of credit would typically be a better alternative with a lower overall cost of borrowing.

Line of Credit (LOC)

- **What it is:** A business line of credit provides the ability for a business to borrow up to a certain limit, repay, and borrow again as needed.
- **Pros:** Flexible access to funds as needed; typically lower interest rates than credit cards; interest charged only on the amount borrowed.
- **Cons:** Variable interest rates can increase; using an LOC can lead to an overreliance on and increase in debt (especially if you use it to "plug holes").
- **CFO Tip:** For those looking for the flexibility of credit cards without the high interest rate, a line of credit can be a great option. An LOC can help a business have cash available to build up inventory and endure seasonality in sales, among other uses.
- **Where to go for more information:** Speak with your business banker or a financial institution about setting up a line of credit, or check our recommended resources at HiddenProfitTheBook.com.

Small Business Administration (SBA) Loan

- **What it is:** SBA loans are offered through the Small Business Administration, a government agency supporting small businesses in the United States. The goal of the SBA is to help Americans start, build, and grow businesses by providing resources to help them, including business loans.

- **Pros:** Lower interest rates; longer repayment terms; guaranteed by the government, which reduces risk for lenders and reduces the rate for you.

- **Cons:** Lengthy application process; strict eligibility criteria; typically requires collateral.

- **CFO Tip:** There are various SBA loan programs based on individual businesses' needs, so research which fits you best. SBA loans can be great for long-term needs, such as expansion, and often offer the lowest interest rates available. The SBA also has a microloan program to provide short-term small loans to businesses, including new businesses. It also offers disaster loans with low interest rates and long repayment terms if you need money due to a declared disaster (typically weather related).

- **Where to go for more information:** Contact the Small Business Administration or a financial institution that offers SBA loans. There are a few different kinds of SBA loans with different requirements and terms, so make sure to inquire which is best for your specific situation. You can also check our recommended resources at HiddenProfitTheBook.com.

Bank Term Loan

- **What it is:** Term loans are provided directly by banks and other financial institutions to businesses without the involvement of the SBA.

- **Pros:** Fixed repayment terms and interest rates; larger loan amounts for significant investments; can improve a business's credit rating if managed well.

- **Cons:** Typically requires collateral; may have a higher interest rate than SBA loans; there is a regular repayment schedule regardless of a business's cash flow.

- **CFO Tip:** If you aren't able to secure an SBA loan, a business bank loan can be an alternative. This is especially true if you are looking to use the money to expand or scale up your business. Fixed-rate loans are generally less risky than variable-rate loans. Make sure to shop around for the best rates.

- **Where to go for more information:** Discuss options with your business bank or a loan officer, or check our recommended resources at HiddenProfitTheBook.com.

The Hidden Cost of Debt

These days, taking on debt is easier than ever—so easy, in fact, that sometimes we don't even realize we're doing it! Any of these "extra services" sound familiar?

- When you transfer money out of your PayPal or Venmo account: *Get it a day sooner for just 1.5%!*

- When you purchase something at an online shop: *Buy now, pay later! Split your payment into smaller payments [for a fee].*

- When you look at your credit card statement online: *You qualify for a cash advance! Just click here!*

While these offers may not feel like traditional debt, they're all variations on debt arrangements, essentially charging you a fee for quick access to cash. It's essential to check the fine print before hitting the "OK" button. Over the course of a year, interest and fees to take advantage of these "easy" offers can quickly climb into the thousands of dollars. And watch out for the allure of "0% interest" offers, which can come with hidden fees or a spike in the interest rate after an introductory period.

We're bombarded with these tempting debt offers daily, and they can add up fast. In fact, you might even be paying fees to access your own money just a bit sooner. Ease of access can be costly, so it's worth slowing down and evaluating the real price of convenience. Be sure to double check how you are transferring money in apps like Venmo and PayPal, and on payment processors like Stripe. Often the "default" comes with an extra charge.

In general, when it comes to borrowing, easy money = expensive money. Easy money is often funds that are available at the push of a button and don't require any documentation, credit check, or collateral. However, the price you pay for that ease can be high. Not only that, but these types of on-demand debt arrangements make it much easier to fall into the bad-debt trap.

To determine which type of debt arrangement to take on, look at the annual percentage rate (APR). The APR of a debt is the total cost of borrowing the money, including interest and any applicable fees. Looking at the APR helps you compare different debt instruments on an apples-to-apples basis. Importantly, not all debt arrangements are required to disclose their APR. While credit cards, personal loans, and mortgages are generally required to be up front about their APR, other debt arrangements such as merchant cash advances and even some business loans may not be required to provide that information, making it harder to compare options.

In general, you'll get the lowest rate for a secured loan. A **secured loan** is backed by collateral (usually business assets in the case of a business loan). Your mortgage is an example of a secured term loan.

Merchant cash advances and credit cards (easy money) are by far the most expensive when looking at the total cost of the debt. In some cases, you could be spending five to ten times as much as necessary if you regularly use these types of debt instruments in your business. There is a better way.

It's true that qualifying for a business line of credit, term loan, or SBA loan can come with higher requirements, like minimum personal credit and proof of your business's profitability. But just because easy-to-get debt is expensive, it doesn't mean that cheaper debt has to be hard to get. Yes, getting a line of credit or term loan at a lower interest rate may mean you have to pony up a few years' worth of tax returns or financial statements to prove your business's profitability. I've already discussed the importance of keeping well-organized financial records and making sure you're maximizing your profit. Access to cheaper capital is yet another reason to take the actions outlined in this book to improve your business's financial health.

For my recommendations on where to get cheaper debt without having to jump through endless hoops, go to HiddenProfitTheBook.com.

To pay down her debt, the first thing Marianne did was examine her direct and indirect costs. Some of the cuts were simple, such as canceling subscriptions to software she wasn't using, while others hurt her heart a little (telling contractors she liked that she no longer needed their services). Once she had reduced her overall expenses, she was able to examine her profit margins and adjust her price. After that, she revisited her sales process so that she could increase her volume.

Next, she created a spreadsheet of the debt she owed. She included each one's current balance, APR, average monthly interest, and minimum payment. Knowing exactly how much profit she could expect to make, she decided to put a majority of the extra money she had created by pulling Profit Levers to paying down debt. Based on her calculations, she would be able to get out of debt completely in twelve to eighteen months.

Even though she wasn't out of debt—yet!—Marianne felt empowered simply by taking action. She added "Debt Paid" to her monthly KPIs so she could see the progress she was making month after month. That simple metric transformed how she felt about her debt. Instead of feeling resentful about all the money that was going to pay for her past mistakes, she felt proud that she was fixing the problem. As a bonus, she knew that someday the money she was spending on debt would become profit to use as she pleased.

The **Debt Lever** is typically one of the last ones to address. Once you've pulled other levers, such as price and costs, you will have more profit available to pay down your debt, which will free up more profit in the future, which will enable you to pay down more debt, and so on.

How to pull the Debt Lever:

1. Make a list of all your outstanding debt, including interest rates, due dates, and minimum payments. Determine which you will prioritize paying off first, second, and so on.

2. Use the tips in chapter 6 to improve your cash flow, which will help reduce your reliance on defensive debt.

3. Use the Direct Costs, Indirect Costs, Price, and Volume Levers first to maximize your profit.

4. Commit a percentage of your profit to paying down debt faster (read more about this in part IV). Each month, allocate a percentage of profit to your debts and make a payoff plan for each.

5. **Optional:** Research lower-interest loans or zero-interest credit cards to consolidate your debt and reduce interest payments. Do this only *after* you have made a repayment plan you know you can stick to.

If your goal is to get out of debt, whether business or personal, it's important to know that the process is typically slow and frustrating, and sometimes you might even backslide. That is *normal*. Thanks to the culture in which we live, debt is incredibly easy to get into and not so easy to get out of. But you can do it. You've already done incredible things; you've built a whole dang business. It's time to show that debt who's boss.

In part IV of this book, I'll discuss more strategies to help you earmark some of your profit for debt repayment, as Marianne did. For now, make that list of your outstanding debt, payoff dates, and interest rates, and decide which one you'll tackle first!

CHAPTER EIGHTEEN

Make Big Profits

You're now familiar with all of the Profit Levers—kudos to you for getting this far! Now it's time to go back into your control room and imagine that the levers are lined up on the wall in front of you. As a reminder, they are:

PROFIT LEVERS

VOLUME PRICE MIX AVERAGE TRANSACTION VALUE

DIRECT COSTS INDIRECT COSTS TAXES DEBT

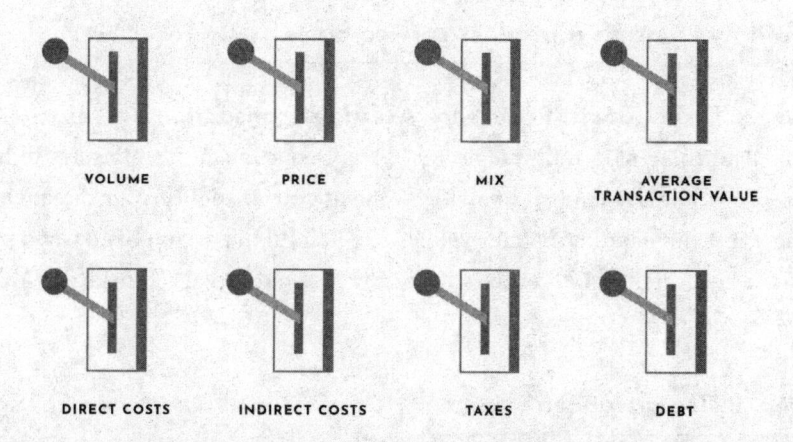

Before you start pulling levers at random, remember that it's usually better to focus on one at a time. It may already be abundantly clear where you need to start, or you may have several levers that all need urgent attention.

Each business is different, and your situation is unique. There isn't one way (or one order) that works best for everyone, so feel free to create the Profit Lever strategy that works best for you. However, if you aren't sure where to begin, starting with the cost levers (Direct and Indirect Costs) is a good way to see an immediate bump in profitability. Below is one example of how you might tackle the Profit Levers one by one.

Small Tweaks = Big Profits

Step 1: Reduce your indirect costs by 2%.

Lever: Indirect Costs
Cutting your indirect costs has the benefit of helping you both now and in the future by plugging the cash leaks in your bucket. Focus on areas where you aren't seeing a return on investment. Starting with your recurring costs will give you the biggest bang for your time.

Step 2: Analyze your prices, sales, and profit margins on a product/service basis.

Levers: Direct Costs, Price, Mix, Average Transaction Value
Calculate the gross profit margin for each of your business's offerings to help you determine if you need to change your pricing or reduce your direct costs. These individual profit margins will also be helpful to have on hand when pulling the next set of Profit Levers, specifically Mix and Average Transaction Value.

Step 3: Use advanced tactics.

Once these levers have been pulled, you know that you are maximizing the value of each and every sale you make. At that point, it's time to:

1. Focus on driving sales (Lever: Volume)
2. Look at ways to reduce taxes (Lever: Taxes)
3. Make a plan to pay down your debt (Lever: Debt)

The first time you go through this process, it will likely feel arduous, and you won't be sure if you're doing it right. Don't worry, that's normal. Just like a muscle, the more you use these levers, the easier it will get. Eventually, you'll make nearly all of your business decisions entirely through the lenses of the eight Profit Levers.

Here's the kicker: Tweaking even a few of these Profit Levers by only 2% can have a compound effect on your bottom line that will result in *much more than* 2% extra profit. Because math is awesome like that!

Let's illustrate this with a hypothetical example. Let's say your P&L looks a little like this before you pull any of the Profit Levers:

PROFIT & LOSS

	BEFORE PROFIT LEVER ADJUSTMENTS	PROFIT MARGINS
Revenue	$ 100,000	
Direct Costs	50,000	
Gross Profit	50,000	50%
Indirect Costs	25,000	
Operating Profit	$ 25,000	25%

While you're pulling in revenue in six figures, you're left with only a fraction of that to pay yourself at the end of the day (only a quarter out of every dollar you make!). Let's walk through the steps above and see how small tweaks can add up to *big* profits:

Step 1: Reduce your indirect costs by 2%.

- **Indirect Costs Lever.** Find the low-hanging fruit—and cut. You don't need to spend hours on this one. Simply pull up your bank statement or accounting software and look at your monthly recurring expenses. Aim to reduce those indirect costs by just 2%. In the case above, 2% of $25,000 in indirect costs amounts to $500 for the year, just $42 per month!

Step 2: Analyze your prices, sales, and profit margins on a product/service basis.

- **Direct Costs Lever.** Review your direct costs, including any cost of goods sold or direct labor costs, including your time. Where might there be opportunities to save money or gain more efficiency? To start, aim to reduce your costs per product/service sale by 2%. If it costs you $100 to service each customer, how could you do it for $98 instead? Challenge yourself and get creative to find that hidden profit!

- **Pricing Lever.** It's time to analyze your pricing. Do your profit margin calculations and identify where there is room for improvement. Aim to increase your prices by just 2%, even if you apply the change only to new customers to start. Combining these price changes with the reduction in direct costs will have an exponential effect on your gross profit margin. Using the example above, a 2% reduction in direct costs coupled with a 2% increase in average prices will yield a 6% increase in gross profit (from $50,000 to $53,000). Not bad for small tweaks!

- **Average Transaction Value Lever.** After you've adjusted your pricing, it's time to look at how you might be able to increase your average transaction value. Let's say your current average transaction value is $200. How could you bump that up to $204 (a 2% increase)? If you offer a $40 upgrade, just one of every ten customers would need to opt in to it to increase your average transaction value by 2%. Bonus points if the upgrade wouldn't have much of an impact (if any) on your direct costs.

- **Mix Lever.** Where might you be able to shift sales from some of your lower-margin products to your higher-margin products? How could you get at least 2% of your customers to opt for the more profitable offer? Alternatively, how could you increase your gross profit by 2% by shifting your sales mix emphasis from one product to another? Consider shifting your messaging and promotional plans to drive people where you want them to go.

Before we move on to the other levers, let's do a quick recap of how these actions alone have improved your hypothetical gross profit margin and bottom line—without your having to bring in *any* new sales. (Note that results are rounded for ease of presentation, and the math may not recalculate easily, in part because each lever builds on the previous one.)

PULLING THE PROFIT LEVERS

	BEFORE PROFIT LEVER ADJUSTMENTS	COSTS LEVERS	PRICE LEVER (2%)	AVERAGE TRANSACTION VALUE LEVER (2%)	MIX LEVER (2%)	AFTER PROFIT LEVER ADJUSTMENTS	MARGIN INCREASE
Gross Profit	$ 50,000	$ 1,000	$ 2,000	$ 2,000	$ 1,000	$ 56,000	12%
Indirect Costs		25,000	(500)			24,500	
Operating Profit	$ 25,000	$ 1,500	$ 2,000	$ 2,000	$ 1,000	$ 31,500	25%

In this example, all of those small tweaks ended up yielding a 12% gross profit increase and a 25% operating profit increase without a single ounce of added hustle. Strategic shifts like these are the keys to finding the hidden profit in your business. Even if you start by pulling just one or two of these levers, it can make a big difference to your overall bottom line—and your financial stability.

The reason I recommend focusing on these levers before you focus on bringing in new sales is that doing so ensures that you are maximizing your profit from each and every one of those new sales. Now every sale you bring in will generate 12% more in gross profit than it would have before! That means it's finally time to pull the final levers.

Step 3: Use advanced tactics.

- **Volume Lever.** Now it's time to focus on bringing in more business, knowing that you are maximizing the profit of every sale you make. In the same example, let's assume that you increase your sales by just 2% annually. Here's what your margins would look like now.

PULLING THE VOLUME LEVER

	BEFORE PROFIT LEVER ADJUSTMENTS	AFTER PROFIT LEVER ADJUSTMENTS	MARGIN INCREASE	VOLUME LEVER (2%)	AFTER VOLUME LEVER	MARGIN INCREASE
Gross Profit	$ 50,000	$ 56,000	12%	$ 1,000	$ 57,000	14%
Indirect Costs	25,000	24,500			24,500	
Operating Profit	$ 25,000	$ 31,500	25%	$ 1,000	$ 32,500	30%

An overall 30% increase in your operating profit margin? Not bad for some 2% tweaks! But what if you want to turbocharge the process even more? If you opt to aim for 2% *monthly* sales growth (instead of annual), your annual operating profit would nearly double (!!!) from your current levels. What could you do with double your current profit?

This is a perfect illustration of the power in numbers: Small ripples can compound to make waves bigger than the sum of their parts, and there isn't as much as you might think that separates a marginally profitable business from a highly profitable one. A little bit of strategy goes a *long* way. And we aren't even through all of the Profit Levers yet!

Now that you've maximized your operating profit, you can look at the "below the line" items such as income taxes and interest on debt. Higher operating profit means more money available to help you pay down your debt faster, thereby reducing the amount of interest you need to pay.

Regarding taxes, you may be wondering "But, Jamie, if I increase my operating profit, doesn't that mean my taxes will go up, not down?" And you'd be correct. A higher operating profit with all else being equal means that the amount you pay in taxes will increase. However, you'll still have significantly more money than you would have had previously, even after taxes. Assuming a 22% marginal tax rate, the extra $7,000 you'd make in the above example would increase your tax liability by about $1,500. However, you'd still have over $5,500 more cash available than you would otherwise have had. That increase in take-home pay is why we don't let the fear of paying taxes hold us back from maximizing our profit.

Plus, as your tax liability goes up, you can institute more of the tax-saving strategies I talked about in chapter 16. For example, the more profit you make, the more likely electing S corporation taxation will save you money. That means it's possible to increase your profit *and* reduce your taxes at the same time! Talk about a win-win!

You don't need to double your prices or drastically cut your expenses to massively impact your bottom line. When you harness the power in numbers and step into the role of CFO, there are endless money-generating opportunities to be discovered. If you want to see what kind of impact pulling the Profit Levers could have on your overall bottom line, head over to HiddenProfitTheBook.com and grab my free Profitability Maximizer template for some plug-and-play fun!

OVERCOMING YOUR FEAR OF "BEING WRONG"

I see so many business owners who are held back from stepping into their role as their own CFO because of the fear that they won't do it right. There are simple, viable business changes that they could make that are sitting not too far into the data, yet they let their *fear* of numbers keep them from realizing the *power* in numbers. And while we do want the numbers on our tax returns to be accurate, being the CFO of your own business is *not* about getting your calculations exactly right. It is more than okay to make educated assumptions based on your experience when you are analyzing possible changes in your Profit Levers or trying to forecast future profit; as a former CFO myself, I know that that's the only way to do it!

I encourage you to bring a sense of fun and even play to your strategic financial decisions. Start to visualize your profit as a puzzle that can be solved in a variety of different and creative ways. Over time, this will feel more and more natural, and you might even find yourself looking forward to it (really!).

Your Next Step

As I'll talk about more in part IV, earning more profit isn't just for profit's sake. Greater profit margin in your business can equate to greater margin (monetary and otherwise) in your life. I want you to feel a level of freedom you've never felt before. I want you to be able to afford to hire extra help as your business grows and be confident that you can still pay yourself well. That is what the Profit Levers can do. At the end of the day, making a greater profit margin isn't just about making more money; it's about creating more *time* margin, too. Isn't that the dream?

In the final part of the hidden profit journey, I'll show you how to use the extra profit you've created to help you achieve the life and business you've always dreamed of, while also making a big impact on the world. (Hint: It's all about creating a personalized plan for how you will *use* your profit.)

PART IV

Create Your PROFFIT Plan™

Whew! Give yourself a pat on the back for making it through all those super fun formulas (unless, of course, you *enjoyed* getting into the numbers weeds—did we just become best friends?).

For most of us, the idea of making more profit is probably enticing. But being more profitable simply for profit's sake may not motivate us enough to put in the level of effort needed to take control of our finances. Maybe you even pride yourself on not being motivated by money or material possessions. That's why, along with the tangible strategies to increase profit we talked about in the last section, it's important to paint a picture of how increasing our profit can change our lives (and the lives of others) for the better.

How can we leverage the hidden profit we find in our business in ways that are truly motivating and exciting? This final section of the book is all about setting up systems that will serve your bigger goals and the greater good, and how the power in numbers can help you live a life defined by freedom and impact.

CHAPTER NINETEEN

Make a Plan for Your PROFFIT

When we're concerned about making ends meet, it can be hard to let ourselves dream. I hope that when you start to uncover the hidden profit in your business, you will also begin to see the possibilities for your life and business more clearly. Give yourself permission to look forward with a newfound hope.

This is where you get the opportunity to pose an exhilarating, albeit sometimes nerve-racking, question to yourself: *What do I really want?*

Maybe you want to grow your business to be a multimillion-dollar business or eventually sell it for a big payday. Maybe you want to have safety and security so you can retire yourself and/or your spouse or help your kids go to college debt-free. Maybe you want to travel the world or invest in a vacation home. Maybe you want to be able to give generously to causes you care about. Maybe you want to pay down your personal debt so you can feel freer. Or maybe you would like to have a little extra cash so that you aren't living paycheck to paycheck.

Maybe you want to do all of that—and more.

What you really want to do is highly dependent on *you* and will likely morph and change as your life changes. What I wanted ten years ago is different from what I envision for my life today. And that's okay. This decision doesn't have to be a forever thing. But knowing what is important to you *now* will help you move in a direction that feels right.

You can start by writing down your goals and dreams for the future. Now isn't the time to censor yourself; this is just for you. If you're a visual person, this might look like a vision board where you utilize pictures and quotes that define what you want your life to look like in the future. Start by thinking about those long-term goals.

Once you create your list of goals, it's time to prioritize based on where you are now. What do you need to be doing today in order to make progress toward that long-term vision? To figure it out, you'll want to ask yourself what is *most* important to you at this stage of your life (think: over the next twelve months). Is it maximizing your current paycheck? Paying down personal or business debt? Saving for retirement or a down payment on a house? Growing your business rapidly? Having more time and money to travel and experience new things?

Not everything can be your top priority, at least in the short term; unfortunately, you have to pick. I know, it can be tough. As I said, this doesn't have to be your forever priority. In fact, you can change your mind next month if you'd like! Define your top short-term priority *right now*, and then rank the rest. For some of you, there may be an urgent need, such as paying yourself enough to cover your bills or paying down high-interest-rate debt or back taxes. Others of you may have more flexibility to prioritize things such as investing in your business to grow it, planning for early retirement, or increasing your free time. Take a few moments to consider what you really want and need at this stage of your life. Resist the temptation to overthink it!

Once you have a good idea of what your more immediate goals are and you've ranked them accordingly, it's time to make your PROFFIT Plan.

What the heck is a PROFFIT Plan? you ask.

Great question. It's a personalized plan for managing your business income (i.e., your profit). I recommend you look at your cash profit (the net cash you made over a given period, after expenses) at least monthly and allocate it into different "reserves" or "envelopes." Essentially, you want to give every dollar of your profit a *job*.

As you might have guessed, each of these reserves is a letter in the PROFFIT Plan acronym. #nerdalert

P: Pay Yourself Fund

R: Rainy Day Fund

O: Opportunity Fund

F: Future Fund

F: Fun Fund

I: Impact Fund

T: Tax Fund

Am I aware that I misspelled "profit"? Yes. However, I insist on including some "fun" in your financial planning—after all, you only live once (YOLO)!

> ### THERE'S AN APP FOR THAT
>
> You may be wondering how to keep track of these reserve balances. Thankfully, you can put your dollar bills and envelopes away. All (or some) of these funds can be set up as separate bank accounts if you prefer, but it isn't necessary. You could also utilize a budgeting app, your accounting software, or even a spreadsheet to keep track of your fund balances. Some banking platforms even have built-in functionality to allow you to segregate funds, either with or without creating separate accounts. In fact, some banking platforms will actually move money automatically from one account to another based on rules you set. At the end of the day, the important thing is what will work for you and what is easiest for you to keep up with.
>
> For recommended banking platforms and other tools to help you track your PROFFIT Plan reserves, check out HiddenProfitTheBook.com.

When I showed my methodology to my husband for the first time, he cleverly coined the tag line "PROFFIT Planning: for people who give two 'Fs' about their finances." While I haven't officially adopted it as a slogan, it doesn't cease to make me chuckle!

The purpose of a PROFFIT Plan is to use the profit your business generates to help you meet your unique personal and business goals. Creating separate "buckets" to which to allocate your cash regularly will help you reach your goals more intentionally.

We'll keep coming back to our PROFFIT Plan in the next few chapters, diving deeper into each of the funds and how to use them. But for now, start thinking about what you want to do with all that profit you're creating!

CHAPTER TWENTY

Build Your P-O-T of PROFFIT

I want to start by focusing on the P-O-T of PROFFIT, specifically: the **P** (Pay Yourself) Fund, the **O** (Opportunity) Fund, and the **T** (Taxes) Fund.

> **CHIEF FINANCIAL OPINION:**
> **Don't Work for Free**
>
> If I had a dollar for every time a business owner told me they don't regularly (or ever!) pay themselves from their business, I'd be a rich woman. This even happens in fast-growing companies with healthy profit margins.
>
> Often, profit made is reinvested into the business to help fuel its growth. While this is typical in the early days of a business, sometimes old habits die hard. But when you aren't paying yourself regularly, you are working for free or close to it.
>
> Would you work for anyone else for free? Likely not. So don't do it for yourself, either.

P = Pay Yourself Fund

The Pay Yourself Fund represents the share of profit that you will pay to yourself as an owner's draw. Note that this is *not* the same as the salary you take from your business as people on payroll do. If you own an S corp or C corp and work actively in your business, you should be paying yourself a reasonable salary in the form of payroll (if that's not happening already, the Profit Levers will help you get there). However, that money is separate from the funds that should be captured here. Think of it this way: Your salary pays you the income you earn from working *in* your business. Any extra profit you make is earnings for being an owner/investor in your business and compensates you for the extra risk you have taken on.

If you don't have a Corporation (S or otherwise), your Pay Yourself Fund will represent the full amount you pay yourself (your owner draw).

Five years into her boutique business, Harper felt as though she was spending all the money that came in on inventory and staff costs. Even after making sure her profit margins were adequate, she still didn't feel that she could pay herself regularly. In fact, she would take a draw from the company only once a year and was nervous about taking too much out in case she needed it later.

She paid herself from the leftovers—if there were any. And it was starting to put a crunch on her family's finances. While Harper struggled, she was also convinced that that was normal. She had heard the statistics that most small businesses don't break even, much less make a profit, for years. She kept telling herself "someday" it would all be worth it, but that someday never seemed to come. As her business grew, she still felt as strapped for cash as she had in the early days.

After going around and around in that cycle for far too long, Harper finally decided to find help. In her search for a plan to help her pay herself, she became a student of mine and learned about making a PROFFIT Plan. Rather than an inflexible plan that felt difficult to implement, she loved that she could customize it to fit her goals, habits, and personality.

Once Harper instituted her PROFFIT Plan, she was able to set a portion of the profit she made toward paying herself. Rather than viewing all her money as one giant pot of cash and spending it all on her business, every dollar in her business finally had a purpose, *including* making sure she was paid. Using her PROFFIT Plan in combination with cash flow forecasting (discussed in chapter 5), she felt confident that she could take out money to pay herself without worrying whether her business would need it later. She committed to paying herself an owner's draw at least once a month, using her PROFFIT Plan as her guide.

What Harper hadn't realized consciously was that after years of not paying herself regularly, she had become quietly resentful of her own business and all the energy it demanded of her for little return. She had even considered shutting it all down and finding a regular J-O-B instead. Instituting her PROFFIT Plan and paying herself every month without fail not only helped her family's financial situation but also gave her a renewed sense of passion for her business. Without the constant financial pressure on her shoulders, she remembered why she had started her business in the first place. Having the extra mental space allowed her to dream again. A year after instituting her PROFFIT Plan, she decided she wanted to open a second location, using money saved in her Opportunity Fund, which I'll discuss next. A year earlier, she had considered shutting it all down, but now she was excited to expand. That's the difference paying yourself regularly can make!

Implementation

The percentage you allocate to the Pay Yourself (P) Fund will be highly dependent on your short-term and long-term goals, as well as your growth goals for your business. A typical range is 25% to 50% of before-tax profit. If your business is seasonal, you may not want to pay yourself the full amount of your Pay Yourself Fund in the good months and instead leave a portion in the Pay Yourself Fund to help cover you in slower months and allow you to take draws even when less income is coming in. Don't leave the money aside for too long, though; you should be paying yourself at regular intervals, preferably taking a draw at least once per month.

Not sure what percentage to set yet? No worries. You can (and should) revisit this percentage once you've gone through the other funds and adjust to make sure that the total adds up to 100%.

O = Opportunity Fund

I mentioned that Harper decided to expand to a second location a year after instituting her PROFFIT Plan. How could she afford to do that, when previously she had been struggling to pay herself? The key was her Opportunity Fund, the O in the PROFFIT Plan.

One of the biggest questions my clients used to ask me was whether they could afford to hire an employee, purchase an asset, take a training course, or hire a coach, among other things. If you've ever wanted to invest in something for your business but wondered if you can afford it, the Opportunity Fund will change your world.

Of course, it's a loaded question and one that is tough for someone else to answer without knowing your goals or the ins and outs of your business. So I developed a system that can tell anyone definitively whether they can "afford" something without going into debt or stealing from other important priorities.

Your Opportunity Fund is what you use to save for the nonrecurring investments you want to make in your business and when you want to take advantage of great opportunities that may present themselves. Each month, a portion of your profit will go into this fund and enable you to save up for larger, more impactful purchases over time. The goal is to help you save diligently toward a larger-ticket item that you may otherwise have to pass on or go into debt for.

Do you need to upgrade your computer equipment? Are you contemplating hiring an administrative assistant? Perhaps there is a course you've had your eye on taking to sharpen your skills? The Opportunity Fund will make those investment decisions more straightforward.

If you're wondering whether you can afford a purchase, check your Opportunity Fund. Not enough in it? It's likely time to pass on that investment for now, but let it fuel you to turbocharge your profit so you can grow your Opportunity Fund quickly. Make note of any missed opportunities that you want to revisit later. Remember, the answer isn't "no"; it's only "not yet." The right opportunities have a way of coming back around.

The Opportunity Fund is a great way to save up for growth. Before her new store was ready to open, Harper was able to save for the costs it would incur. Once she decided she wanted to expand, she set a goal amount to save in her Opportunity Fund to cover the first three months' rent on her new location, plus up-front renovation costs. Though it took a little longer than if she had decided to take on debt to expand, it was the best choice for the risk-averse Harper. It also meant that she could become profitable quicker, since she wasn't paying interest on a business loan.

You can use the Opportunity Fund for hiring, too. When I hire a new contractor or employee, I generally aim to have one to three months of their pay saved up in my Opportunity Fund before hiring them. This helps cover the time it takes before I begin to see the Return on Investment of a new hire, and having funds already set aside for their paycheck reduces the financial pressure of hiring. If I'm hiring for a more administrative position, I'll often aim to have saved at least three months' worth of their pay in the Opportunity Fund first, since the ROI is less direct and immediate. However, if I'm hiring a new salesperson, client service person, or someone else with a direct line to revenue generation, I might keep only one month's worth of their pay in my Opportunity Fund, as the expectation is that I'll see a Return on Investment faster.

Having an Opportunity Fund completely transformed my business. The fund has paid for my taking valuable educational programs, upgrading my equipment, hiring my team, experimenting with new marketing and advertising strategies and software, and hiring experts such as a search engine optimization (SEO) strategist and YouTube agency. Had I not been intentional about putting money into this fund, I likely would have spent it in other ways without even realizing it, and my business would not be what it is today.

How do you know when to pay for an expense out of your Opportunity Fund and when to pay from your regular operating account? Most recurring expenses needed to run your business will come from your regular operating account. Your Opportunity Fund is generally for reinvesting to grow. It's important to get into the habit of paying for one-off expenses from your Opportunity Fund so you don't unintentionally balloon your business's indirect costs. Remember, I said you *don't* need a budget—*if* you are following your own money rules and regularly keep tabs on your financial situation. If you always utilize your Opportunity Fund for costs *outside of* the normal course of business, you won't need to budget meticulously.

While the fund can help unintentional overspending (as my Romantics, Celebrities, or even Mavericks might be prone to doing), as an Accumulator, I also find it quite helpful for other reasons. Given that I can skew toward hoarding my money "just in case," I tend to shy away from opportunities that present themselves, even when they could be good investments. Having an Opportunity Fund with money specifically earmarked for reinvesting makes trying something new feel significantly less risky. In fact, I now actively look for the best ways to use my Opportunity Fund money and have a list of possible next investments to make when I have enough saved.

While there are money management systems that will help you prioritize paying yourself and saving for taxes, a PROFFIT Plan is unique in that it also helps you to be intentional about using your money to reinvest and grow (plus have a little fun *and* help others, which I'll discuss later in this section). Paying yourself doesn't have to mean sacrificing your business's growth opportunities. Plus, a PROFFIT Plan allows you to decide how much to allocate to each fund based on your goals. No more trying to squeeze a square peg into a round hole. Woo-hoo!

Implementation

How much should you set aside in your Opportunity Fund? Remember, it all comes down to your goals for your business. If you have big dreams and are hoping for super-fast growth, a higher percentage saved in your Opportunity Fund can help you achieve them without taking on the added stress of debt. An Opportunity Fund will usually amount to 10% to 20% of your operating profit (20% for companies with supercharged growth goals). If growth isn't a priority for you right now, you could go as low as 5%.

Putting more money into your Opportunity Fund will often reduce the amount available to pay yourself right now, so make sure to balance your short-term and long-term goals to figure out the right mix. Remember, you can change your PROFFIT Plan percentages at any time if they aren't working for you, so feel free to play around with them!

T = Tax Fund

Remember when I said that paying taxes isn't that much of a hassle as long as you're prepared to do so? The Tax Fund is how you prepare.

When setting up your PROFFIT Plan funds, it's critical to allocate a percentage of your total profit to paying your income and self-employment taxes, as well as any applicable state and local income taxes. You can then use the amounts that you put into this fund to pay your quarterly estimated taxes and perhaps save some extra "just in case" (depending on your risk tolerance, as discussed in chapter 8) so you'll be prepared for any unforeseen tax increases come April 15. Additionally, because the pass-through nature of small-business taxes (discussed in chapter 16) makes it difficult to determine exactly how much of the tax you owe is related to your business, this "just in case" money can be a welcome gift to your future self.

Because of the level of detail it takes to get an accurate estimate, accountants often use last year's tax return as a basis for this year's estimated taxes to be paid quarterly. If your income situation significantly changes from one year to the next, though, this could result in a significant over- or underpayment of taxes. This is why it's often a great idea to meet with your accountant in the fall each year to do some more detailed calculations of your taxes, especially if you want to make sure you're not under- or overpaying significantly (and why it could be a welcome gift, if you can swing it, to put a little "just in case" money into your Tax Fund!).

Determining Your Effective Tax Rate

If you don't expect your situation to change much year over year, you can do a quick calculation of your personal effective tax rate by looking at your most recently filed tax return.

On the second page of your Form 1040, look for the "This is your total tax" line. This is your total tax liability for the year related to all income on that return. Then divide that figure by the "This is your taxable income" line, which is typically on the first page of your tax return.

For example, if your total tax is $25,000 and your total income was $125,000, your federal effective tax rate is 20% ($25,000 divided by $125,000). Using this as a proxy for how much of your profit to put aside for taxes is a good place to start for federal income and self-employment taxes, especially if you expect your income to be the same as or lower than last year. If you live in a state with higher state taxes, you'll want to add a little extra to that estimate.

When you pay estimated taxes, the IRS does not generally assess interest or penalties as long as you pay at least 100% of last year's taxes by January 15 of this year (when the last quarterly estimated payment is due). That means that if you paid $20,000 in federal taxes last year, as long as you pay $5,000 in estimated taxes per quarter this year, you won't be assessed fees for underpayment (at higher income levels, the IRS requires you to pay at least 110% of last year's tax to avoid penalties, which would be $22,000 in this example).

However, that doesn't mean you won't owe a big tax bill if you simply match last year's taxes owed. This is where the Tax Fund comes in.

If you expect to make much more than you did last year, it's important to realize that the additional money you make will likely be taxed at a much higher rate than last year's effective tax rate. That's because your **effective income tax rate** is an average of all the rates you pay on your taxable income. The first money you make is taxed at the lowest rate (zero for the amount of money that's less than the standard deduction). As you make money above and beyond what you did last year, you'll pay a **marginal income tax rate** on the additional income, which is the tax rate on the last dollar of income you earn. If you estimate your taxes based on last year's effective tax rate but make more money this year than you did last year, that can lead to those unexpected tax bills we all know and definitely don't love.

Consulting with a qualified tax expert (CPA or EA) will help you better estimate your tax burden for the current year. This is especially important if you have had significant changes in your tax situation (tax filing status, an income change, or changes in credits you are eligible for).

If you want to make sure you'll be covered, you'll want to save extra in your Tax Fund, especially if your business is growing. Doing this allows you to give yourself a "refund" if you don't wind up needing it, without having to give the government an interest-free loan. I tend to pay my estimated taxes quarterly based on last year's actual taxes paid but save additional funds in my Tax Fund just in case (especially if I expect my income to grow!).

Implementation

So what's a typical range for the Tax Fund? Anywhere between 15% and 30% of profit (not revenue) is where I see most business owners land. If you have a Corporation and you're already withholding taxes on your paycheck separately from this fund, you'll likely be on the lower end of that range. If you have significant income and/or live in a state with higher income taxes, you'll likely fall on the higher end.

Paying taxes will probably never be fun (even I can't help that), but the better prepared you can be, the less headache-inducing they will be. Your PROFFIT Plan will help make sure you are prepared.

When people have just started their PROFFIT Plan, this is the account I recommend that they start with. While you don't *have* to have separate bank accounts to execute your PROFFIT Plan, it may make sense to put your tax savings into a separate account to ensure that you don't inadvertently spend that money.

CHAPTER TWENTY-ONE
Prepare for the Future

Brenda owns a well-known farm in the country where she teaches horseback riding to kids. Summer is her busiest time of year because that's when she runs a full-day horseback-riding camp each week. The rest of the year, her teaching is limited to a few hours each week after school and on Saturdays. From a revenue perspective, she makes 50% of her annual revenue during just ten weeks in the summer. However, she still has to feed, house, and care for her horses and the farm all fifty-two weeks in the year.

Every year the same cycle repeats: In the summer Brenda is flush with cash, but by the middle of the winter she's scraping by trying to make ends meet. She felt ashamed and blamed the situation on herself. She told herself that clearly, she just isn't good with money.

What Brenda didn't realize was that she was dealing with an issue that many, if not most, small-business owners struggle with in some way: seasonality. It's actually quite rare for businesses to have a perfectly steady stream of revenue every month of the year. Even businesses that are highly profitable on paper likely have times of the year when they're strapped for cash.

The problem wasn't Brenda. And if, like her, you struggle with seasonality in your business, the problem isn't you. Brenda's problem was her system of managing cash (or lack thereof). She needed to implement a plan—a PROFFIT Plan!—to protect herself during those lower-income winter months.

R = Rainy Day Fund

This is where the letter R comes in. R is for Rainy Day Fund. The purpose of the Rainy Day Fund is to put money aside so you'll be prepared for things that will try to knock you off course.

You'll notice that this fund is *not* called an "emergency fund." This is on purpose—and not just because there isn't an E in the word *profit*. Psychologically, an emergency fund feels like something we should never use unless we're in the direst of circumstances (especially for those of us who are Accumulators). True emergencies will, hopefully, be few and far between. However, rainy days aren't abnormal. In business, a rainy day could be a low sales month or unexpected expenses popping up.

The Rainy Day Fund is also a perfect place to save extra cash in a seasonal business. You can use it to put aside cash during the higher-sales months to cover costs during the lower-sales months.

When Brenda first started to use the Rainy Day Fund, she wondered how much of her profit she should put into it to prepare for her business's seasonality. Of course, the answer was in her data. When she pulled her quarterly Profit and Loss Statement for the year, it looked a little like this:

PROFIT & LOSS

	Q1	Q2	Q3	Q4	FULL YEAR
Revenue	$ 8,000	$ 28,000	$ 32,000	$ 10,000	$ 78,000
Direct Expenses	800	2,800	3,200	1,000	7,800
Gross Profit	7,200	25,200	28,800	9,000	70,200
Indirect Expenses	10,000	12,000	12,000	10,000	44,000
Total Profit (Loss)	$ (2,800)	$ 13,200	$ 16,800	$ (1,000)	$ 26,200

Based on her numbers, she realized that she would likely need to save at least an extra $3,800 in her Rainy Day Fund during Q2 and Q3 to cover her during the other two quarters of the year (−$2,800 + −$1,000). She saw that her Q2 and Q3 profits added up to $30,000. With a little back-of-the-envelope math, she determined that putting 15% of her profit into the Rainy Day Fund during the good quarters should give her $4,500 extra to work with during the slower quarters ($30,000 × .15 = $4,500, slightly more than the $3,800 minimum needed; building in a buffer is always a good idea!).

By knowing her numbers and planning ahead, Brenda was finally able to avoid running up her credit card bills during the lower-cash-flow months and feel more in control of her money. She also broke out of the feast-and-famine cycle by looking ahead and planning for the future.

I use this strategy in my business, too, and it has been a great way to relieve pressure during lower-cash-flow months. Since I create digital products related to organizing and managing small-business finances, it's not surprising that my sales peak is between September and April, when most people are focused on getting their numbers into order and prepping for tax season. Practically no one is motivated to work on their finances during the summer months, and I don't blame them. Even I tend to be more lax with my discipline (both financial and otherwise) in the summer. But if you happen to be reading this book in a beach chair, I award you a gold star!

Having a Rainy Day Fund can help you plan for future foreseen events, such as seasonal business trends, as well as unforeseen events such as economic downturns, changes in regulations, and other events out of your control. Even a popular ice cream business in sunny Florida can struggle because of unfavorable weather trends that reduce daily foot traffic. In that case, the business owner can use the Rainy Day Fund to quite literally save for a rainy day when sales are down due to weather. A healthy Rainy Day Fund is the key to a resilient business that can withstand tough times when they come.

Oftentimes, business owners see falling revenue and assume that the cause must be something *they* did (or didn't do). But a lot of the time, it's less about you and your product and more about what consumers are going through. In tougher economic times, your target customers' average discretionary spending might decline. If yours is a business that relies on tourism, for example, it will likely be impacted by economic conditions that make people less likely to travel. Economic cycles are normal, but many businesses don't make it through prolonged downturns. In fact, the U.S. Bureau of Labor Statistics reported that about 1.8 million small businesses closed during the "Great Recession" between 2008 and 2010.[1] The biggest factor that determines a business's fate in tough times? Not surprisingly, it's its cash reserves—or lack thereof.

That's why it's important to be intentional about how you use your Rainy Day Fund. While it doesn't require a five-alarm fire for you to use the money you have saved there, spending from it should be purposeful.

Below are a few examples that will help you determine when to cash in your Rainy Day Fund and when to hold out.

Do use your Rainy Day Fund for:

- Planning for inherent seasonality of sales (like our horseback-riding instructor, Brenda)
- Unexpected expenses that are required for your business to function properly (you own a catering company and need to fix your refrigerator that suddenly broke)
- Economic downturns or other uncontrollable events that could affect your sales

Don't use your Rainy Day Fund for:

- Discretionary business spending
- Expenses that should be paid from other funds (such as your Opportunity Fund)

The Rainy Day Fund is there to create more safety and security in your business and thus more resiliency and sustainability. It will also help you feel freer to do things such as pay yourself or reinvest in your business without worrying that you may need the money for an emergency down the line. If you think it's helpful, putting your Rainy Day Fund into a separate savings account (preferably accruing interest) can put it far enough out of reach that you are less tempted to dip into it for just any old reason.

Implementation

How much money should you put into your Rainy Day Fund? For most businesses, you'll want to accumulate about one to three months' worth of base indirect expenses (i.e., the recurring monthly expenses needed to run your business). Once you've saved that target amount, you can stop adding additional money until you use it and need to replenish it. Remember, the PROF-FIT Plan is made to be dynamic, so it can (and should) change along with your changing business needs.

Putting that much money aside may seem like a pipe dream, especially if cash flow is a struggle right now. If that's the case, you'll want to start with the Profit Levers first and focus on fixing any of the cash flow timing issues covered in chapter 6.

After pulling those levers, building your Rainy Day Fund should be your second-highest priority (after paying your taxes, of course!). I suggest starting with a higher percentage of your profit going to the Rainy Day Fund, and then reducing the percentage later once you've built up some reserves. Starting at 10% to 15% and reducing it to 2% to 5% as your savings grow is a great potential strategy. Aim to have your Rainy Day Fund fully funded within six months if you can. Once you have saved your target amount, you can reallocate that percentage to another fund until you want or need to build your Rainy Day Fund up again.

F = Future Fund

When I ask most business owners, especially women, what they really desire when it comes to their finances, they rarely mention private jets or yachts. Instead, I often hear the same word, whether I'm talking to a sixty-year-old or a thirty-year-old: freedom.

Freedom to retire when they want to.
Freedom to travel.
Freedom to enjoy life.

Freedom to have options.

Freedom to *breathe*.

Even if you love what you do, you'll likely enjoy your work more knowing that you have the option to stop if you'd like.

The first *F* in PROFFIT Plan stands for Future Fund, but it's really about creating freedom. Money put into the Future Fund helps secure your financial future and give yourself options. Depending on your personal situation, preparing for your future may include putting money into a retirement account, paying down debt (personal or business), or possibly saving for your kids' future educational expenses.

You may wonder why I don't include these future savings in the Pay Yourself Fund. After all, this money is likely going to be used personally rather than in your business unless you are paying down business debt or putting money into a company-sponsored retirement plan. But there's intentionality behind this. Separating your Future Fund money from the money you pay yourself keeps you accountable for how this money is used. If I pay myself one lump sum from my business, it's less likely that the money will be used in the way it was originally intended. Keeping the money earmarked for a specific purpose until it's time to use it (or contribute it to a retirement account, etc.) is a great way to ensure that you don't undermine your future goals. You mustn't inadvertently use this money to pay today's bills. This is about moving closer to the future you *really* want.

Implementation

What percentage of profit should you put into your Future Fund? As with the other funds, the answer will be highly dependent on your circumstances and goals. My friends Susan and Joe are married and have operated a home power washing business together for the last twenty years. They love being business owners but are now in their midfifties and looking toward the future. They would love to step back from their business within the next few years so that they can travel the world as they've always dreamed of doing. Susan and Joe have retirement funds but haven't always been diligent about their savings goals in the past.

Because their goal is to either partially or completely retire within the next five to ten years, they've decided to heavily prioritize their Future Fund and use it to make catch-up contributions to their retirement accounts. To achieve this, they've decided to put 20% of their profit into their Future Fund.

You may also choose to prioritize your Future Fund if you have significant levels of personal or business debt and use it to help ease that burden. However, if you don't have much debt or aren't planning to retire anytime soon, you may not need to put such a high percentage of your income into this fund.

At a minimum, however, saving 5% of your income in your Future Fund will serve you well in the long run. Remember, contributing to a retirement plan can also be a great way to save on taxes, so the more you contribute to a traditional retirement plan such as a 401(k) or SEP-IRA, the less you'll need to put aside in your Tax Fund.

CHAPTER TWENTY-TWO
Make It Fun

Wait, a whole chapter about having fun in a book about finances?
Yes. As far as we know, we have just one life to live. One life to enjoy. One life to explore. One life to make memories. Thus, any system of managing your finances that doesn't help you live a richer life is missing something essential.

In the last chapter, I talked about how most of us are striving to find freedom, however we define it. Yet weeks, months, and even years go by without our feeling that we're truly experiencing life.

So many of us say that we'll take that trip or go to that fabulous five-star restaurant we've heard so much about "someday." We push it off and push it off and find any number of excuses for why we can't do it yet. And while preparing for the future is incredibly important, as we discussed previously, so is living in the *now*. We can't let life pass us by. Beans and rice be damned.

Not only that, but studies have shown that taking time away from work to unclutter your mind leads to increased creativity, which is essential to business success.[1] The numerous health benefits of rest are well researched, including a reduced incidence of health issues such as heart disease and enhanced life satisfaction. Relaxation is not the opposite of productivity; it's an essential ingredient of it.

Yet most business owners struggle to take a vacation, not just because of the cost but also because of the time they'd have to take away from their business. If you are a service-based solopreneur, it can be difficult to justify losing your income for a week or even a few days to go on a trip "just because." Or perhaps you are an owner-operator and worry that the ball will be dropped if you leave for more than a day or two.

Consider: What's the maximum amount of time you'd spend away from your business at one time? If you answered "No limit," that's amazing. I hope you are reading this book in Bali with a piña colada in your hand. But if you are like most small-business owners, you may feel uncomfortable leaving for more than a week—or even just a few days.

In this chapter, we're going to talk not only about how and why to earmark money specifically for fun but also about how to make taking time away *actually* happen. Let's start by looking at a few of the "barriers to fun" that you might be facing and how to overcome them.

Barrier to Fun 1: Trading Hours for Dollars

You are a mighty business of one. You charge customers based on the work you perform, which means that if you aren't working, you aren't making money. Not only that, but the client work might even pile up if you are gone, or you might risk missing delivery dates. While you're away, you might miss inquiries from potential new clients or be slow to respond to existing clients—which could later affect your revenue, maybe even your reputation. There's no one else who can do the work, and the idea of hiring someone to do it sounds daunting. Taking a vacation seems like more trouble than it's worth.

What's a solopreneur to do? After going through the Profit Levers to maximize your profit, it might be time to think about how you charge for your services. Are you charging an hourly rate? If so, you risk falling into the dangerous "trading hours for dollars" trap that leaves you perpetually busy chasing your monetary goals.

Often, charging based on your inputs (i.e., hours worked) is counterproductive for both the service provider and the client. On your side, there is no incentive to be more efficient, as improving your processes will actually reduce the amount of money you make. Additionally, on the client side, the amount they'll need to pay isn't dependable, and the actual hours you spend on jobs could vary from estimates, making it hard for them to forecast their own cash flow. Not only that, but charging by the hour can also limit your income, as the amount customers will pay for work quoted on an hourly basis is limited. For example, customers may balk at paying $1,000 a month for a service that "takes you only three hours." However, they aren't considering the costs involved, including the time and money spent gaining an education and the experience to perform the services well and become an expert. Hourly pricing commoditizes your services and caps what you can realistically charge.

To combat these challenges, consider switching to a "value-based" pricing model, where the amount you charge is tied to the value you provide (your output) rather than the hours you put in (your input). Instead of selling your time, you are selling the end result. If customers deem what they receive (your output) to be worth it, they don't care how much time it takes you to complete the work. In this way, you could possibly justify charging $1,000 a month for work that takes you a few hours, if the output is worth at least that much to the customer. This would better align your interests with those of the clients you serve and incentivize you to continuously improve your processes without reducing your pay as a result.

Barrier to Fun 2: Seasonality of Income

Another reason small-business owners may find it difficult to take a vacation is the seasonality inherent in their income. Perhaps they have one or two busy seasons during the year, which coincide with when the bulk of their income comes in. A tax preparer may have an extremely busy time from January through April and then have several slow months until tax-filing extension season kicks off in September. However, this also means that they see a large decline in revenue during the months they are free to travel, which may make them hesitant to take a vacation.

To overcome this, saving in a Fun Fund (which we will discuss later in this chapter) can help you save vacation funds. Additionally, moving away from one-off pricing to a subscription-based system (or retainer pricing) that is charged year-round can help smooth those peaks and valleys. Understanding the needs of your clients year-round and offering a compelling solution is key to making this switch. This solution will give you more income to have a little fun during your less busy months, enabling you to recharge for the next busy season.

Barrier to Fun 3: Ineffective Systems

Creating streamlined systems is the key to gaining freedom from your business. The best systems are "set it and forget it." The second-best systems are the ones that require some degree of human interaction but are optimized for efficiency.

We've come to equate the word *systems* with technology, but the concept of systems is much broader than that. Even if you feel as though you don't have systems in your business, you likely do. Even a fully manual way of doing things is a system. It's not a particularly great system, but it's a system nonetheless.

Even when a business's systems are intentionally designed, it's not abnormal for the business owner to be the biggest bottleneck. Because in the beginning, systems (whether they're related to sales, product delivery, or customer support) are often designed around the owner, it can be hard to redesign them later. But if you do, you will go a long way to removing the barriers to freedom.

Let's consider your system for taking payments from customers. How do they pay you? Do they pay in store at the point of sale? Do you invoice them? Do you send them to an online checkout cart? Do they send you a check? Do you take orders over the phone and manually key in the purchase (horrors!)?

When evaluating your systems and processes in your business, ask yourself these questions.

- Where are manual touch points currently required in your business? List them. Especially consider those that are administrative in nature, such as receiving payments, scheduling appointments, and sending contracts.

- How could you simplify and systematize these to reduce the manual touch points required? Are there things you are doing that could be eliminated entirely?

- What software systems are available that could automate some of the required tasks, taking yourself out of the process in part or in whole?

- Where you can't automate, how could you effectively delegate some or all of these tasks to someone else?

While making systems more efficient takes some up-front time and energy, it can save you big in the long run. Remember, time is money, so investing in efficiency often provides a worthwhile return—especially if that return includes a much-needed vacation for you!

Barrier to Fun 4: Ineffective Teams

Perhaps you feel you can't leave because if you do, everything will fall apart while you are away. If you've automated what you can and are still worried about the ball being dropped, it may be time to invest in a team you can count on.

If you are a solopreneur, it may be time to hire someone to help you, even for just a few hours a week. You could start with a virtual assistant and train them on the essential activities of your business that keep it running smoothly. Just knowing that someone is keeping the lights on while you are away and can reach out to you in an emergency can give you the peace of mind you need to take a much-needed break.

If you have grown an organization with two or more employees but you are still functioning largely in the role of Manager, it's time to hire someone for (or promote someone to) that role. Not only does functioning as the day-to-day Manager mean it's harder for you to take a vacation; it's also harder to grow and scale up your business. That's because the time you spend managing and overseeing would be more effectively spent on being the CEO and CFO of the business.

When you operate as a Manager, there is almost always something to call your attention away from your highest and best use. Whether it is dealing with a dispute between employees, delegating tasks, or project management, that's time you aren't spending on the big-picture tasks and strategy that will move your organization forward.

Hiring a Manager is a game-changing method of leveling up your business. It also means that you aren't completely necessary for the day-to-day operations to function well, which will give you more time to recharge. Someone with great managerial skills can help you hire and supervise others, delegate work, research and implement new systems, and make sure projects get done on time.

It's true that good employees are hard to find. But they do exist. And good employees are drawn to work that they believe in, not just work that pays them well (though you should do that, too!). More and more, people are drawn to companies that align with their values and have a clear mission they can get behind. A mission isn't what you do; it is *why* you do what you do. Not only will having a clear mission help you attract the right people; it will also give you clarity of direction in your business and a framework to help you make decisions.

Once you have someone you can trust on board, you can take time off without worrying that your business will grind to a halt if you're not there.

Barrier to Fun 5: Lack of Funds

Perhaps you have a great team, fine-tuned systems, and a business model that enables you to earn money even when you are away. That's amazing! You're effectively making the move from being an owner-operator to being a true entrepreneur, with all the freedom that comes with it.

Even then, there's one more thing you need in order to have some guiltless fun in your free time: funds.

Obviously, using the Profit Levers to maximize your profit will help you generate the extra money you need to execute your PROFFIT Plan. However, as with the Future Fund, I've found that if I don't intentionally put money away for that purpose, it invariably ends up being used for something else. This is why my PROFFIT Plan has two *F*'s—because I believe we should be as intentional about having fun as we are about everything else.

When my business started generating revenue, I realized that making money wasn't enough motivation for me, even as an Accumulator. I needed something else to get me excited about my results, and I also wanted to involve my family in my entrepreneurship journey (and perhaps distract them from the far too many hours I was working at the time).

That was when I added the extra *F* to the word *profit* in my PROFFIT Plan.

I told my husband that I would start putting aside 5% of profit to go toward something just for fun. We had always talked about getting a hot tub (well, *he* had always talked about it), but my practical nature prevented me from purchasing something that felt so "frivolous." Our very first **Fun Fund** was born, and less than a year later we were lounging on our patio in our new hot tub (and I can't lie, he was *totally* right).

Since then, the Fun Fund has helped fund restful retreats, home improvement projects, and memorable family vacations. The best part is that I haven't had to sacrifice financially in any other area to make it happen. Saving for a specific "fun" thing has spurred me to make more profit in my business than I otherwise would have. It has given me a more exciting reason to be judicious with my business expenses and to get creative with new ideas to earn revenue. Having a specific goal that is all about fun is generally going to be more motivating than just trying to earn a living, pay bills, or save for retirement.

Pick one specific goal you have and write it down. You don't have to start at the hot tub level. Maybe your first Fun Fund goal is a sixty-minute Swedish massage at your favorite spa. Figure out how much money you need to make it happen, then watch your Fun Fund grow as you allocate a portion of your profit to it over time. As soon as you hit your desired goal, it's time to celebrate (and book that massage!). Then pick your next Fun Fund goal. How big or small a goal you choose is up to you; just make sure it's something motivating and exciting!

Your Money Personality and the Fun Fund

Depending on your money personality type, the Fun Fund can serve different—but equally important—purposes.

For Celebrities and Romantics, the Fun Fund can serve as an important boundary and motivator. Think of this as your YOLO fund. If you have money in this fund, it's yours to freely spend as you wish. Spending this money won't put any of your other goals (or your ability to pay Uncle Sam) in jeopardy. You'll feel motivated to stockpile money in your Fun Fund so you can live life the way you want to.

For Alchemists and Mavericks, the Fun Fund can encourage you to tap into your inherent creative moneymaking skills. If you have a specific goal to work toward, you can use your moneymaking superpowers to make it happen in no time. Always dreamed of taking a trip to Greece? Figure out how much extra profit you need and use your money magnetism gifts, and you'll be on a plane to Santorini in no time.

For Nurturers and Connectors, the Fun Fund gives you permission to spend money on yourselves, which you may otherwise be hesitant to do. You often live your life for others, but filling your own cup regularly will mean that you have more to give. You can also use the Fun Fund to take family vacations or travel with friends you care about, creating memories you will cherish forever.

For Rulers and Accumulators, the Fun Fund gives you the permission you didn't know you needed. Rulers need to give themselves permission to step away from the hustle, and Accumulators need to permit themselves to spend some money just for enjoyment's sake. By saving money in your Fun Fund, you can quell the worry and fear that might otherwise rear their ugly heads when you spend money or do something just for you. The key is making sure you don't rob yourself; once the money is in the Fun Fund, it stays there until it's time to have some fun!

Implementation

How much should you allocate to your Fun Fund? As much as you want! Though practically speaking, you probably want to prioritize some of the more "practical" reserves, such as the Tax Fund and Rainy Day Fund. Just as in Abraham Maslow's famous hierarchy of needs, you want to make sure you meet your physiological and safety needs first. But so long as you have that base level of security, you can begin to allocate profit to your Fun Fund.

If you don't have money in your Fun Fund, does that mean you can't have *any* fun? Not in the least. This is about saving for something above and beyond whatever you consider to be your "norm." You aren't using this as a budget for discretionary spending in your personal life. Instead, it's a motivating factor to save up for something *super* cool.

If you are early on in your business or it isn't very profitable yet, you may choose to start this fund at just 1% of your profit. As your profit grows, so can the percentage that you allocate to it. For those with very profitable businesses and/or dreams to see the world, you may choose to go as high as 10% (or more!).

Another way to determine how much to put into your Fun Fund is to decide what you want the money to go toward and set an ideal time frame in which to get there. Then you can calculate what percentage of your profit you need to save to achieve that goal.

Let's say you want to take a trip to northern Italy with your family of four so you can feast on homemade pasta and wine for days (my dream vacation). You do your research on flights (don't forget to utilize those credit card points!), hotels, and transportation. You determine that you will need to save around $10,000 in cash to make it happen, and you'd love to be able to book the trip in about eighteen months. That means you'd have to save about $555 in profit each month to hit your goal. If you currently make $11,000 in profit each month, that means that putting aside 5% of your profit per month should get you to your goal in the desired time frame.

Remember, the hope is that having a specific goal for what you will do with your Fun Fund will give you extra motivation that may not exist when your only goal is to pay your bills and pay down debt. In my experience, this motivation keeps me from overspending more than any "budget" possibly could. Would I rather have that high-end state-of-the-art equipment that I don't really need and will cut into my profit or a delicious gelato on a balcony overlooking Lake Como? Talk about a no-brainer.

As an Accumulator and Ruler myself, it seems fitting that I'm writing this chapter two thousand miles from home on an island in the Caribbean, overlooking endless palm trees and ocean. Travel is something I've always loved, and now that my kids are out of the baby/toddler stages, I dream of taking them to see more of my favorite places around the globe. I'm thankful for my amazing team and the systems we have in place that enable my business to run without interruption even when I'm away. I'm also thankful for the Fun Fund that helps make vacations like these a reality instead of a perpetual "someday" dream.

I can't take my money with me when I leave this earth, but I *can* take the priceless memories of twirling my daughter around in the ocean waves and climbing rocks above the crystal blue water with my son. I can keep the memories of greeting the huge tortoise that wanders into our open-air kitchen daily and watching the orange sunset over the water each night. I'm still here living in the moment, yet the memories I know we are creating in real time already bring tears to my eyes. I'm so filled with gratitude just to be here right now.

For a long time, the Accumulator side of me tried to keep me at home. She said we'd travel "someday" when we "had enough to spare." It's taken a lot of mindset work for her to let go and live a little. Sometimes she still balks at menu prices and gets sticker shock in local souvenir shops. But then she realizes that the Fun Fund exists for just this reason and that this money isn't being taken from any of those big, important long-term goals. And she sighs, takes a sip of her glass of rosé, and allows herself to enjoy the beautiful view.

CHAPTER TWENTY-THREE
Make an Impact

The simple act of running your business well can make a difference in the world. Successful small businesses can create jobs, stimulate the economy, and provide needed goods and services to their communities.

Whether you run a neighborhood coffee shop, a local plumbing service, or a tutoring business, you have the opportunity to impact others in a positive way. That's one of the great gifts of business ownership: It enables us to be part of something bigger than ourselves. Running a financially successful business can also enable us to give more generously than we could ever have imagined.

I = Impact Fund

While this book has focused largely on how to maximize profit, profit really matters only when it has a worthy purpose. That's why I've talked about using profit to create more financial security, prepare for your future, and even have a little fun. But that's only scratching the surface of what profit can do.

For too long in my life, I told myself that I'd give more money away someday, "when I could." But in truth, I never felt as though I could. Even though my family was financially stable, I continued to delay charitable giving. There was always a new mile marker to achieve first. It was in my heart to help others, but I never felt financially secure enough to do it the way I truly wanted to. I struggled to put my money where my mouth was.

Eventually—and with the help of my wonderful hubby—I decided it was time to stop making excuses and get into the game. We started giving a percentage of our income first, before we even got the chance to spend it.

We began with just 2% and steadily increased that percentage as we became more financially comfortable. It was stunning to realize that we didn't miss that money. We barely notice that it's gone, then or now. Automating our giving—which most charities enable—was a game changer, as the money never felt like "ours" in the first place, which made it much easier to part with. I've never regretted a single dollar I've given away to a worthy cause, and my guess is that you likely feel the same way.

Today, my business sets aside 10% of its profit to give back and support causes that align with our core values as part of our PROFFIT Plan Impact Fund. For us, that includes organizations impacting women, children, and underrepresented communities. We routinely offer our employees the ability to pick the organizations we support through this fund.

We've also rolled out a charitable match program as an employee benefit, in which the company donates $2 for every $1 an employee donates to a cause that aligns with our mission. We've also offered scholarships to our programs and are involved with our local communities through volunteer activities. For myself and my team, the idea of what our business profit can do fuels our drive more than the pursuit of personal gain ever could.

The purpose of discussing this is not to toot my own horn or guilt others; I simply want to show that it is possible to prioritize *both* profit and purpose. While you may assume that these goals are in opposition to each other, they

HOW TO GIVE–SUSTAINABLY

Giving a percentage of your profit is more sustainable and predictable for a business than is giving a percentage of overall revenue. This approach ensures that you don't inadvertently make the business unprofitable or unable to pay its bills as a result of giving back. You can be extremely profitable *and* give generously; it's not an either/or choice.

are actually inextricably linked. The more profitable our business is, the more opportunities we have to do good things. Not only can a profitable business give more money, but business owners also have the margin necessary to give more of their time to the causes that matter to them.

It's important to note that there are *innumerable* ways to make an impact as a business owner. While giving money is one, it isn't the only one. Here are a few ideas to get your juices flowing.

- **Offer free or discounted services** for those who may not otherwise be able to afford them.

- **Utilize sponsorship opportunities** to support causes you care about. For example, your business could help sponsor a local 5K charity run, a nonprofit booth at a community festival, or a fundraiser for your local schools. Unlike with many other giving methods, you can often deduct money spent on sponsorships as marketing expenses for your business, especially if you are able to display your logo, thus decreasing your taxable business income.

- **Donate extra inventory** to shelters or other nonprofits that could benefit from it.

- **Partner with charities** in your brick-and-mortar store to donate a percentage of sales to their cause on a particular day. This can help drive traffic to your business, introduce you to potential new customers, and build goodwill in the eyes of your community.

- **Become a mentor** for others who could use your guidance and expertise.

- **Use your business to bring awareness** to important causes through social media, newsletters, or flyers.

- **Join local clubs and organizations** with a mission to make a positive impact.

- **Give your employees time off** for the purpose of volunteering or participate in a group volunteer event together.

- **Help your company "go green"** by minimizing waste and adopting environmentally friendly policies and practices.

- **Become a leader in your community.** You can put your business management skills to use by organizing fundraisers or other events to support important causes.

Consider what causes you care about and how you can engage with your community. Decide how you will make an impact, and remember that it is okay to start small. How can you use your talents to make this world better? How can you contribute to the greater good through your business? Trust me: The world desperately needs your leadership and generosity.

Impact Compounds

As I mentioned earlier in this chapter, the simple act of running a profitable small business makes an impact. Even a 2% increase in average small-business profit across the nation would have a massive impact on the economy as a whole, and not just for those at the top.

Some of that is due to what economists call the "multiplier effect." Small businesses tend to spend their profit locally, and those dollars are recirculated in the local economy many times over, creating a huge upward spiral for the area. Remember, making more money doesn't have to mean that someone else makes less. Making money is not a zero-sum game. Instead, by running financially successful businesses, we can create an exponential effect that will lift us *all* up. In this way, supporting small and local businesses is a way to give back that keeps on giving.

Tax Impacts of Giving

Since this is a book about finances, it makes sense to go a little deeper into how charitable gifts do (and don't) impact your taxes. There are some nuances for business owners to be aware of. Knowing the rules can help you make the most of your giving! Remember, any donations must be given to qualified charitable organizations and may be limited based on your income level or other personal tax circumstances.

Donations that are typically deductible for pass-through entities (make sure to document them!) include:

- **Sponsorships.** If you provide support to nonprofit organizations or events, you can generally deduct it directly as a marketing expense. Just ensure that you are given some kind of recognition (display of your logo, etc.) to justify that the sponsorship was promotional in nature.

- **Inventory donations.** These are deductible to the business, but the deduction is typically limited to the amount you originally paid for the inventory, not what you would have sold it for.

- **Services donation.** If you are donating services, you can write off salaries paid to staff for this work or any other expenses incurred, just as you could if you did the work for a fee. However, you can't get a deduction for what you would have charged if someone had paid full price.

- **Property donations.** You can donate equipment, machinery, vehicles, and other items from the business to a charity and get a deduction for it. The deduction the business receives is equivalent to the value of the property on the Balance Sheet. If the fair market value is higher than what is on the Balance Sheet, you may be able to get a personal deduction for the excess. If you're donating property, make sure to let your tax accountant know so they can maximize your deductions.

Donations for which you may get a personal tax deduction as a pass-through entity include:

- **Cash donations.** Any donations of cash you make that aren't related to marketing purposes likely won't be deductible to your business (cash donations are currently directly deductible to the business only for C corps). However, those deductions are deductible at the personal tax level. Unfortunately, you'll see the benefit of this only if you itemize your deductions. Since most taxpayers don't itemize their deductions because it would cost them more in taxes than using the standard deduction, many donors don't see a tax benefit from the cash donations they make.

- **Property donations.** As noted above, if you donate property with a higher fair market value than the value shown on your Balance Sheet, the excess may be deductible at a personal level. As with cash donations, you'll see the benefit of this tax incentive only if you itemize your deductions.

- **Stock or securities donations.** If you donate stock or securities, you can get a deduction for the value of that stock on your personal tax return (again, only if you itemize!). If you have significantly appreciated stock, you may want to set up a *donor-advised fund*. This type of fund allows you to donate your appreciated stock and get a tax deduction for the current value of the stock without having to pay capital gains taxes on the increase in value (when and if certain conditions are met, including owning the stock for over a year).

There are also some donations that don't have any kind of preferential tax treatment. But that doesn't mean you shouldn't make those donations if you enjoy doing so. Tax deductions are great, but they aren't the primary reason to give. After all, being charitable, financially or otherwise, is about making this world better! The following are generally *not* eligible for tax deductions (business or personal).

- **Donations with a personal benefit** (not a business benefit). If you purchase an item at a silent auction (for example, concert tickets), it generally isn't deductible. However, if you paid in excess of the market value of the item, you may be able to get a personal deduction for the amount you paid, above and beyond the value of what you received (if you itemize your deductions).

- **Donations to individuals.** Giving money directly to those in need, as opposed to a qualified charity, is not deductible as a charitable contribution.

- **Donations of your time.** If you are donating services, only your actual costs incurred (salary costs, etc.) are deductible, not the typical retail value of the service you would otherwise have charged.

- **Contributions to political campaigns.** The IRS doesn't allow deductions for political contributions to candidates, parties, or political action committees. That said, there are qualified charities that advocate for legislation related to particular causes that could be deductible alternatives.

If your head is spinning at these donation rules, I'm right there with you. That's why I'm actively working to help get legislation passed that would simplify these rules significantly, allowing small-business owners who run pass-through entities to deduct cash donations they make to charity as an expense to their business (just as C corporations can). This would allow more business owners to "get credit" for the donations they are already making and encourage more generosity by small businesses through favorable tax treatment.

With over 30 million pass-through entities in the United States, a change in the tax rules could spur billions of dollars in additional charitable giving that would help our communities, our country, and the world. Even if every one of those entities gave just $100 more to charity, that would be $3 *billion* in additional funds to good causes! It would also allow business owners who are already making charitable donations to reduce their taxes, thereby freeing up more money available for giving.

Creating change isn't quick or easy, but it's a fight worth conducting. When small-business owners are empowered to make a greater impact, we not only strengthen our communities, but we also build a future where generosity and opportunity go hand in hand. Together, we can make a lasting difference.

> **TAKE THE PIN PLEDGE**
>
> If you are dedicated to making a profound impact through your business and want to be part of a dynamic community doing big things, we invite you to take the Power in Numbers® pledge. Share the positive changes you are bringing to your local area and the world, and get inspired by the stories of other entrepreneurs making a difference at HiddenProfitTheBook.com.

Implementation

What you decide to allocate to your Impact Fund is up to you, but 2% is a great starting point. If giving money isn't feasible for you just yet, review the list above and pick another way to give back that resonates with you. Not only will you help others, but making a positive difference is incredibly motivating and rewarding and will ultimately bring you a greater sense of purpose and satisfaction.

While you may not feel that you can make much of a difference as an individual, can you imagine what we, small-business owners, could do together? In the next and final chapter of this book, I want to paint a vision of our collective future that will fill you with hope. After all, the power in numbers is about much more than making more money.

CONCLUSION
There's Power in Numbers

One night two years ago, I woke up from an extremely vivid dream. In the dream, there were thousands and thousands of birds surrounding my house, trying to get in. Somehow, my subconscious knew they were starlings, even though I had never knowingly seen one. I wrote it down in my notes app and went back to sleep.

The next day I couldn't stop thinking about the dream. I just couldn't shake it. While by nature I'm very analytical and grounded (I'm an accountant, for goodness' sake), I do believe that God or the universe or fate sometimes gives us signs that we are meant to follow. We can ignore them, but those signs will keep popping up over and over again until we finally decide to pay attention to them. I had a distinct feeling this was one of those times. The dream felt as though it was meant to tell me something incredibly important.

The dream came at a time when I was contemplating my next steps in my professional life. I had scribbled down the phrase "power in numbers" six months earlier, and felt a connection with it but had no idea what to do next. I felt undeniably restless, and I knew that something greater was calling me, but I didn't know what. That dream kept nagging at me, until I finally decided to look up starlings. Perhaps there was a hidden message I was meant to find. As soon as I began to learn more and watch videos, I realized exactly what the dream was trying to tell me.

Harnessing the power in numbers isn't just about unlocking the money-making potential of tracking metrics, managing your cash flow, or maximizing your profit; it's also about how much we can do collectively.

Starlings travel in groups of thousands. They move together, making gorgeous patterns across the sky called *murmurations* (if you want a moment of Zen, google "starling murmuration video" and prepare to be mesmerized). Because of that, starlings are symbolic of unity and communication. Despite their outward appearance, these small birds aren't docile or quiet creatures. A starling will protect other members of its group at all costs. And as beautiful as they are, you *don't* want to mess with a starling.

A starling murmuration has no leader. Instead, each bird coordinates its movements with the six or seven other starlings around it, and in turn, each of those with the six or seven around it. This enables tens of thousands of starlings to move as one, united through their shared goal. They never run into one another; there is no competition, only collaboration.

This is what power in numbers means to me—and to you. Like starlings in the sky, flying high together with a common purpose, we can, as entrepreneurs, use our united power to create change. What I realized when thinking about that dream is that we are a little like starlings in our businesses. By ourselves, alone, we can be vulnerable to attack. But no predator can stand up to the collective.

Power in Numbers® is a business I founded to be more than just an educational program or membership; it was created as a movement to help women who lead businesses thrive financially for themselves, their families, their communities, and the world. The goal of Power in Numbers is to democratize small-business financial education, provide affordable access to financial experts, and come together in community with a common purpose; pooling our resources, supporting one another with the goal and intention of putting more economic power into the hands of women and marginalized groups around the globe; flying toward a better future, together.

Alone, we can accomplish only so much. But collectively, we are a murmuration of starlings across the night sky, creating something beautiful out of nothing; inspiring awe in those who watch us from the ground; defying convention and paving our own creative way; defending and protecting one another with all we have, because we can do so much more together than we can apart.

I hope that reading this book has given you practical steps to help you gain control of your finances and start seeing your money differently. Financial education is often the best place to start, but strategies alone won't be everything you need to keep you going. Having a support system around you means you don't have to navigate the stresses of business ownership all by yourself. You can lean on others, because there truly is power in numbers. Help and community exist that can lift you so much higher than you could go on your own.

Let's fly together.

ACKNOWLEDGMENTS

Through writing this book, I've come to understand that when a book author puts pen to paper—or in this case, fingers to keyboard—they are never doing it alone. I am deeply aware of what a privilege it is even to have this opportunity, and I want to acknowledge all the women who came before me, determined to challenge the status quo, paving the way for a book like this to exist.

To my husband, Kemper: Thank you for your unwavering faith in me, even when doubt, fear, and anxiety tried to tell me I wasn't good enough. Without your optimism and encouragement, I would never have taken the risk of starting this business. Without your willing partnership in our home life, I wouldn't have had the space to chase my dreams. And without your love, I couldn't have overcome the obstacles in front of me, including the ones inside my own head. I don't know how I can ever truly show my appreciation, but hopefully that hot tub is a good start.

To my son, Miles, the boy who made me "Mom": Having you changed everything about my life for the better. You gave me a deeper reason for everything I do. It makes my heart smile when you proudly tell your friends that your mom is "famous" (even though your idea of fame is having a YouTube channel). Your empathy for others and desire to make the world a better place are constant reminders that none of this matters if we aren't doing it to help others. Please never change.

To my daughter, Norah, my fearless, tenacious girl: When I look at you, I see myself times 100. I hope no one ever dulls your fire. The world is yours, and my biggest wish for you is that you know you can do whatever you want to do and be whoever you want to be. Keep being you, and never take "no" for an answer (unless I'm the one asking!).

To my dad, Jim, the man who taught me about money: Thank you for the lessons that led me here, but more than that, thank you for your belief in me along the way. Even way back when you used to display my report cards on your office door, I always felt how proud you were of me. I hope I continue to make you proud.

To my mom, Judy: You've always seen the real me. Thank you for always being my first call when I needed to vent, for grounding me, and for reminding me that life is more than just achievements; it's also about how we can love those in our lives well.

To my sister, Jenny: Sorry for the years of being that bratty little sister who threw books at you to get you to leave my room. Who knew that someday I'd have a book of my own? I'll try not to throw this one at you (at least not the hardcover version). Love you, Sis!

To my entire extended family: The support from you has been instrumental in my life and my arrival at this point. A special thank-you to my in-laws, Steve and Sonya, who treated me as one of their own from the very beginning. Thank you for your words of encouragement along the way!

To my incredible team and all of those who have helped grow this business over the years: I count my lucky stars daily that I have you. Sarah, Danielle, Lyndsey, Crystal V., Crystal W., Melissa, Regen, Emilia, Lupita, Rosie, Alejandra, and so many others who have been a part of building this: Thank you for being an instrumental part of spreading this mission. Sarah, my right hand, thank you for burying all the exposed wires I leave behind and always challenging me to be better. Danielle, thank you for believing in the vision and loving our students so well. I wouldn't have been able to do this without the support of this amazing team!

To Amy Porterfield: Your mentorship changed the trajectory of my life. Thank you for guiding me to where I am today.

To my dear friends: Thank you for encouraging me, checking in on me, and celebrating with me. For much of my life, I prided myself on being able to do things on my own, but your support has taught me to feel safe leaning on others.

To Liza: You have helped me see the world beyond my practical black-and-white box. Your influence has helped me grow as a human and a friend, and I'm forever grateful.

To Bree and Kellie, my encouragers: Every woman deserves a cheerleading squad like you.

To Rockvale Writers Colony and the writers I met there: Thank you for creating a place where I could be inspired, clear my head, and write from my heart.

To Dr. Aldhizer, my professor who encouraged me to join the Accounting program at Wake Forest: Thank you for seeing my potential and helping set me on this path.

To everyone who helped me get this book out into the world, I'm beyond grateful:

To Meghan Stevenson, my book guide: Thank you for sending me that fateful email asking if I was ready to start the book. Your help and guidance in this process have been invaluable.

To my agent, Leila Campoli: Thank you for advocating for me and helping me navigate this brand-new (and somewhat intimidating) world of publishing.

To my editor, Kimberly Melium, at Simon Acumen: Thank you for believing in this book and helping make it the best it could possibly be.

To my amazing students, FLWBO group members, YouTube subscribers, and everyone else who has allowed me to be part of your financial journey: Thank you from the bottom of my heart. Your trust, openness, and willingness to share your challenges and successes have inspired the stories in this book. Whether you've worked with me directly, joined my programs, or simply shared my content with others, your support has made it possible to create something I hope will empower and uplift others on their own financial paths.

And last, to Skip, my loyal writing buddy: Thank you for your moral support while curled up at my feet while I wrote this book (just as you are right now).

NOTES

Introduction

1. Karrin Sehmbi, "Small-Business Statistics 2024," Nerdwallet, February 8, 2024, https://www.nerdwallet.com/article/small-business/small-business-statistics.

2. J. Jarpa Dawuni and Jordan Frazier, "The Future of Black Women in Corporate Leadership: Opening Doors to Move Up," TIAA Institute, October 2022, https://www.tiaa.org/content/dam/tiaa/institute/pdf/insights-report/2022-10/tiaa-institute-the-future-of-black-women-in-corporate-leadership-wvoee-dawuni-october-2022.pdf.

3. Aimee Picchi, "Even 'Breadwinner' Wives Do More Housework Than Husbands," Moneywatch, CBS News, April 13, 2023, https://www.cbsnews.com/news/women-breadwinners-tripled-since-1970s-still-doing-more-unpaid-work/.

4. Kiah Treece, "Small Business Loan Statistics and Trends 2024," Forbes Advisor, April 18, 2024, https://www.forbes.com/advisor/business-loans/small-business-loan-statistics/.

5. Belle Wong, "Average Salary by State in 2024," Forbes Advisor, May 1, 2024, https://www.forbes.com/advisor/business/average-salary-by-state/.

Chapter 3: When Numbers Lie

1. Morgan Housel, *The Psychology of Money: Timeless Lessons on Wealth, Greed, and Happiness* (Harriman House, 2020), 43.

Chapter 5: Manage Your To-Do List

1. Bernard D. Beitman, "The Resonating Dance of Intention and Synchronicity," *Psychology Today*, March 10, 2024, https://www.psychologytoday.com/intl/blog/connecting-with-coincidence/202403/the-resonating-dance-of-intention-and-synchronicity.

Chapter 6: Manage Your Cash Flow

1. "Nearly Half of Small Businesses Feel the Impact of Inflation on Their Cash Flow," Xero, September 7, 2023, https://www.xero.com/us/media-releases/half-small-businesses-feel-impact-inflation-cash-flow/.

2. "Closing Strong: Year-End Cash Flow Strategies, Monitoring, and the Role of Spend Management Platforms," U.S. Bank, November 16, 2023. https://spend.usbank.com/blog/closing-strong-year-end-cash-flow-strategies-monitoring-and-the-role-of-spend-management-platforms/.

3. "49 Cart Abandonment Rate Statistics 2024," Baymard Institute, July 11, 2023, https://baymard.com/lists/cart-abandonment-rate.

Chapter 8: Manage Your Risk

1. Kit Yarrow, "This Is Your Tax Return on Behavioral Economics," *Psychology Today*, March 15, 2011, https://www.psychologytoday.com/us/blog/the-why-behind-the-buy/201103/this-is-your-tax-return-on-behavioral-economics.

Chapter 10: Become Profitable

1. Muqsit Ashraf et al., "How to Grow Your Return on Resilience," Accenture Strategy, 2024, https://www.accenture.com/content/dam/accenture/final/accenture-com/document-2/GrowYourReturnResilience.pdf.

Chapter 16: Pay Less Taxes

1. "Small Business Statistics," Chamber of Commerce, July 24, 2024, https://www.chamberofcommerce.org/small-business-statistics/.

Chapter 17: Carry Less Debt

1. Yaqub M., "90+ Small Business Statistics: Ultimate Numbers in 2024," BusinessDasher, November 4, 2024, https://www.businessdit.com/small-business-statistics/.

Chapter 21: Prepare for the Future

1. "Small Business Statistics," Chamber of Commerce, July 24, 2024, https://www.chamberofcommerce.org/small-business-statistics/.

Chapter 22: Make It Fun

1. Christine J. Syrek, Jessica de Bloom, and Dirk Lehr, "Well Recovered and More Creative? A Longitudinal Study on the Relationship Between Vacation and Creativity," *Frontiers in Psychology* 12 (December 2021): article 784844, https://doi.org/10.3389/fpsyg.2021.784844.

INDEX

A

Accenture, 134
accountability and ownership, 134
accounting
    accrual method of, 25, 83
    cash method of, 83
    funny business in (profit on paper but shortage of cash), 24, 80–83
    matching principle in, 81
    outsourcing of, 36–37, 82, 110, 198, 237
    and reconciliations, 41–42
    rules of, 24, 33, 80–81
    software for, 35–36, 41
    See also taxes
adaptability, 135
AI (artificial intelligence), 35, 57
assets
    on Balance Sheets, 25–27, 32–33, 82–83
    depreciation of, 81
    long-term, 81

Average Transaction Value, 135, 169–75, 218, 220

B

Balance CFO, 6
Balance Sheets
    assets on, 25–27, 30, 32–33, 35, 82–83
    draws from your business (paying yourself) on, 33–34, 83
    equity on, 25–26, 30, 32–34, 83
    inventory on, 25–26, 30–32, 82
    liabilities on, 25–27, 32–33, 82–83
    and P&Ls, 27–34
    print shop (case study), 23–32, 34, 80
    transactions' impacts on, 27–32
    who must file them, 25

Baymard Institute, 88
billing (invoicing), 84–85, 88–89
bookkeeping
    outsourcing of, 36–37, 43, 110
    software for, 41
budgeting, 91–105
    expenses, monitoring/managing, 91, 93, 101–02
    flexible, 101, 105
    and industry standards, 100
    margins (breathing space), 94–96
    no-need approach to, 92–93, 235
    profit margins, calculating, 96–97
    profit margins, monitoring, 101–02
    profit margins, using, 97–98
    reactionary, 92–93
    return on investment (ROI), evaluating, 102–05
    run rate (baseline monthly expenses), 99, 101
bulk pricing discounts, 180

C

cash flow/management, 79–90
    accounting funny business, 24, 80–83
    and accrual vs. cash accounting, 83
    and asset purchases, 82
    billing, 84–85, 88–89
    causes of shortages, 79, 82–83
    and debt, 82–83
    defined, 66
    forecasting, 72–74, 76, 102
    and growth of business, 83, 85–86
    importance of, 79
    inventory, 85–87, 90
    and inventory purchases, 82
    music therapy business (case study), 84–85, 87
    optometry business (case study), 85–86
    and owner's draws, 82
    and paying employees, 90
    prepayment/deposits, 88
    quick ways to improve, 87–90
    and shopping cart abonnement, 88–89
    timing of cash collection, 83
    on your to-do list, 71–74
C corporations (C corps), 25, 195, 203, 233
CEOs (Chief Executive Officers), 66
CFOs (Chief Financial Officers), 66, 77
channel mix, 161
charitable giving, 259–66

Chief Executive Officers (CEOs), 66
Chief Financial Officers (CFOs), 66, 75
CLV (Customer Lifetime Value), 58, 163, 172–73
Coca-Cola, 159
competition vs. collaboration, 145
compliance
    costs related to, 186
    defined, 66–67
    as a financial duty, 66–68, 91
    and financial statements, 22
    outsourcing, 37, 70–71, 127–28
    with tax requirements, 68
    on your to-do list, 65–71, 76–77
confirmation bias, 46
correlation vs. causation, 49–50
covid pandemic, 94–95
credit cards, 210, 214
Customer Lifetime Value (CLV), 58, 163, 172–73
customers
    average price of transactions by, 58
    cost of acquiring, 58
    loyalty and retention of, 58, 172–75
    satisfaction of (net promoter score), 58
customization, 172

D

data, 39–51
    accuracy of, 40–42
    analysis as intimidating, 14
    anecdotal, 49–50
    assuming cause-and-effect relationships in, 49–50
    avoiding financial problems (ostriching), 43–45
    completeness of, 41–43
    and confirmation bias, 46
    and cutting your losses, 47–48
    defined, 13
    and ego, 45–49
    failure/mistakes as, 18, 48
    importance of, 13–19
    vs. metrics, 54–55 (*see also* performance metrics)
    organization of, 42, 59–60
    overview of, 11
    on profitability, 14–15
    quantitative and qualitative, 50
    and reconciliations, 41–42
    subjective vs. hard (numbers), 14
    and the sunk cost fallacy, 47
    therapy business (case study), 42–43
    truth testing of, 50–51
    wedding venue business (case study), 43–45
    winery (case study), 39–40, 46, 48–49

debt
- annual percentage rate (APR), 214
- bank term loans, 212–13
- business loans, 114
- cash from, 82
- cheaper, 214–15
- credit cards, 210, 214
- good vs. bad, 208–9
- hidden cost of, 213–15
- lines of credit (LOCs), 115, 211
- merchant cash advances (MCAs), 207–8, 210–11, 214
- payments of, 83
- as a Profit Lever, 135, 215–16, 218–19
- purpose and payoff plan, 117
- reducing, 207–16
- and risk, 114–15, 117
- secured loans, 214
- shopping for a bank, 114
- Small Business Administration (SBA) loans, 211–12
- toy store (case study), 207–8, 215–16

delegating tasks, 179–180
depreciation, 24, 81–83
direct costs
- determining, 148–51
- few to no, 155–56
- vs. indirect costs, 148–49
- as a Profit Lever, 96, 103, 135, 177–82, 218, 220
- reducing, 178–81

donations, 260, 263–65
draws from your business (paying yourself), 33–34, 82, 154, 231–33, 246

E

email open rate, 58
equity, 25–26, 30, 32–34, 82, 119

F

Federal Insurance Contributions Act, 69
finances
- assumptions, guesstimates, and rounding, 8
- being "bad with numbers," 5–6
- being "good with numbers," 8
- mastering, importance of, 1–3
- motivation for mastering, 10
- responsibility for, 110

Financial Control Room (duties and management)
- overview of, 63–64
- skin care business (case study), 65, 67, 76
- *See also* cash flow/management; Profit Levers; risk; to-do list

financial statements, 21–38
  action to take, 38
  importance of, 21–22
  outsourcing tasks, 36–37
  print shop (case study), 23–32, 34, 80
  spreadsheets/accounting software for, 35–36
  and taxes, 22
  See also Balance Sheets; P&Ls
free shipping, 171
fun, barriers to, 249–55
  ineffective systems, 252–53
  ineffective teams, 253–54
  lack of funds, 254–55
  seasonality of income, 251–52
  trading hours for dollars, 250–51
Fun Fund, 251, 255–58
Future Fund, 245–47

G

Great Recession (2008–2010), 243

H

HiddenProfitTheBook.com, 37–38, 63, 70, 74, 121, 199, 202, 215, 223
hierarchy of needs, 257
Housel, Morgan: *The Psychology of Money*, 40

I

Impact Fund, 258–66
Income Statements. *See* P&Ls
indirect costs
  80/20 rule of, 186–89
  expenses to keep, identifying, 185–86
  expenses vs. investments, 182–85
  as a Profit Lever, 135, 181–89, 219–20
  strategies for reducing, 191
industry budgeting standards, 100
inventory
  on Balance Sheets, 25–26, 30–32, 82
  and cash flow, 85–87, 90
  managing, 180–81
  stocking vs. just-in-time/drop-ship model, 86, 90
  turnover of, 58, 86
invoices outstanding, days of, 58
IRAs, 192–94, 200–201, 205
IRS, 81, 109, 111–12, 192–93, 239
  See also taxes

K

KPI Dashboard, 59–60
KPIs (Key Performance Indicators), 55–56, 58, 60

L

leads, 57
liabilities, 25–27, 32–33, 82–83
lines of credit (LOCs), 115, 211
liquidity of a business, 27
LLCs, 195–96, 199
LOCs (lines of credit), 115, 211

M

margins (breathing space), 94–96, 224
margins (in business). *See* profit margins
marketing, 138, 140–41
Maslow, Abraham, 257
Medicare, 196
merchant cash advances (MCAs), 207–8, 210–11, 214
metrics. *See* performance metrics
mix (of products and services), 135, 159–67, 218, 221
money
    and emotions, 146
    positive impacts of, 7
    as a tool, 7
money personalities
    eight distinct personalities, 122–24
    experts on, 121
    Money Personality Quiz, 121, 125
    quick cash based on, 128–29
    yours, 120–21, 125–26, 128–29
    See also self-reflection and management
money personalities, types of
    Accumulators, 122–26, 128, 191, 257
    Alchemists, 122–23, 126–28, 257
    Celebrities, 122–23, 126, 128, 257
    Connectors, 122–24, 126–27, 129, 170, 257
    Mavericks, 122–23, 125–26, 129, 257
    Nurturers, 122–23, 126–27, 129, 170, 257
    Romantics, 122–23, 126, 129, 257
    Rulers, 122–23, 125–26, 129, 257
motivation for helping others and ourselves, 10
multiplier effect, 262

N

needs, hierarchy of, 256
NerdWallet, 6
net worth of a business. *See* equity
numbers. *See* data

O

occupancy rate (percentage of appointments booked), 58
"101 Jobs Kids Can Do in Your Business," 202
Opportunity Fund, 234–36
order bumps, 171
ownership and accountability, 134

P

package bundles, 171
package mix, 161
Pareto principle (80/20 rule), 141, 186–86
partnerships, 115–17
The Path Made Clear (Winfrey), 48
PayPal, 213–14
Pay Yourself Fund, 231–33, 246
performance metrics, 53–61
    action to take, 61
    and anxiety about the future, 53, 56
    common, 57–58
    KPI Dashboard, 59–60
    KPIs (Key Performance Indicators), 55–57, 59, 60–61
    lagging indicators, 54–55
    leading indicators, 54–55
    metrics vs. data, 54
    monthly review of, 59–60
    revenue, 99
    swimsuit business (case study), 53, 56
    types of, 54–55
personality. *See* money personalities, types of
P&Ls (Profit and Loss Statements)
    and Balance Sheets, 27–34
    equation for, 22, 24
    frequency of, 21–22
    home organization businesses (case study), 15–17
    importance of, 21–22
    monthly review of, 98, 101–02
    organization of, 42–43
    past performance measured by, 54
    print shop (case study), 23–32, 80
    transactions' impacts on, 27–32, 80
    See also profit margins
Plum Paper, 169–70
political campaigns, contributions to, 264
Power in Numbers, 266, 268
prices, 143–58
    advice from coaches or "media experts," 147
    based on competitors' prices, 144
    based on feelings, 146
    based on what you're worth, 143

prices (*cont.*)
- calculating, 147–57
- direct costs, determining, 148–51
- direct costs, few to no, 154–56
- direct costs, reducing, 178–81
- direct costs vs. indirect costs, 148–49
- discounts, 146
- dog grooming business (case study), 150–51, 153, 158
- equations for, 147, 149
- formula for setting, 150–51, 153
- furniture company (case study), 146
- gross profit margin, determining, 149–50
- hourly pricing, 248–49
- indirect costs, determining, 149–50
- inflexible pricing, 156
- minimum, 147, 150–51, 181
- overanalyzing, avoiding, 152–53
- and paying yourself, 154
- as a Profit Lever, 135, 219, 220
- raising, conditions for, 156–57
- raising, strategies for, 157–58
- subscription-based (retainer) pricing, 250–52
- value-based pricing, 251
- and the value of owner labor, 153–54

product mix, 161

PROFFIT Plan
- boutique business (case study), 228–31
- creating, 227–30
- Fun Fund, 251, 255–58
- Future Fund, 245–47
- horseback riding camp (case study), 241–44
- Impact Fund, 259–66
- importance of, 86–87, 225
- meaning of, 230
- Opportunity Fund, 234–36
- overview of, 9
- Pay Yourself Fund, 231–33, 246
- power washing business (case study), 246–47
- Rainy Day Fund, 242–45
- and seasonality, 241–42, 251–52
- Tax Fund, 237–39

profitability
- becoming profitable, 133–36 (*see also* Profit Levers)
- dog grooming business (case study), 133, 136, 139, 142
- equation for, 14–15, 80
- and tax avoidance, 14–15 (*see also* cash flow)
- *See also* P&Ls

Profitability Maximizer, 223
Profit and Loss Statements. *See* P&Ls
Profit Levers
    artisan soap business (case study), 137, 139
    Direct Costs (*see also under* prices)
    dog grooming business (case study), 133, 136, 139, 142, 150–51, 153, 158, 161, 163–65, 173–74
    overview of, 9, 135–36
    Price (*see also* prices)
    promotions, timing of, 162
    sales coaching business (case study), 177–78, 182, 187–89
    winery (case study), 138
profit margins
    calculating, 96–97
    and direct costs, 96
    equations for, 96–97
    gross, 96–97, 149–50
    home organization businesses (case study), 17–18
    importance of, 224
    monitoring, 101–02
    net, 97
    operating, 97–98
    overanalyzing, avoiding, 152–53
    by product or service, 57
    using, 97–98

The Psychology of Money (Housel), 40
Psychology Today, 113

R

Rainy Day Fund, 242–45
resilience, 134
reticular activating system (RAS), 75
return on investment (ROI), 102–105, 180–81, 185
risk, 107–18
    action to take, 117–18
    and debt, 114–15, 117
    overview of, 107, 118
    in partnerships, 115–17
    of personal equity in your business, 117–18
    and taxes, 109–14
    tolerance for, 108, 113–14
Roth IRAs, 189–90, 196–97, 201

S

Sacred Money Archetypes, 9, 120, 122–24
    See also money personalities, types of
salary, average, 7
SBA (Small Business Administration) loans, 211–12
scarcity mindset, 126
S corporations (S corps), 25, 194–98, 203, 233

seasonality, 241–42, 251–52
self-reflection and management
    action to take, 126–28
    coffee shop (case study), 123–24, 126–27
    financial gaps, finding and bridging, 127–28
    importance of, 119
    nonnegotiables, identifying, 127
    online education business (case study), 124
    personal organizing business (case study), 124
    strengths, reflecting on, 128
selling more, 137–42
    See also Average Transaction Value; Profit Levers
Small Business Administration (SBA) loans, 211–12
Social Security, 196
sole proprietorships, 195–96, 199
sponsorships, 261, 263
standard operating procedures (SOPs), 179
starlings, 267–68
Statements of Operations. *See* P&Ls
Stelmaszak, Dr., 45–46, 49–50
streamlining your processes, 179
Stripe, 214
subscriptions, 171, 187
SummerHawk, Kendall, 9, 121
sunk cost fallacy, 47
suppliers, 180

T

taxes
    audits, 109, 111–12
    bank account for paying, 117
    charitable gifts' impacts on, 262–65
    compliance with requirements, 68
    deductions, 108–13, 117
    effective income tax rate, 237–38
    excise, 70
    federal income and payroll, 68–69
    FICA, 69
    local, 68
    marginal income tax rate, 238
    overpaying vs. underpaying, 113–14, 237
    as a Profit Lever, 135, 203–05, 218–19
    quarterly estimated, 113, 273–38
    receipts/expense records, 111–12, 117
    and risk, 108–14
    self-employment, 69, 113, 196
    state income, 68–69
    state sales tax, 68–70
    See also accounting
taxes, reducing, 191–205
    business entity types, 194–99

    deductions, 191–92
    hiring your children, 199–205
    income shifting, 199
    retirement accounts, 193–94, 200–201, 204
    tax loopholes, 192
    travel expenses, 192–93
Tax Fund, 237–39
time-saving technology, 179
to-do list, 65–77
    compliance, 65–71, 76–77
    monthly money list, 77
    strategy, 66, 74, 76
    See also cash flow
Twain, Mark, 45

U

upselling, 170–71
    See also Average Transaction Value

U.S. Bank, 79
U.S. Bureau of Labor Statistics, 243

V

Venmo, 213–14
VIP upgrades, 171
volume (sales), 135, 139–42, 218–19, 222–23

W

waste reduction, 180–81
website traffic, monthly, 58
wholesale purchasing, 180
Winfrey, Oprah: *The Path Made Clear*, 48

X

Xero, 79

ABOUT THE AUTHOR

Jamie Trull, CPA, is a financial literacy coach and profit strategist dedicated to helping small-business owners maximize profitability, achieve sustainable growth, and make a positive impact. Jamie holds a bachelor's degree in Analytical Finance and a master's in Accounting from Wake Forest University, credentials that have shaped her expertise in business finance and strategy.

With a background as a Finance Leader at Coca-Cola Enterprises, Jamie transitioned from the corporate world to focus on serving small businesses as a Virtual CFO. During that time, she noticed a critical gap in accessible financial education tailored to small-business owners and self-employed individuals. Determined to bridge the gap, she created a series of educational programs that simplify complex financial topics and equip business owners with actionable strategies to improve profitability, reduce taxes, and achieve financial confidence. Her mission is to empower entrepreneurs to create wealth, freedom, and opportunities to make a positive impact.

Jamie is also the founder of Power in Numbers® (PiN), a movement designed to connect financial professionals with small-business owners to create a stronger, more collaborative ecosystem. With a focus on creating community and supporting women and marginalized entrepreneurs, Power in Numbers® provides affordable access to financial experts and tools, bridging the gap between entrepreneurs and the financial guidance they need. Learn more at www.PiNtheMovement.com.

When she's not empowering business owners, Jamie can be found enjoying a Broadway musical, getting hooked on a true crime documentary, or hitting the pickleball court. At home, she treasures spending quality time with her husband, Kemper; their two children, Miles and Norah; and their beloved pups, Skip and Deacon.